HISTORY
OF THE
𝕭𝖎𝖌 𝕾𝖕𝖗𝖎𝖓𝖌
𝕻𝖗𝖊𝖘𝖇𝖞𝖙𝖊𝖗𝖎𝖆𝖓 𝕮𝖍𝖚𝖗𝖈𝖍

NEWVILLE
PENNSYLVANIA

1737-1898

by
Gilbert Ernest Swope

with an
Introduction by Rev. Ebenezer Erskine, D.D.

HERITAGE BOOKS
2008

HERITAGE BOOKS
AN IMPRINT OF HERITAGE BOOKS, INC.

Books, CDs, and more—Worldwide

For our listing of thousands of titles see our website
at
www.HeritageBooks.com

A Facsimile Reprint
Published 2008 by
HERITAGE BOOKS, INC.
Publishing Division
100 Railroad Ave. #104
Westminster, Maryland 21157

Originally published 1898 by Times Steam Printing House
Newville, Pennsylvania

— Publisher's Notice —
In reprints such as this, it is often not possible to remove blemishes from the original. We feel the contents of this book warrant its reissue despite these blemishes and hope you will agree and read it with pleasure.

International Standard Book Numbers
Paperbound: 978-1-58549-530-6
Clothbound: 978-0-7884-7732-4

PREFACE.

In presenting this little history of the Big Spring Presbyterian Church, we feel quite safe in saying that we are giving all that is obtainable regarding the congregation, and more than we expected to find when we began our work. Owing to the fact that there were no records in possession of the congregation prior to 1830 except an old trustees minute book, the prospect for obtaining data was not very encouraging. However, by careful inquiry among the old families of the church and other means, we were enabled to find that herein given. Through the kindness of Miss Jennie W. Davidson, a great granddaughter of Rev. Samuel Wilson, we were given permission to examine a great mass of old family papers, the accumulation of more than a century. Among these papers we were fortunate enough to find much valuable matter, relating not only to the ministry of Rev. Samuel Wilson but also to that of some of his predecessors. No regular session books seem to have been kept by the early pastors, all the records found being on detached pieces of paper. The earliest record found bears date Dec. 12, 1768, and records a case of discipline.

We are indebted largely for the matter contained in the sketches of the pastors of the church to the "Centennial Memorial of the Presbytery of Carlisle." We greatfully acknowledge the interest shown and the assistance given by the pastor of the Big Spring Church, the Rev. Ebenezer Erskine, D. D. We are pleased to append the address delivered by Dr. Erskine at the celebration of the founding of Log College.

It is valuable as an historic document, and finds here a fitting place because of its treatment on the Presbyterian church in the Cumberland Valley.

Our thanks are also due and very cheerfully given to Mr. John W. Strohm, editor of the "Newville Times," whose interest in local history and genealogy is well known, and whose co-operation has made the publication of this volume possible.

GILBERT E. SWOPE,
NEWVILLE, PA.

Aug. 17, 1898.

Introduction.

This brief and comprehensive volume may be very properly styled a documentary history of the Big Spring Presbyterian Church and congregation, and a genealogy of many of its families.

Its author, Mr. Gilbert E. Swope, is an enthusiast on the subject of genealogy and an expert in the discovery and use of old documents bearing on the history of families and churches.

As the result of his patient and laborious researches, the names of nearly all the families of this venerable church and congregation have been rescued from an impending oblivion, and a list of most of its elders, trustees and families have been preserved. No sessional records are in possession of the congregation prior to 1830. It was the custom of many pastors prior to that date to keep a roll of members, of admissions to the church, of baptisms and marriages, and to make a record only of cases of discipline and to submit the same to presbytery for examination and approval, then to consider it of no further value nor worthy of preservation.

Mr. Swope, discovered papers left by the Rev. Samuel Wilson, pastor from 1787 to 1799, stored away in an old trunk and found in the garret of one of his descendents, and gained access to certain other papers which had been left by Rev. Dr. Joshua Williams, pastor from 1802 to 1829, and found in possession of some of his relatives in the distant west. These documents have thrown a flood of light upon the history of this church from 1775 to 1830, more than half a century, and which if not discovered, would have soon been lost sight of forever.

It is a great matter to have recovered thus the names of all the families of that period, many of them reaching back to the origin of the church, the divisions of the congregation into districts, the names of the parents and children, and members of the church in each district; and also the names of the elders to whose supervision these districts were assigned, and still more several lists of theological questions given out annually by Mr. Wilson for the careful study of the people, and for an examination on the same, by pastor or elder.

The character of these questions indicate not only a high degree of religious intelligence upon the part of the minister but also imply corresponding intelligence on part of the people. These, in connection with regular examinations of the young on the catechism, and of the more advanced on chapters in the Confession of faith, go to show the modes of religious instruction and training peculiar to that period of the church and widely prevalent in other congregations of that day, and which in connection with the faithful preaching of the word on the Sabbath, had a most important influence in the way of awakening the minds of the people in relation to religious subjects, in the quickening of religious thought and inquiry, and in the development of well instructed and stable Christians as to matters of doctrine and duty, all leading to exemplary and consistent Christian living.

To trace the origin and progress of individual churches, whose history runs back to the first settlement of the country, to give the names, individuals and families which have composed the same, to put on record reliable accounts of the origin, lives and characters of the ministers, the distinctive characteristics of their faith and modes of conducting the worship of their congregations, and of their general pastoral services; to give a true and reliable history of their growth and progress, as has here been done by Mr. Swope, is to render a very important service in relation to the foundation and character of the church in this country.

The Big Spring Presbyterian Church, as indicated by the lists of admissions to its membership, has been blessed with revivals of religion from time to time, through all its history, giving increased vitality to the church as well as considerable accessions to its membership. Such seasons, of greater or less power have been enjoyed in 1794, 1822, 1832, 1833 and 1834. The revivial of 1877 was doubtless one of the most remarkable awakenings of the whole community in the history of the church, resulting in the admission of over one hundred and twenty members to the church of all ages, on confession of their faith, and of some two hundred more to the churches in the town. A careful examination into the origin of our early congregations, as to their ministers and people, and as to their standards of doctrine and form of government and modes of worship, as learned from their history and records, is of special importance, as throwing light upon the actual character of the church in these respects from the beginning. Whatever difficulty may be experienced in some parts of the country in this respect, none need be felt in regard to the churches of this valley, nor of the State of Pennsylvania.

The settlement of the Cumberland Valley and the constitution of its churches, is directly traceable to that great providential movement which took place among the Scotch Irish Presbyterians settled in the province of Ulster, in the north of Ireland, which runs back to near the beginning of the 18th century, and which led to a steady and increasing stream of emigration from that Province to this country, and which added greatly to the strength and character of the Presbyterian Church in America. And this state of things in Ulster, was only a part of that wider movement which took place in Scotland, England, France and Holland, as well as in Ulster. The history of Presbyterian colonization in America, is largely the result of papal and prelatic persecutions in Europe. By the act of uniformity passed in 1662, two thousand Presbyterian ministers were cast out of the Church of England. A considerable number of whom found refuge in this country, chiefly in New England.

By reason of the persecutions of the Reformed Churches of France, which were strictly Presbyterian in government and Calvinistic in doctrine, and which was consummated under Louis XIV. by the revocation of the edict of Nantes in 1685, two hundred thousand French protestants suffered martyrdom, and about seven hundred thousand were driven from the kingdom, many of whom found their way to this country. Two thousand churches, with their ministers, were nearly extirpated by that cruel and bloody persecution.

"Modern history," it is said, "hardly affords a parallel to the cruelty and oppression under which Scotland groaned for nearly thirty years," under the reigns of James II. and of Charles I. and Charles II. and all in support of Episcopacy and under the instigation of the Bishops. Multitudes of learned and pious ministers were ejected from their parishes, and ignorant and ungodly men substituted in their places, upon whose ministrations, unedifying as they were, the people were forced to attend under severe penalties.

The ejected ministers were prohibited from preaching or praying in public, even in fields or other retired places. To enforce these oppressive laws, exorbitant fines were imposed, torture was freely resorted to to extort evidence, the prisons were filled with victims of oppression, soldiers were quartered upon defenceless families, and allowed the greatest license and many were massacred upon the public highways. It is no wonder that the Scotch Presbyterians abhorred episcopacy. In their views and experience, it was identical with oppression, despotism and impiety.

Considering their long continued persecution, the wonder has been expressed, that they did not rise up *en masse* and forsake the country. The hope of overthrowing episcopacy and of regaining their liberties, constrained the majority of them to withstand their oppressors. Emigration from Scotland by reason of such oppression, while not so great as might have been expected, was yet considerable. Four thousand Presbyterians are reported to have come into New England prior to 1640, many of whom were from Scotland. In 1729 a church was organized in Boston, composed of Scotch and Irish Presbyterians. The

VI

First Church in New York City, composed chiefly of Scotch and Irish Presbyterians, was organized previous to 1716, and called the Rev. James Anderson, a Scotch Presbyterian minister from New Castle, Delaware, to become their first pastor.

The emigrants from Scotland to east New Jersey were many and influential. They came in such numbers, says Bancroft, as to give to the rising commonwealth, a character which a century and a half have not effaced. But it was to Pennsylvania and the Carolinas, that a larger and increasing stream of emigration from Scotland and the North of Ireland came. The latter in much larger numbers than the former.

The Presbyterians in Ulster were rendered exceedingly uncomfortable by reason of the tyrany and exactions of their despotic monarchs, by the restrictions and penalties imposed by parliament, the intolerance and persecutions instigated by the Bishops and the rapacity and greed of the landlords. Among the laws enacted intended to harass and annoy them, was what was called the Test Act, which prohibited them from holding any office in Dublin or the province. This was followed by the Marriage Act by which they were forbidden to be married by their own ministers, and rendered liable to arraignment for immorality in the ecclesiastical courts for such marriage. Worse than all, what was known as the Schism Act, was passed in 1714, which would have swept the Presbyterian Church of Ireland well nigh out of existence, had not Queen Anne died before it could be enforced.

These and other like acts estranged the people from their country, and caused them to turn their attention to the new colonies then being planted in America, where they might secure for themselves and familiies' future homes, and the blessings of civil and religious liberty, denied them in their own land. The consequence was that as far back as 1713, both ministers and people began to come to America. In this great movement, the Rev. Thomas Craighead, a minister of considerable prominence, with some others led the way. In 1715 he came to New England, in 1724 he removed to Pennsylvania and 1737, became the first pastor of the Big Spring Church. Some six thousand Scotch Irish are said to have come in 1720. Later on they are reported to have come at the rate of twelve thousand from year to year. Cumberland County, which in the outset included Franklin, was chiefly settled by them. From 1736 onward, they crossed over at Harrisburg in great numbers and settled in this vicinity along the Conodoguinit and the Big Spring more numerously than elsewhere, by reason of the junction of these two streams of water at nearly right angles. Out of these sturdy, rugged Scotch Irish people, this church was originally organized.

From here they spread on down the valley into Virginia, the Carolinas and Tennessee, many crossing the mountains over into Western Pennsylvania and farther down across into Kentucky. A thousand families are said to have arrived in the state of North Carolina from the more northerly settlements in 1764. No other country, says Dr. Ramsey, furnished the province of South Carolina with so many citizens as the North of Ireland. These strict Presbyterians driven here largely by the persecutions to which they had been subjected at home, the Scotch, the Scotch Irish, the Dutch from Holland and the French Huguenots, laid the foundations of the Presbyterian Church in Boston, New York, New Jersey, Pennsylvania, Maryland, the Carolinas and Georgia, through all which sections of country they settled in great numbers. In 1705, the first Presbytery was organized in Philadelphia. In 1716 the first Synod was formed. In 1729 the Westminster Standards were adopted by the Synod.

This last event took place eight years before the organization of this church. The Rev. Thomas Craighead, its first minister, was a member of that Synod and voted for the adopting act.

Before the settlement of the second pastor, the Rev. John Blair, in 1742, the church had divided into two branches, the Old and the New Side. Both sides, however, adhered with equal tenacity to the Standards adopted, and regarded themselves as identical in doctrine, government and worship with the Church of Scotland.

While adopting the Confession of Faith as containing the system of doctrine set forth in the Holy Scriptures, and approving the form of government and the directory for worship, as conformable to the word of God, at the same time all who held to the essential doctrines of Christianity were cordially invited and freely welcomed into the communion of the church. An important distinction has always been made between Christian and ministerial communion. We are bound to regard and treat as Christians all who make a credible profession of faith in the Lord Jesus Christ and accept of the essential doctrines of the Christian religion. The lowest terms of salvation are the highest terms of Christian communion. What will take a soul to Heaven should take it in the Church on earth.

The terms of ministerial communion are different. The conditions upon which ministers are admitted to office in the church is not merely acceptance of the essential doctrines of the Gospel, but the sincere adoption of the Confession of Faith as containing the system of doctrine taught in the Scriptures. Those called and chosen to be teachers and rulers must be sound in the faith, and therefore accept the standards of the church as the church's authorized and accepted interpretation of the teachings of God's most holy word.

No one applying for admission to the Presbyterian Church will be rejected, nor any one already a minister of the church be subjected to discipline who is not supposed to reject some of the distinctive doctrines taught in this system set forth in the Confession of Faith and Catechisms of the Church. That system is the Reformed or Calvinistic sys-

VIII

tem in contradistinction to the Armenian, Pelagian, semi-Pelagian or Socinian systems held by other branches of the nominally Christian Church.

It was on this basis the Presbyterian Church was organized in this country. On this basis the church has had a remarkable growth. From an organization of five ministers and three ruling elders in 1705, it has grown in less than two centuries into a Church extending over all this wide spread land and into all heathen countries on the same doctrinal basis. This church contains 7,429 ministers, 1,423 candidates for the ministry, 477 licentiates, 7,631 churches, 27,874 ruling elders and 960,-911 church members. May it ever continue to live and prosper on the same divine basis. EBENEZER ERSKINE.

NEWVILLE, PA., August, 1898.

The Big Spring
Presbyterian Church.

THE lands in the "Kittochtinny", or present Cumberland Valley, were not purchased from the Indians until October 1736, and were not, therefore, before that time open for sale. But for several years prior to that period the agents of the proprietors knowing the feelings of the Indians to be favorable had encouraged settlers to come hither, and had issued to them special licenses for the securing and settlement of such lands beyond the Susquehanna as might please them. *

After the lands of the valley were finally thrown open to settlers, there was a great influx of emigrants, many coming from the old-settled counties of Lancaster and Chester, and many directly from Ireland. Most of the settlers being Irish and Scotch Irish, very few of other nationalities were found here until a much later date. These people first sought the land bordering on the streams of water because of the convenience of an abundance of water, and of timber which grew along the water courses. Thus we find that very soon after the land was thrown open for settlement, the inviting lands of this vicinity attracted a large population to the borders of the Conodoguinet Creek and the Big Spring. One of the first acts of our forefathers after locating land and building homes for themselves and families was to provide a spiritual home or place for the worship of God.

* Note Hist. Franklin Co. McCauley.

The Presbyterians who settled in the neighborhood of the Big Spring organized a congregation not later than the spring of 1737. On the 22nd of June the people of Hopewell petitioned Presbytery for their concurrence in drawing a call to the Rev. Thomas Craighead. About this time the name of this people was changed from the people of the Conodoguinet to the people of Pennsboro and Hopewell, the line having been run in 1735 from the north to the south mountain by way of the Big Spring dividing the valley. All east of that line was called Pennsboro and all west of it Hopewell. By the "people of Hopewell" referred to in the call to Mr. Craighead no doubt were included the congregation at Middle Spring as well as Big Spring. They were both known by the general name of "Hopewell" and individually Big Spring as Lower Hopewell, and Middle Spring as Upper Hopewell. The congregation of Upper Pennsboro objected to the call to Mr. Craighead and the establishment of a church on the Big Spring as an encroachment upon their territory, as there was a rule of Presbytery not allowing congregations to be located within ten miles of each other. The Presbytery appointed a committee to look over the territory and confer with the people on the calling of a pastor and the location of a house of worship. This conference was held at the house of James McFarlane on the Big Spring in 1737. The committee reported to Presbytery in November 1737, and notwithstanding the urgency of the congregation and the impatience of Mr. Craighead, action was deferred until the next year. On Aug. 31, 1738, Presbytery appointed Mr. Alexander Craighead to install Mr. Thomas Craighead the second Friday in

October and that he "send an edict to be published timeously before." Mr. Craighead's pastorate was a short one as he died the following year. At this time he was well advanced in life, but his mental powers continued in their full vigor. "He still preached with great power and impressiveness. Under his discourses the people were at times deeply and powerfully moved and often when dismissed were unwilling to leave.

On one of these occasions near the close of April 1739, at a communion season in the Big Spring Church, when having preached until quite exhausted, he waved his hand being unable to pronounce the benediction and exclaimed: 'Farewell! Farewell' and sank down and expired in the pulpit." Tradition says that his remains were buried beneath the present church edifice, but this is very doubtful as this church was not built until fifty years after his death. It is more probable that he was buried beneath the church he built and in which he preached, as was the custom at that time.

PASTORATE OF REV. JOHN BLAIR, D. D.

After the demise of Rev. Thomas Craighead the Big Spring congregation was without a regularly installed pastor until 1742. They had been supplied however during this time by Mr. James Lyon of Ireland, who was then under the care of the Presbytery of New Castle, and by others sent out by Presbytery of Donegal. On the 27th of December, 1742, Rev. John Blair was installed pastor of the Big Spring Church in connection with the Middle Spring and Rocky Spring congregations. The records kept during his ministry are the earliest positive evidence we have of the three churches being under one pastor. Although it is very probable that Rev. Thomas Craighead preached in those churches at the same time he ministered to the people at Big Spring. Rev. S. S. Wylie, in his history of the Middle Spring Church, seems quite positive of the fact, and cites very plausible evidence to sustain his position. If the people of Big Spring were unable to support a pastor alone in 1742, and later, it is not very probable that they could do so in 1738.

We learn from the sessional records of the Middle Spring Church (1742) that "the minister and elders of Big Spring, Middle Spring, and Rocky Spring, met at Middle Spring in order to settle the division of the ministers' labors among the three congregations." They agreed upon the following arrangement, "that the ministers' labors be equally divided in a third part to each place, as being most for the glory of God and good of his people." It was also, "upon motion of the elders of Big Spring, left to them, the people, and Mr.

Blair, to converse among themselves in respect to the subscriptions of the Big Spring Congregation." Mr. Blair during his ministry here resided at Middle Spring on a farm of two hundred and twelve acres the warrant of which bears date October 5th, 1743. It is said that "he and his wife, with their hired servants, lived in a style quite above their plain country parishioners. The people were extremely kind to Mr. Blair and his young wife, so that they often had a superabundance of the good things of this life." Just how long Mr. Blair continued in this field of labor is uncertain. Webster in his history, and Sprague in his annals of the American Pulpit, who, quotes from Webster, both give the date of his leaving the "Three Springs" as December 28, 1748. The last record in the session book kept during his ministry at Middle Spring is dated February 8th, 1749. All agree that Mr. Blair was driven from his field of labor by the incursions of the Indians. There were no Indian troubles in 1749, but after the defeat of Braddock July 9, 1755, and the retreat of Dunbar, this valley was swept by fire, sword, scalping knife, and the tomahawk of the cruel savage. Hundreds of people left the valley for the interior counties and others took refuge in the larger towns and forts of the valley. It is not improbable that Mr. Blair was among those who left the valley for safety, and we are inclined to accept the opinion of those who give his departure as being 1755, or even later. Another evidence of his presence here at a late date is the following receipt in the hands of Rev. S. S. Wylie. "September 11th, 1757, received from John Johnson, 2 £ and 2 d. which appears to me to be in full of stepens due Rev. John Blair "by me, David Megaw."

PASTORATE OF REV. GEO. DUFFIELD, D. D.

Probably owing to the distracted condition of the country resulting from the Indian troubles a successor to Rev. John Blair was not called until 1759. In that year the congregations of Carlisle and Big Spring united in a call to the Rev. George Duffield, D. D., but he was not installed until the third Wednesday of September, 1759. According to the terms of his call, one third of his time was to be given to Big Spring and two thirds to Carlisle. In 1761, an effort was made by the Big Spring congregation to obtain the one half of Mr. Duffield's labors. To this, the congregation of Carlisle objected and gave notice by commissioners that if Presbytery would not allow them the two thirds of his time they would at the next meeting make application for all his time. At the next meeting of Presbytery after considering the claims of each party it was decided in view of Mr. Duffield not being physically able to endure the fatigue of giving one-half his time to Big Spring, that he should give one third of his time to Big Spring and two thirds to Carlisle as agreed upon when the call was made out, and that the salary should be in the same proportion. This arrangement continued until 1769 when Mr. Duffield's relation to Big Spring was dissolved on account of the salary promised, having been allowed to fall in arrears.

PASTORATE OF REV. WILLIAM LINN, D. D.

The successor of Rev. Dr. Duffield as pastor of the Big Spring congregation was the Rev. William Linn. He received a call from this congregation April 9, 1777, and was installed October 3, 1777. The congregation at this time seems to have increased sufficiently to justify them in securing the services of a pastor for themselves alone. Mr. Linn remained as pastor of the congregation until 1784 when he resigned to become Principal of Washington Academy, in Somerset County, Md. The relations of Mr. Linn and the Big Spring congregation seem to have been very pleasant. In letters in my possession written by him to his friend John Heap then living in Baltimore he expresses much affection for his late parishioners the congregation of Big Spring. In one of these letters written from Washington Academy June 28, 1785, he gives the impression that the congregation of Big Spring recalled him to become their pastor. We quote from it as follows "The invitation from Big Spring is singular and unexpected, and lays me under additional obligations to that people. I would fain enough, if it was prudent and consistent with duty, return to my old walks and old field. I have not refused the invitation from Big Spring, nor have I greatly encouraged it. The same line I have persued as to prospects held out from Elizabethtown. I am really undetermined and know not what to do. Big Spring is most eligible because most obscure and retired." We regret very much that a very careful search has failed to reveal a record of the ministerial acts of Dr. Linn or either of his predecessors.

THE PASTORATE OF REV. SAMUEL WILSON.

After the resignation of Rev. William Linn there was a vacancy of three years in the Big Spring Church. Just why the pulpit was vacant for so long a time we are unable to state, but we know that efforts were made to secure a pastor. On the 21st of March, 1786, a call was extended to the Rev. Samuel Wilson. The call was accepted and Mr. Wilson was installed June 20, 1787. His pastorate was one of activity and prosperity for the congregation. The different departments of church work were well organized and good results followed. Many accessions were made to the church, a new church building was erected, and the Borough of Newville laid out on the church lands. Mr. Wilson was pains-taking and accurate in keeping a record of his church work, and fortunately the records have been preserved although hidden in a garret for a century, and just brought to light. These records we are glad to give as they are valuable not only to the church but to the community. Mr. Wilson after a faithful ministry of almost thirteen years closed his life as pastor of the congregation, Mar. 4th, 1799.

CALL EXTENDED TO REV. SAMUEL WILSON.

"We, the subscribers of this paper, members of the Presbyterian Congregation of Big Spring, taking into consideration that we have been for a considerable time without a gospel minister, by the removal of the Rev. Mr. William Linn, our late worthy pastor, and being satisfied with the piety, learning, character and ministerial qualifications of Mr. Samuel Wilson, preacher of the gospel, of whom we have had trial by his preaching among us, do hereby invite, call and entreat you, the said Samuel Wilson, to become our minister, and to take charge and oversight of our souls in the Lord. We promise you all due obedience in the Lord, and that we will attend the divine ordinances, administered by you, and submit to your discipline according to the rules of our Society, and we entreat the Reverend Presbytery of Donegal, to take the said Mr. Samuel Wilson on trial for the holy ministry, and on his being found qualified, to ordain him as a minister. In witness whereof we have subscribed this paper at Big Spring, this twenty-first day of March, in the year of our Lord, one thousand, seven hundred and eighty-six."

John McKeehan.	John Reid.
Samuel McCormick.	John Hodge, Sr.
Hugh Laughlin.	William Duncan.
David Ralston.	James Irwine.
Robert Patterson.	John Brown.
John Bell.	John O'Neal.
S. Cunningham.	William Douglass.
James Graham.	Alexander Officer.
Hugh Patton.	James Officer.
Margaret McKean.	Thomas Espey.
Jno. Ewing.	James Gillespie.
Solomon Lightcap.	Samuel Hawthorn.
William Giffen.	James Robinston.
Robert Bovard.	Alexander Leckey.
William Hodge.	John McFarland.
Charles Leiper.	Richard Woods.
Wm. McFarlane.	James Johnson.

Robert Bell.
Alex. Laughlin.
Sam'l. Finley.
Samuel Blair.
Thomas Jacob.
Thomas Buchanan.
Joseph McKibben.
John Allison.
John Bell.
Jos. Pollock.
Jas. Laughlin.
Robert Hutchison.
Atchison Laughlin.
John Mitchell.
Samuel Mathers.
William Wilson.
Francis Donald.
James McQuon.
James Wilson.
George Little.
John Brown.
Jarmon Jacobs.
John Davidson.
Alexander Thompson.
Robert Shannon.
Joseph Parks.
William McCracken.

Samuel Lindsay.
Matthew Wilson.
William Lindsay.
John Whiten, Jr.
Elizabeth McCullough.
Thomas Grier.
Ann Browster.
John Lusk.
David Lusk.
William Lusk.
Alexander McBride, Jr.
William Milligan.
Agnes Irwine.
William Hunter.
William Walker.
Robert Walker.
Robert Patterson.
James Turner.
Adam Bratton.
Joseph Walker.
William Hunter.
James Huston.
Catherine Brown.
Margaret McClure.
James Armstrong.
Jared Graham.
Margaret McFarland.

SUBSCRIBERS TO THE SALARY OF REV. SAMUEL WILSON.

"Big Spring, Cumberland Co. Pa., March 21, 1786. We, the subscribers of this paper and members of the Presbyterian Congregation of Big Spring, do hereby bind and oblige ourselves to pay annually to Mr. Samuel Wilson, preacher of the gospel, on his being ordained to be our minister, and while he shall discharge the duties of the said office, the sum of one hundred and fifty pounds, Pennsylvania Currency in specie. We will also allow him the use of the house and glebe possessed by our former minister, with sufficient security for the payment of the above sum during his incumbency."

	£.	s.	d.
Alexander Laughlin,	1	10	
John Davidson,	1	15	
Robert Shannon,	1	5	
David Williamson,	1	10	
Thomas Buchanan,	1	5	
Alexander Thompson,	1	10	
James Jack,	1	5	
William Denning,	1		
Andrew Bell,	1	10	
John Allison,		15	
Robert Patterson,	1	10	
David Ralston,	1	10	
John McKeehan,	1	5	
Hugh Laughlin,	1	10	
John Bell,	1		
Jeremiah McKibben,	1		
James Graham,	1	10	
Joseph Parks,	1		
Charles Luper,	1	15	
George McKeehan,	1	5	
Hugh Patton,	1	10	

	£.	s.	d.
Margaret McKean,		10	
William Giffin,		15	
William Hodge,	1	5	
Alexander McKeehan,	1		
William McCracken,	1	10	
William McFarlane,	1	10	
Samuel McCormick,	1	5	
William Laughlin,	1	15	
Thomas Jacob,	1		
Andrew Walker,		15	
Rannuel Blair,	1	3	
Samuel Findley,	1	10	
S. Cunningham,	1		
Jno. Ewing,	1		
Robert Bovard,		10	
Hannah Bovard,		10	
Solomon Lightcap,	1	5	
Jas. Pollock,	1		
Jas. Laughlin,	1	10	
Atchison Laughlin,	1		
Robert Hutchison,	1		
John Mitchell,		7	6
Samuel Mathers,	1	5	
Jarmon Jacobs,	1		
John Reed,		15	
John Hodge, Sr.		5	
William Duncan,		8	6
James Irvine,	3		
John Brown,	2		

MEMBERS RECEIVED INTO THE BIG SPRING PRESBYTERIAN CHURCH BY THE REV. SAMUEL WILSON.

PRESBYTERIAN CHURCH.

This list is not complete as it does not begin until four years after he was installed pastor of the church.

JUNE 1791.

Samuel Anderson and William McNicholas admitted from Ireland.

Isaac Shannon.
Jean Shannon.
Margaret McFarlane.
Jennie Adams.
John Connelly.
Thomas Glenn.

Alexander Glenn.
Jean Glenn.
John Laughlin.
Margaret Carson.
Ann Espey.
Ruth Hamilton.

SEP. 29, 1791.

Martha Ewing.
Samuel Fenton.
John Parks.
Eleanor Reid.
John Boyd.
Jean Ewing.
Ann Fenton.

Mary Morrison.
Katherine Jacob.
William Porterfield.
Mary Walker.
Robert Morrison.
John Reid.
John Adams.

MAY 23, 1792.

Joseph Gourd.
Isabel Anderson.
Robert Officer.
Margaret Gourd.

Mary Laughlin.
David Officer.
John Anderson.
Mary Mathers.

OCT. 18, 1792.

F. Work.
Robert Sterrit.
Mrs. Sterrit, his wife.
A. Elliott.
James Fenton.

Jennie Hannon.
Hugh Bryson.
Daughter of John Purdy.
Hannah Carson.
Mary Laughlin.

MAY 29, 1793.

Gabriel McKimins.
John Carson, Jr.

Rosanna McFarlane.
Peggy Johnson.

John Patton.
Hezekiah Patton.

OCT. 19, 1793.

Sidney Forhner.
Betsy McKeehan.
Martha Gillespie.
Daughter of W. Ewing.
Katherine Forhner.
Jennie Johnson.
Alexander Work.

Samuel Moyer and wife.
Elizabeth Martin.
Betsy McFarlane.
Nathaniel Gillespie.
Rosanna Work.
Jared Martin, Jr.

MAY 1794.

Robert Gillespie.
George Gillespie.
Thomas Jacob.
Elizabeth Jacob.
M. Thompson.
Mary Johnson.
Eliz. Sterrit.
Jane McCormick.
Mary Wilson.
James Patton.
Saml. Emit.
Robert Johnson.
John Shannon.

Mary Shannon.
Margaret Shannon.
Joseph Shannon.
Jane McKinsey.
Mary Shannon.
Samuel Bryson.
Sarah McEntire.
Thomas McCormick.
James Lindsey and wife.
Joseph McCormick.
———McGoffine.
Major Finley.
Polly Finley.

SEPT. 30, 1794.

Matthew Laughlin.
Phebe Laughlin.
Priscilla Forhner.
Mary Forhner.
Jean Blain.

James Moor.
Martha Adams.
Rob. Kilgore and wife.
James McGoffine.

MAY 20, 1795.

Thomas Morton and wife, Joseph Morton and wife,

PRESBYTERIAN CHURCH.

Miss Ramsey, James Purdy.

OCT. 20, 1795.

Mary Pollock, Ruth Cook, Nancy Hughs, wife of Alex. Glenn.

JUNE 8, 1796.

Mary Green.
Adam Wilson.
Andrew Taylor.
Hugh Thompson.
Samuel Thompson.
Margaret McKeehan.
Elizabeth Espy.

John Davidson.
Elizabeth Davidson.
Elizabeth Geddes.
Dr. John Geddes.
Nancy Roberts.
Sam. Lightcap and wife.
Obadiah Patterson and wife.

OCT. 1796.

Betsy Work.
Susanna Work.
Nancy Brown.
Alexander Thompson.
Leary McCormick.
Peggy Thompson.
David Williamson.

Tamar Williamson.
Nancy Shannon.
Daniel McGuire.
Theo. McClure.
Ginny Bell.
Susanna Hutchison.
Martha Hutchison.

JUNE 14, 1797.

Elizabeth Johnson.   Samuel McElheny.

OCT. 25, 1797.

Mrs. Isaiah Graham.   Jenny Eliot.

AUG. 29, 1798.

James Montgomery.
Wm. Connely and wife.
John Green.
Sally Green.
Mary Ramsey.
John Peeples and wife.
Nancy Douglas.

Mrs. Bryson.
Elizabeth Espey.
Robt. Peeples and wife.
Isaiah Graham.

A PETITION FOR THE ELECTION OF AN ELDER.

"To the Rev. Samuel Wilson and the session of the Big Spring Congregation.

The humble petition of the subscribers showeth that in consequence of the death of Mr. John Lusk, elder of this quarter, we were, and still continue to be in want of such a guardian to preside over us as a ruling elder. We therefore petition your honors to grant us your consent to nominate and appoint one of our number for our elder. And in consequence of our return of an elder your wisdoms will be pleased to confirm our choice, if no legal objections appear to hinder. And your petitioners as in duty will ever pray &c.

James Ramsey.
Nathan Ramsey.
Thomas Woods.
Andrew Huston.
Samuel Woods.
William Woods, Jr.
Alexander McBride, Jr.
William Gladen.
Andrew Browster.
William Browster.
John Huston.
Thomas Norton.
Archibald McCullough.
Joseph Turner.
John Turner.
William Roan.
Nathaniel Eckels.
William Lusk."

* * * * * * *

"To The Rev. Mr. Wilson :—Reverend Sir,

I enclose you the petition of the Southern part of the Big Spring Congregation, with a desire that they should be heard, and if so it will be convenient for the quarter to meet at the house of Mr. James Ramsey to have the election, and the sooner the better with conveniency. This from your sincere friend, Alexander McBride, Jr.

Dec. 10, 1789."

PROCEEDINGS OF A MEETING OF SESSION.

"The session of the Big Spring Congregation seriously affected on the one hand with the declining state of religion, the decay of real piety, and on the other with the prevalence of vice and profanity, view it as a matter truly distressing the many professors of Christ's holy religion who attend upon the distinguishing ordinances of his church manifest such a disposition to encourage balls and other criminal amusements. Also that they allow themselves in drunkenness, in the profanation of God's name, in various species of gambling, a neglect of family worship, as well as attending upon the public means of grace, and notwithstanding live in the belief that they have a continued right to the sealing ordinances of the church and are offended if these are refused to them. Session, very sensible that there is a fault in such conduct, and not desirous to clear themselves, afraid that a charge of unfaithfulness to God and the souls of men should justly fall on them lest they partake in the sins of others, unanimously agree to endeavor a reformation in these things. They know well that wherever the fault may lie it is not in the discipline of the church which makes all the errors enumerated censurable, but rather in a lack of discipline among ourselves. In order to a reform, they are assured that some change must take place with respect to the mode of admission. They have no doubt that the evil in many cases may be traced to a delicacy in members with persons applying on the Sabbath for the baptism of children. If reports have been in circulation unfavorable to Christian character, there is then little time or opportunity to inquire into them, and it has been feared that if persons were then kept back, offense would be taken, and no doubt reports are sometimes groundless. To prevent then the growing evil and the prostitution of holy ordinances, the members of session respectively engage that they will use every lawful means which belongs to their office in order to a knowledge of those who are members of their own district, that they will not recommend any one chargeable with any of the glaring crimes above taken notice of. It is unanimously agreed in session that in the future that any persons who have in view to attend upon the ordinances of baptism some time before, signify their intention to the member of session in the district in which he lives, or if there be no member of session in the district, the one most convenient, so that the member previous to his recommending him may have an opportunity of conversing with him before he recommends him, and that the blessing of God may succeed this attempt for the reformation of this society, upon whose account it is essayed, is the earnest prayer of the respective members."

MEMBERS AND ADHERENTS OF THE BIG SPRING CHURCH, 1789.

About 1789 Rev. Samuel Wilson made lists of members and adherents of the church dividing them into districts, and over each district, an elder was placed. The lists give the ages of the persons, and states whether they were in communion, not in communion, and whether they were baptized. The communicant members of the church are shown in these lists by a star following a name. There is no date attached to the lists, but comparing the ages given of persons whose ages we positively know, we feel quite safe in saying, the lists were made in 1789. Dating back from that time, the number of years given to each person, will give about the year in which they were born.

One of the duties of the elder, was, to visit the people and catechise them. Questions having been previously prepared by the pastor and given to the members to commit to memory, or, at least to obtain a correct understanding of them. These visitations of the elder were made annually.

JOHN CARSON'S DISTRICT.   QUESTIONS AND MEMBERS.

1. Who was the penman of the Book of Genesis? When is it generally thought to have been written, and what length of time does that history contain?

2. What are the principal doctrines and events recorded in this book?

3. What do you understand by creation, and is it a work peculiar to God only?

4. What seems to be the order of creation, and what was the work of each day?

5. What are those called who do not acknowledge divine revelation? What objections do they offer against Moses and his writings, and how are their arguments confuted?

6. What rational arguments can be offered in favor of Moses, that his mission was from God and that his writings were of divine inspiration?

7. What scripture prophesies have been fulfilled and what are at present fulfilling or yet to be fulfilled?

28 THE BIG SPRING

These with the ninth chapter of the Confession of Faith to be examined upon.

Robert Mickie	68, *	Mary McGuffine	7,
Agnes Mickie	64, *	Robert McGuffine	4,
David Mickie	22,	William Leman	*
Elenor Mickie	20,	Samuel Leman	7,
Hannah Mickie	18,	Martha Leman	29, *
Phillis, a negro.		William Leman	5,
Thomas E. Fullerton	21,	James Johnston	23,
Isabel Fullerton	18,	Margaret Johnston	22,
John Ackman	30,	Robert Johnston	20, *
Mary Ackman	28,	William Auld	30, *
Elenor Laughlin	70, *	Christiana Auld	25, *
Matthew Laughlin	30,	Mary Auld	7,
Paul Laughlin	27,	Martha Ewing	70,
Doctor Laughlin	24,	Samuel Findlay	35,
Peggy McCune	17,	James Denny	21,
Samuel McCune	16,	William McCracken	35,
John McCune	12,	Elizabeth McCracken	*
William M. Flin	7,	Betsy Peoples	16,
Isabel McCune	50, *	Robert Peoples	14,
Robert McCune	17,	Martha McCracken	9,
Rebecca Parks	13,	Jenny McCracken	7,
William Parks	11,	Jonathan, a Negro,	
David Parks	9,	Prudence Farhner	19,
Priscilla Carson	35, *	Robert Mickie	45,
Elisha Carson	20,	Isamiah Mickie	35,
John Carson	18,	Andrew Mickie	12,
Hannah Carson	16,	Mary Mickie	10,
Joseph McGuffine	32,	Thomas Mickie	7,
Jane McGuffine	27, *	John Smith	20,
William McGuffine	9,	Jonathan Kilgore	27,

Ruth Kilgore	22,	John Caldwell	20, *
John Caldwell a member of session.		Elizabeth Caldwell	
		Samuel Caldwell	14,
Anne Caldwell	45, *	Ann Caldwell	12,
James Caldwell			
Families,			24
Persons in full Communion,		.	14

WILLIAM LINDSAY'S DISTRICT. QUESTIONS AND MEMBERS.

1. What are the different kinds of faith taken notice of in the scripture?

2. What are the marks by which true faith is distinguished from all other kinds?

3. Whither does saving faith lie in assent or consent?

4. What reason would you assign why no actions are acceptable to God, but such as flow from faith?

5. Will it then follow, that wicked and unregenerate persons, may as well transgress the law of God, as endeavor the observance of it?

6. Must we turn from sin in order to come to Christ by faith?

7. Seeing faith is the act of the believing soul, in what sense then, is it said to be the gift of God?

These, with the eighth chapter of the Confession of Faith, to be examined upon at John Woods' Wednesday, Dec. 30th.

William Hunter	60, *	David Shannon	55, *
Jane Hunter	60, *	Sarah Shannon	47, *
John McIntire		Lenard Shannon	21,
Sally McIntire	18,	Samuel Shannon	19,
Joseph Hunter	14,	Patty Cowley	8,

William Warrington	9,	Rachel Mills	24, *
William Walker	50, *	Gabriel Glen	50,
Jane Walker	50, *	William Glen	9,
Elizabeth Walker	25,	Jenny Glen	7,
James Walker	19,	Jared Graham	24,
William Walker	18,	Jenny Graham	20,
Rachel Walker	16,	John Brown	55, *
Jane Walker	15,	Martha Brown	50, *
Samuel Walker	10,	Mary Brown	20, *
Joseph Walker	45, *	John Brown	18,
Rachel Walker	40, *	William Brown	15,
Mary Walker	18,	Agnes Brown	16,
Elizabeth Walker	16,	James Brown	11,
Jane Walker	12,	James McGovern	35,
Isabel Walker	9,	Ann McGovern	20,
Hannah Walker	7,	Mary McGovern	8,
James Walker	6,	Francis Donnel	
Andrew Walker	40,	George Lightel	
Mary Walker	38, *	Sarah Lightel	
James Walker	18, *	William Hunter	50, *
Joseph Walker	11,	Jane Hunter	50, *
Jane Walker	9,	James Hunter	17,
Betsy Walker	7,	Agnes Hunter	17,
Robert Walker	56, *	William Hunter	15,
Margaret Walker	50, *	Lathie Hunter	13,
Mary Walker	19,	Jane Hunter	11,
John Walker	17,	Lathie Wilson	
Elizabeth Walker	14,	John McTeer	23, *
Margaret Walker	8,	Agnes McTeer	20, *
Robert Walker	6,	Adam Brattan	35,
Gabriel Glen	55, *	Martha Brattan	9,
Jane Glen	40, *	John Gilmore	

PRESBYTERIAN CHURCH. 31

William Wilson	60, *	David Ewing	24, *
Mary Wilson	59, *	Elizabeth Ewing	22,
Samuel Wilson	25,	James Graham	60,
Mary Wilson	20,	Susannah Graham	45,
Margaret Sayers	17,	Thomas Graham	21,
James Wilson	27,	Arthur Graham	19,
Margaret Wilson	22, *	Isaiah Graham	18,
William Giffin	35, *	James Graham	14,
Elenor Giffin	30, *	Elizabeth Moor	18,
Betsy Giffin	11,	Margaret Moor	12,
Sally Giffin	5,	Robert Boyd	16,
Joseph Pollock	30,	Margaret McFarlane	55, *
Mary Pollock	28,	Robert McFarlane	22,
Thomas Jacob	30,	Ann McFarlane	19,
Elizabeth Jacob	27,	Mary McFarlane	16,
Elenor Jacob	12,	Elizabeth McFarlane	13,
Mary Jacob	9,	Hannah McFarlane	10,
William Patton	25,	William Brisby	40, *
Mary Patton	25,	Sarah Brisby	35, *
William Ferguson		Nancy Brisby	13,
James Marshbank	25,	Betsy Brisby	12.
William Patton	80, *	William Brisby	10
Janet Patton	78, *	John Brisby	8,
John Patton	30,	Elizabeth Wilson	70, *
William Patton	27.	Matthew Wilson	28,
Margaret Patton	25,	Prudence Penwell	16,
William Devinport	23,	Joseph Edmonston	25,
Robert Patton	12,	Agnes Edmonston	22,
Samuel Bayle	30,	Adam Conelly	17,
Martha Bayle	25,	James McFarlane	27,
Horace Brattan	17,	Elizabeth McFarlane	23,
Anne Brattan	15,	Ceasar and Dick,	

THE BIG SPRING

James Johnson	30, *	Joseph Woods	14,
Martha Johnson	28, *	Adam Hays	86,
Peggy Johnson	10,	Joseph Hays	23,
Jenny Johnson	6,	Anne Hays	18,
Samuel Lindsy	60, *	John Green	16,
Nancy Lindsy	55,	Nancy Allen	13,
Samuel Lindsy		Patrick Gibson	*
Robert Lindsy		Martha Gibson	*
Jenny Lindsy	20,	James Connelly	22,
Nancy Lindsy	16,	William Connelly	20,
William Lindsy	27,	Elizabeth Connelly	18,
Jane Lindsy		Charity Connelly	17,
Robert Huston	50,	Joseph Means	26, *
Martha Huston	50, *	Nancy Means	24, *
Nancy Huston	20,	John McFarlane	60,
Peggy Huston	18,	Elizabeth McFarlane	50,
John Espy	20, *	Sarah McFarlane	20,
William Clark	24, *	James McFarlane	16,
John Love	27,	Robert McFarlane	14,
Margaret Love	25,	Andrew McFarlane	14,
James Love	25,	Thomas Buchanan	30,
Thomas Love	22,	Agnes Buchanan	28,
William Clark	67, *	Robert Buchanan	8,
Agnes Clark	*	William Buchannan	6,
John Clark	13,	Jenny McClellan	14,
John Woods	80, *	William McFarlane	56,
Jane Woods	80, *	Elizabeth McFarlane	50,
Richard Woods	27,	David Murray	22,
Isabel Woods	35,	Anne McClellan	16,
Robert Woods	25,	James Hall	9,
Polly Woods	18,		
Families,			44.

JOHN BELL'S DISTRICT.   QUESTIONS AND MEMBERS.

1. What do you understand by creation? Is it a work peculiar to God?

2. How will you prove from scripture and reason, in opposition to Aristotle and others, that the world is not eternal?

3. How will you prove both from scripture and reason, that the world neither came by chance, nor yet made itself?

4. How will you defend the Mosaic account, which asserts, that the world has not existed 6000 years, against ancient history, which tells us of Egyptian records for more than thirteen thousand years, and the Babylonians, speak of things done four hundred and seventy thousand years before, and the Chinese tell of things, still longer done.

The third chapter of the Confession of Faith also to be examined upon.

Elleanor Gillespie	67,	Mary Johnston	14,
Geo. Gillespie (absent)	25,	John Johnston,	10,
James Gorly	7,	Jane Johnston	8,
Sal, a negro,		James Johnston	5,
James Gillespie	38,	Robert Dunbar	*
Jane Gillespie	30,	Samuel Wilson	26,
William Gillespie	7,	Samuel Hawthorn	32, *
Mat. M. Gillespie	5,	Margaret Hawthorn	28, *
John Talbart	10,	James Hawthorn	9, *
Rebecca Armstrong	50 *	George Kelsy	60,
James Johnston	78, *	Elizabeth Kelsy	28, *
James Johnston	38, *	Jane Kelsy	20,
Alexander Johnston	16,	George Kelsy	22,

Elizabeth Bell	52, *	Jennet McClure	25,
Katharine Brown	50, *	Hannah Anderson	23,
Robert Bell	24, *	Margaret McClure	19,
Jane Bell	22,	Andrew McClure	21,
William Bell	24,	James Laird	34, *
Joseph Bell	17,	Jane Laird	24, *
George Bell	15,	Joseph Halbert	20,
John Bell	13,	John O'Neil	40, *
Thomas Bell	12,	Thomas Espey	50, *
Katharine Bell	10,	Ann Espey	42, *
Alexander Officer	60, *	Margaret Espey	20, *
Mary Officer	67, *	William Espey	18, *
James Officer	36, *	Rachel Espey	16,
Mary Officer	30, *	Ann Espey	13,
Jane Gordon	19,	Robert Espey	11,
Katharine Gray	20,	Elizabeth Espey	9,
Samuel Miller	17,	James Espey	7,
William Douglas	47, *	Robert McClure	55, *
Mary Douglas	41, *	Margaret McClure	20,
Margaret Douglas	16,	Nancy McClure	16,
Agnes Douglas	14,	Robert McClure	14,
John Douglas	12,	Mary McClure	12,
Mary Douglas	10,	Betsy McClure	7,
William Douglas	7,	Alexander Leckey	26, *
Margaret McClure	55,	Elizabeth Leckey	29, *

    Families, 16.
    In full communion, 27.
    Total number of persons. 79.

ROBERT PATTERSON'S DISTRICT.

This was called the Yellow Breeches district, and

PRESBYTERIAN CHURCH.

extended south from the turnpike, to the Yellow Breeches Creek, east, to the Cumberland Furnace, on the Yellow Breeches, and west to Jacksonville.

QUESTIONS AND MEMBERS.

1. What description would you give of Heaven?
2. Upon what is the believers' title to Heaven founded?
3. Has God promised Heaven to believers absolutely, or does he require conditions on their part?
4. Can believers under the new covenant dispensation, who have once a right to Heaven, by their misconduct, lose it and forfeit their right?
5. Is the doctrine of the saints perseverance founded on scripture? If so, how will you prove it, and defend the doctrine against those who deny it?
6. How will you make it appear from scripture and experience, that there is no such thing as sinless perfection in this life?
7. Seeing Heaven is an holy place, and nothing unclean can enter into it at any time, then are believers made completely holy and fitted for Heaven?

These, with the sixth chapter of the Confession of Faith to be examined upon.

Thomas Glen	60, *	Deborah Patterson	18,
Elizabeth Glen	54, *	Daniel Kelly	30, *
Thomas Glen	21,	Elizabeth Kelly	36, *
Alexander Glen	19,	Christian Kelly	50, *
John Glen	17,	William Kelly	16,
Sarah Patterson	60, *	Ann Kelly	14,
Obediah Patterson	25,	Richard Kelly	12,
Zacheus Patterson	20,	James Houston	70, *

THE BIG SPRING

John Huston	24,	Mary Woods,	20,
Andrew Huston	22,	Mat, a negro.	
Sarah Huston	26, *	William Woods	25, *
Jane Huston	18,	Jane Woods	22, *
Thomas Norton	40,	Nathan Woods	8,
Sarah Norton	36,	Samuel Goodling	15,
Betsy Norton	9,	John Mitchel	10,
Thomas Norton	7,	Janet Ramsey	60, *
Elizabeth McCulloch	56, *	Nathan Ramsey	25, *
James McCulloch	20,	Mary Ramsey	13, *
Robert McCulloch	12,	Agnes Ramsey	17,
Rosian Adair	8,	Elizabeth Ramsey	16,
William Wagstas	30,	Margaret Ramsey	14,
Charity Wagstas	19,	Alexander McBride	26,
Agnes Irwin	70, *	Tabitha McBride	24,
Thomas Grier	35, *	Mary Patterson	60, *
Jane Grier	25, *	Esther Patterson	20,
Ann Browster	60, *	Ann Patterson	18,
William Browster	25,	Sarah Patterson	16,
Alexander Browster	22,	Elizabeth Patterson	14,
Mary Carithers	28, *	Thomas Patterson	12,
Charles McConel	56, *	Robert Johnston	30,
Isabel McConel	46, *	Ann Johnston	35,
Eleanor McConel	17,	Margaret Harper	28,
Martha McConel	16,	John Lemon	45, *
Mary McConel	13,	Elizabeth Lemon	35, *
Jenny McConel	10,	Jane Lemon	14,
John McConel	7,	Nancy Lemon	12,
William Woods	60, *	Polly Lemon	10,
Samuel Woods	26,	Robert Fowler	30,
Jenny Woods	24,	Elizabeth Fowler	19,
John Woods	22,	John Fowler	23,

PRESBYTERIAN CHURCH.   37

William Ewing	40, *	Jane Ewing	44, *
Jane Ewing	35, *	Thomas Ewing	16,
Nancy Ewing	14,	Rebecca Ewing	14,
Robert Ewing	9,	Anna Ewing	11,
William Ewing	7,	James Ewing	7,
Alexander Ewing	5,	Thomas Adams	30, *
Katharine Crawford	12,	Agnes Adams	28, *
Thomas Ewing	45, *	Jenny Adams	14,
Mariana Ewing	40, *	Samuel Adams	10,
John Ewing	15,	Richard Adams	7,
Rebecca Ewing	6,	David McCurdy	60, *
Alexander Clark	12,	Mrs. McCurdy	57, *
Elenor Reigh	60, *	James McCurdy,	25,
Samuel Reigh		Mary Morris	*
Mary Reigh	16,	David McCurdy	20,
Joseph Gourd	25,	Janet McCurdy	19,
Margaret Gourd	24,	Nancy Lowry	18,
Nancy Homes		Adam Clelland	35, *
John McCurdy	20,	Jane Clelland	45, *
Elizabeth McCurdy	24,	John Calvert	20,
Joseph Van Horn	30, *	Eleo Galbraith	9,
Annie Van Horn	25,	William Appleby	35, *
John Ewing	50, *	Nancy Appleby	28, *
Sarah Ewing	48, *	Eliza Appleby	14,
Jane Ewing	22,	J. Appleby	12,
William Ewing	20,	Jane Appleby	10,
Martha Ewing	18,	John Appleby	9,
Matthew Ewing	16,	James Leeper	45, *
Mary Ewing	12,	Mary Leeper	40, *
James Ewing	10,	Allen Leeper	16,
Rebecca Ewing	8,	Martha Leeper	13,
James Ewing	52, *	James Leeper	11,

Sally Leeper	9,	William Hunter	23,
Jack, a mulatto.		Elizabeth Hunter	21,
Families,			33.
Persons in full communion,			46.
Total number of persons,			148.

ROBERT LUSK'S DISTRICT.

Robert Lusk, was one of five brothers, who emigrated from Ireland at an early date, and settled in this vicinity. He bought a farm in Mifflin township, known as the "Fountain of Health Farm," which had been warranted to Andrew McElwain, about 1730. Robert Lusk married Martha McClure of Adams County.

QUESTIONS AND ANSWERS.

1. Upon what account was the feast of pentecost observed, and what remarkable things happened at that time?

2. What were the different laws God gave to His people, and what were their various uses?

3. Why are the ten commandments called the moral law?

4. With what different forms hath God clothed the moral law?

5. What do you understand by the law of nature?

6. What do you understand by the law as a covenant of works?

7. What do you understand by the law as a rule of life?

These, with the seventh chapter of the Confession of Faith, to be examined upon.

Mary Sterret	80, *	David Sterret	50, *

PRESBYTERIAN CHURCH.

Rachel Sterret	48, *	Robert McElwain	22,
Robert Sterret	24,	Elizabeth McElwain	20,
Bryce I. Sterret	22,	John Paten	50, *
David Sterret	20,	Francis Paten	*
Elizabeth Sterret	18,	William Paten	20, *
John Sterret	16,	James Paten	18,
William Sterret	10,	John Paten	16,
Elizabeth McMullan	8,	Joseph Paten	14,
Sandon, a negro.		Mary Paten	12,
Ned, a negro.		Thomas Paten	9,
Andrew Patterson	35, *	Robert Paten	7,
Mary Patterson	*	Fanny Paten	7,
Jane Patterson	15,	Joseph Shannon	25,
Nathan Patterson	13,	Mary Shannon	26,
Samuel Patterson	11,	John Morrow	30, *
James Patterson	9,	Hannah Morrow	29, *
Sarah Patterson	8,	Mary Morrow	8,
William Stephenson	40, *	David Ramsey	110, *
Jane Stephenson	33, *	Sarah Ramsey	13,
Elizabeth Stephenson	12,	Anne Ramsey	11,
James Stevenson	10,	Margaret Ramsey	9,
James McElwain	37, *	Mary Ramsey	7,
Mary McElwain	12,	David Ramsey	5,
John McElwain	10,	Robert Lusk	27, *
Ruth McElwain	7,	Martha Lusk	21, *
Andrew McElwain	33, *	Jane Lusk	4,
Elizabeth McElwain	30, *	Thomas Martin	
Elizabeth Mason	17,	Mary Martin	25,
Mary McElwain	8,	Rosanna Martin	18,
Robert McElwain	7,	John Martin	16,
Jane McElwain	5,	Jane Martin	14,
Mary McElwain	70,	James Hamilton	*

George Hamilton		* Betsy Johnson	
Ruth Hamilton		Robert Bell	48, *
Andrew Bell	40,	Jane Bell	49, *
Betsy Bell	13,	Walter Bell	16,
Samuel Bell	10,	William Bell	15,
Matty Bell	7,	David Bell	13,
John Bell	17,	Peggy Bell	11,
John McClure	17,		
Families,			16.
In full communion,			22.
Total number of persons,			81.

SAMUEL M'CORMICK'S DISTRICT.

Samuel M'Cormick, was born 1726, and died Sept. 4th, 1803. He married Eliza Bowman, who was born 1727, and died Oct. 7th, 1811, He settled in Mifflin Township, prior to 1781. He first purchased the farm, now known as the Asper farm. This he sold, and bought from William McFarlane, the farm below Doubling Gap, on which he died, now owned by W. H. McCrea. That he was greatly concerned for his own, and the spiritual welfare of the people over which he had charge, is evinced by his many letters to his pastor, on these subjects.

LIST OF MEMBERS.

Isabella Hall	67 *	John Montroe	62, *
Ruth Cook	14,	Mary Ann Montroe	31, *
John Reed	50, *	Margaret Montroe	14,
Sarah Reed	34, *	William Montroe	9,
Elizabeth Long	10,	Reuben Montroe	6,
Samuel Lowry	9,	Sarah Denison	84, *

PRESBYTERIAN CHURCH. 41

Martha French	45, *	Isaac Durbara	50, *
Thomas Mathers	54, *	Jane Durbara	20, *
Mary Mathers	50, *	Reuben Durbara	20,
Margaret Mathers	20,	John Durbara	18,
William Mathers	18,	Alexander McClin-	
Jane Mathers	16,	tock	40, *
Mary Fenton	80, *	Sarah McClintock	39, *
Samuel Fenton	40,	David Dougherty	19, *
Ann Fenton	30,	John Stars	19, *
James Fenton	13,	Elizabeth Palm	11, *
Robert Fenton	11,	James Brannan	40,
Samuel Fenton	9,	Mary Brannan	19,
John Fenton	7,	John Brannan	16,
Andrew Thompson	40, *	Thomas Brannan	12,
Mary Thompson	40, *	William Brannan	9,
Mary Ann Thompson	18,	John McFarlane	50, *
Hugh Thompson	16,	Mary McFarlane	50, *
Samuel Thompson	14,	James McFarlane	26,
Hannah Thompson	12,	Margaret McFarlane	24,
Andrew Thompson	10,	Elizabeth McFarlane	15,
James W. Thompson	8,	John McFarlane	13,
James Walker	26, *	Alexander McFarlane	11,
Jane Walker	25, *	Ann McFarlane	10,
George Taylor	60,	William McFarlane	8,
Elenor Taylor	55,	John Shannon	33,
George Taylor	24,	Agnes Shannon	30,
Nancy Taylor	20,	Mary Shannon	12,
James Patterson	40, *	Ann Shannon	11,
Mary Patterson	38, *	Andrew Shannon	9,
Nancy Patterson	15,	Sarah Shannon	7,
Thomas Patterson	12,	John Wallace	32,
Robert Patterson	10,	Elizabeth Wallace	30,

William Mophet	36, *	Nelly Gallespie	10,
Rebecca Mophet	38, *	Grace, a negro.	
Jane Mophet	12,	Nathaniel Gallespie	33,
Phoebe Mophet	10,	Martha Gallespie	32,
Thomas Barnes	70,	Millie Gallespie	10,
Grizel Barnes	55, *	Mary Gallespie	8,
Margaret Barnes	27,	Ann Gallespie	6,
David Barnes	20,	Thomas Pennel	16,
Robert Barnes	17,	Sarah Majoirs	45,
Elizabeth McCormick,		Elizabeth Majoirs	21,
wife of the elder	60, *	Isaac Majoirs	11,
Joseph McCormick	23,	Nancy Majoirs	9,
Thomas McCormick	21,	Hugh Ramsey	30,
Ann McCormick	18, *	Margaret Ramsey	25, *
Jane McCormick	16,	John Mitchel	25, *
John Purdie	40, *	Margaret Mitchel	
Margaret Purdie	40, *	Samuel Mitchel	35, *
Thomas Purdie	18,	Mary Mitchel	34, *
James Purdie	14,	John Mitchel	14,
Rachel Purdie	12,	Ezekiel Mitchel	11,
Mary Purdie	10,	James Mitchel	7,
John Purdie	8,	Alexander Elliott	35, *
Robert Gallespie	45,	Agnes Elliott	35, *
Elizabeth Gallespie	40,	Jannet Elliott	13,
William Gallespie	19,	Mary Elliott	10,
Samuel Gallespie	14,	Catharine Elliott	8,
Nancy Gallespie	12,		

In full communion, 38.
Total number of persons, 123.

DAVID RALSTON'S DISTRICT.

David Ralston, was a son of Andrew Ralston, who

settled, 1728, on the farm now owned by Mrs. Parker, opposite the Newville station. David was one of five children, and came into possession of his father's farm, where he lived until 1806, when he moved to Westmoreland County, and died near Greensburg, 1810. He was twice married, first to a Miss Scott, second to Miss Elizabeth McClintock. Both wives died at Big Spring. By his first wife, David Ralston had issue: Elizabeth married Thomas Jacob; Jane married, first, a Mr. McDonald, and secondly, a Mr. Taylor; Elenor married a Mr. Miller; James married Ruth Carson; Andrew married Miss Kirkpatrick. By his second wife David Ralston had issue: Agnes married a Mr. Allsworth; Margaret married a Mr. Moorhead; Ann married Mr. Banks; Mary unmarried; Sarah unmarried; David married Lacy McAllister.

LIST OF MEMBERS.

John Brown	40,	John Turner	60,	*
Elizabeth Brown	38,	Mary Turner	56,	*
Adam Brown	18,	Joseph Turner	20,	
Mary Brown	16,	Sally Turner	6,	
Margaret Brown	14,	Thomas Moore	60,	
Elizabeth Brown	12,	Saml. Moore		
Hannah Brown	10,	John Mitchel		
Joseph Brown	8,	Lacy Mitchel		
Ann Brown	6,	Jennet Mathers	50,	*
William Smith	32, *	Samuel Mathers	35,	*
Sarah Smith	30, *	Isabella Mathers	33,	*
Robert Smith		John Mathers	12,	
John Smith		Thomas Mathers	10,	
Elizabeth Smith		Joseph Mathers	25,	
Mary Smith		Eleanor Mathers	23,	

THE BIG SPRING

Robert Hutchison	50, *	Rosannah Hutchison,	18,
Mary Hutchison	48, *	Martha Hutchison	16,
Nancy Hutchison	14,	Mary Laughlin	*
Robert Hutchison	12,	Margaret McKein	35, *
Mary Hutchison	10,	William McKein	19,
Walter, a negro.		Mary McKein	17,
John Adams	27,	Elizabeth McKein	14,
Jenny Adams	20,	Mary Patton	30, *
Elizabeth Ralston,		Elizabeth McEntire	28, *
wife of the elder	45, *	James Mitchel	50, *
Nancy Ralston	14,	Mary Mitchel	48, *
Margaret Ralston	12,	Eve Mitchel	
Amy Ralston	10,	Elizabeth Mitchel	
Mary Ralston	8,	Rebecca Mitchel	13,
Sally Ralston	7,	James Mitchel	9,
David Ralston	5,	Mary Mitchel	7,
John Reed	20,	William Duncan	26,
Eleanor Reed	25,	Margaret Duncan	23,
Sally Reed	7,	Charity Davis	12,
Grant, a negro.		James Irwin	
John Hodge	81, *	Isabel Irwin	
Agnes Hodge	60, *	John Irwin	
William Laughlin	69,	Mary Irwin	
Mary Laughlin	48,	Mary Irwin	
James Laughlin	17,	Eleanor Irwin	
John Laughlin	15,	Caleb Ardiler	30,
William Laughlin	9,	Jane Ardiler	28,
Rachel, a negro.		Francis Morris	9,
Catherine Atchison		Garman Jacobs	29,
Atchison Laughlin	*	Katherine Jacobs	24,

Families, 14
Persons in full communion, 19

PRESBYTERIAN CHURCH.   45

Persons not in communion,   70.
Total number of persons,   89.

HUGH LAUGHLIN'S DISTRICT.

Jane Laughlin	34, *	David Williamson	35,
Buhard Brines	12,	Samuel Williamson	13,
David, a negro.	25,	Hugh McElhenny	30,
Alexander Laughlin	52, *	Margaret McElhenny	33,
Charity Laughlin	37, *	Hugh Kirkpatrick	13,
Susana Laughlin	15,	Richard Nicholdson	73, *
Ann Laughlin	10,	Mary Nicholdson	77, *
John Laughlin	8,	James Nicholdson	33,
Eve, a negro.		Mary Nicholdson	33,
Jack, "		Isaac Shannon	18,
Hall, "		James Steen	13,
Robert McCormick	30,	Sal, a negro.	
Esther McCormick	38,	Pomp, "	
Wm. Nisbit, (absent)	28,	Robert Shannon	64, *
Esther Nisbit	19,	Jane Shannon	63, *
James Stewart (absent)	28,	Sarah Shannon	30, *
Thomas Martin		John Shannon	33,
Eleanor Stewart	22,	Mary Shannon	20,
Thomas Montgomery	20,	Mary McGuffin	5,
Rebecca McMullin	13,	Robert Morrison	56, *
John Allen	26,	Elizabeth Morrison	58, *
Isabella Allen	20,	Robert Morrison	20,
Hugh Allen	57, *	Mary Morrison	16,
Jennet Allen	50,	William Morrison	13,
Elizabeth Allen	18,	Samuel McElhenny	40,
Alexander Allen	19,	Mary McElhenny	38, *
Jenny Allen	14,	George Sully	16,
David Allen	13,	Rebecca McElhenny	66,

THE BIG SPRING

Martha McCasland	47,	Samuel Bryson	19,
William Montgomery	14,	Hugh Bryson	15,
Sarah McGlaughlin and family,		Ellenor Donoway	10,
		Allen Means	24, *
Robert Barr and family,		Alexander Wier	24,
		William Carnahan	77, *
John Gorrel	47,	Martha Carnahan	66,
Isabella Gorrel	50,	Joseph Carnahan	29,
Isabel Moor	9,	Robert Carnahan	25,
Joseph Shannon and family		Judith Carnahan	24,
John McGuffine	30,	Rob't Mathers and family,	
William Hanna	60, *	John Wright	30,
Samuel Morrow	60, *	Jennet Wright	30,
Jane Morrow	50, *	Margaret Wright	18,
William McGuffine	20, *	William Thompson	81,
John Bell	45, *	Ellenor Thompson	71,
Martha Bell	38, *	Aaron Hains	12,
Walter McClure	16,	Tom, a negro.	
Jenny Bell	8,	Hannah "	
William Bryson	60, *	Matthew Thompson	30,
Margaret Bryson	53, *	Ann Thompson	23,
Rebecca Bryson	26, *	Mary Allison	9,
Families,			25.

JOHN ROBINSON'S DISTRICT.

James Laughlin	68,	Esther Robinson	50,
Mary Laughlin	30,	Mary Robinson	10,
Robert Laughlin	24,	Esther Robinson	7,
Hugh Laughlin	18,	John Robinson	5,
William Laughlin	20,	William Thompson	25,
Elizabeth Laughlin	15,	Jane Thompson	24,
Robert M. Gopock	8,	Sally Chapman	8,

PRESBYTERIAN CHURCH.

Susanna Thompson	56, *	Elizabeth Work	23,
Alexander Thompson	28,	Alexander Work	20,
Leacy Thompson	24,	James Work	18,
Peggy Thompson	22,	Susanna Work	16,
Hugh Thompson	20,	S. Work	14,
Sally Grier	10,	John Work	27,
Adam Carnahan	50,	Mary Work	23,
Agnes Carnahan	36,	James Carson	39,
James Carnahan	17,	Mary Carson	31,
Agnes Carnahan	14,	Janet Carson	9,
Adam Carnahan	20,	Solomon Lightcap	60,
Elizabeth Carnahan	8,	Mary Lightcap	55,
Joseph Wilson	82, *	Samuel Lightcap	25,
Mary Wilson	66, *	Solomon Lightcap	24,
Joseph Wilson	28,	Levi Lightcap	22,
William Wilson	23,	Nancy Lightcap	21,
Ann Wilson	21, *	Elizabeth Lightcap	20,
Ann Kennedy	10,	William Lightcap	18,
Jane Jack	60, *	Godfrey Lightcap	16,
James Jack	25,	Thomas Lightcap	14,
Cynthia Jack	23,	John Morain	65, *
Andrew Jack	21,	Sarah Morain	76, *
Hannah Jack	17,	John Morain	30,
John Wilt and family		John Laughlin	30,
Agnes McGoffine	60,	Margaret Laughlin	28, *
James McGoffine	35,	James Carithers	8,
John McGoffine	33,	Jeremiah McKibben	31,
S. Work	53, *	Mary McKibben	29,
Sal, a Negro.		Fan, a Negro.	
William work	25,		

Families, 16.   Persons in full communion, 11.
Total number of persons   72.

JOHN MCKEEHAN'S DISTRICT,

John McKeehan, was one of four brothers, who settled in West Pennsboro township, at an early date. His brothers were, Benjamin, James and Alexander. He died March 7, 1813, aged 75 years. His wife Elizabeth, died June 20, 1822, aged 77 years.

LIST OF MEMBERS.

James Turner	29,	Rebecca Rippet	10,
Mary Turner	29,	Mary Rippet	8,
James Walker(absent)	30,	Matthew Davidson	
—— Johnson	43, *	and family,	
Thomas Johnson	57, *	George McKeehan	40,
Mary Johnson	21 *	Mary McKeehan	30, *
Jean Johnson	17, *	Mary McKeehan	6,
Margaret Johnson	13,	Jenny McKeehan	7,
—— Johnson	8,	Randle Blair	40, *
William Miller	21,	Charity Blair	38,
John Miller	20,	John Blair	16,
James Houston	33,	Daniel Blair	13,
Isabel Houston	25,	Jenny Blair	9,
Robert Houston	6,	Elizabeth McKeehan	45,
John Davidson	42 *	George McKeehan	18,
Leacy Davidson	38, *	James McKeehan	16,
John Davidson	16,	John McKeehan	14,
James Davidson	14,	Samuel McKeehan	11,
Ann Davidson	9,	Alexander McKeehan	9,
Bill, a negro.		Mary Ann McKeehan,	
David Glen	36, *	James Atchison	68,
Mary Glen	26, *	Elizabeth Atchison	66, *
William Hanna	11,	Jacob Atchison	23,
John Rippet	40,	Benjamin Atchison	20,
Elizabeth Rippet	34,	Deborah Boyd	45, *

PRESBYTERIAN CHURCH. 49

John Boyd	19,	Peggy McKeehan	14.
George Boyd	15,	John McKeehan	13,
James Boyd	13,	Betsy McKeehan	10,
Eleanor Boyd	10,	Margaret Eager,	
Benjamin McKeehan	30,	Robert Beard,	
Margaret McKeehan	27,	Elizabeth Beard	35,
Elizabeth McKeehan	25,	Margaret Beard	17,
James McKeehan	35, *	James Beard	12,
Mary McKeehan	30, *	Anne Beard	10,
Nancy McKeehan	16,		

Families, 17.
In full communion, 14.
Total number of persons, 68.

MARRIAGES BY REV. SAMUEL WILSON.

Appleby, William, and Agnes McCurdy, Feb. 7, 1787.
Atchison, Joseph, and Elizabeth Moor, Mar. 26, 1789.
Alexander, James, and Margaret Harper, Oct. 25, 1792.
Armstrong, James, and Nancy Lemond, Apr. 8, 1794.
Armstrong, James, and —— Liggat, Nov. 4, 1794.
Armstrong, Robert, and Mary McDowell, Apr. 30, 1795.
Anderson, James, and Eleanor Crow, June 27, 1797.
Barr, Robert, and Elizabeth Allen, May 27, 1788.
Bell, Robert, and Rachel Espey, May 29, 1788.
Browster, William, and Margaret Robison, Mar. 1, 1790.
Blair, —— and ——Hunter, Oct. 23, 1792.
Blain, Robert, and Mary Craig, Feb. 17, 1795.
Bell, Joseph, and Elizabeth Sharp, Apr. 30, 1795.

Barr, John, and Sarah Gailly, (?) May 5, 1795.
Brown, Alexander, and Mary Jacob, Dec. 8, 1795.
Brown, William, and Rachel Walker, July 28, 1796.
Bell, William, and Elizabeth Stephenson, Sept. 15, 1796.
Boyd, George, and Elizabeth Brown, Mar. 2, 1797.
Brandon, Thomas, and Mary Fertig, Jan. 9, 1798.
Clark, Henry, and Mary Lowry, Oct. 25, 1788.
Crowel, —— and —— Walker, July 24, 1789.
Carson, Elisha, and Margaret Eager, Mar. 29, 1791.
Carnahan, Robert, and Agnes Wallace, (?) Oct, 10, 1791.
Cowden, William, and Eliza Whitelock, Apr. 29, 1793.
Crowel, Samuel, and Mary Walker; May 26, 1795.
Carnahan, James, and Katharine Drugon, (?) Jan. 20, 1797.
Crow, George, and Margaret McElwain, Aug. 17, 1797.
Culver, Levi, and Nancy Agnew, Dec. 22, 1796.
Durbarrow, —— and —— Martin, May 13, 1793.
Duncan, William, and Nancy McKeehan, May 31, 1792.
Davidson, John, and Betsy Young, Sept. 30, 1794.
Davidson, Francis, and Elizabeth Myler, Apr. 30, 1795.
Douglas, John, and Nancy McDowell, Mar. 1, 1798.
Duncan, James, and Mary Ewing, June 5, 1798.
Emmett, Samuel, and Rebecca Bryson, June 19, 1788.
Espey, John, and Margaret Huston, Nov. 10, 1789.
Elder, John, and —— Monemy, (?) Aug. 15, 1793.
Fullerton, Thomas Elder, and Isabella McCune, Mar. 27, 1788.

PRESBYTERIAN CHURCH.

Fowler, John, and Eleanor Mickie, Feb. 19, 1789.
Finley, Samuel, and Polly Brown, May 5, 1789.
Fox, John, and Rachel Crowell, Nov. 22, 1796.
Fleming, James, and Jenny Cloyd, July 17, 1798.
Frother, Joseph, and Nancy Liggate, Nov. 20, 1798.
Graham, Francis, and Margaret Randles, May 22, 1788.
Graham, Isaiah, and Nancy Lindsay, Feb. 12, 1793.
Geddes, Dr. John, and Elizabeth Peebles, June 17, 1794.
Green, John, and Barbara Ridsbaugh, Feb. 24, 1794.
Glenn, Alexander and Susanna McKinstre, June 11, 1795.
Geddes, James, and Margaret Douglass, Mar. 1, 1796.
Graham, Arthur, and Nancy McClure, Feb. 14, 1797.
Gillespie, David, and Rebecca Rippet, Mar. 8, 1798.
Glendenning, James, and Rebecca Armstrong, June 12, 1798.
Huston, John, and Deborah Patterson, Dec. 15, 1789.
Huston, Robert, and Agnes Bell, Sept. 2, 1793.
Harper, William, and Esther Patterson, Apr. 1, 1794.
Hughs, Thomas, and Nancy Crawford, May 1, 1794.
Hanna, James, and ―――― Reed, June 10, 1794.
Hemphill, James, and Cynthia Jack, Sept. 3, 1795.
Hawkes, John, and Christian Espey, Aug. 16, 1796.
Hadden, (?) Thomas, and Mary Dridge, Mar. 14, 1797.
Holmes, George, and Sarah Armstrong, Aug. 14, 1798.
Jones, Hugh, and Anne Gamble, June 21, 1787.
Johnson, Andrew, and Elizabeth Johnson, Dec. 18, 1788.
Jones, James, and Betsy Bell, June 10, 1794.
Johnston, Alexander, and Mary Armstrong, Dec. 30, 1794.

Kennedy, John, and Martha Graham, Apr. 22, 1787.
Ker, William and Mary Woods, May 12, 1789.
Kilgore, Robert, and Margaret Kelly, Jan. 20, 1791.
Kirkpatrick, James, and Margaret McKeehan, Apr. 7, 1791.
Kerr, Matthew, and Elizabeth Work, Jan. 1, 1793.
Kelly, James, and Sarah Lauderdale, July 15, 1794.
Laughlin, Dr. Thomas, and Betsy Laughlin, Jan. 24, 1791.
Leecock, William, and Margaret Falkner, May 30, 1793.
Laughlin, Matthew, and Phebe Piper, Apr. 29, 1794.
Lightcap, William, and Mary McElwain, Feb. 23, 1796.
Lindsy, Robert, and Betsy Connelly, Feb. 21, 1797.
Laughlin, Dr. Thomas, and Nancy Piper, July 18, 1797.
McCleary, John and Elizabeth Ewing, July 5, 1787.
McRory, Samuel and Anne Spence, Dec. 4, 1788.
McGlaughlin, Daniel, and Elizabeth Lightcap, Feb. 5, 1789.
McCurdy, David, and ——— Appelby, Aug. 25, 1789.
McElwain, R., and ——— McGlaughlin, Oct. 7, 1789.
Mayes, Samuel, and Barbara Harper, Dec. 17, 1789.
McCormick, Joseph, and Leacy Thompson, Jan. 19, 1790.
McElwain Andrew, and Margaret Bell, Aug. 26, 1790.
McGuffine, William and Elizabeth Porter, Jan. 25, 1791.
McCausland, Mark, and Sally Hunter.

Morrison, Robert and Susanna Work, Oct. 11, 1791.
McClaran, Thomas, and Hannah Mickey, Oct. 20, 1791.
Moor, Samuel, and —— McConnel, Jan. 7, 1792.
Mason, Isaac, and Elizabeth Kirkpatrick, June 7, 1792.
Martin, Thomas, and Widow Stewart, Aug. 16, 1792.
McCune, Samuel, and Hannah Brady, Dec. 26, 1793.
McFaden, John, and Nancy Harper, June 10, 1794.
Michal, John, and Katharine Carrick, June 10, 1794.
Murdock, Robert, and Elizabeth Cummins, Nov. 18, 1794.
McCormick, Robert, and Elizabeth McCullough, Nov. 27, 1794.
Marshall, John, and Jane Leacock, Apr. 21, 1795.
McGoffine, —— and Sarah Crair, May 4, 1795.
Martin, John, and Hannah Thompson, Jan. 14, 1796.
McKean, William, and Sarah Auld, June 30, 1796.
McKeehan, John, and Betsy McKeehan, Oct. 25, 1796.
Murphy, Philip, and Jane —— Apr. 21, 1797.
McCormick, Joseph, and Charity Connelly, Apr. 27, 1797.
Mathers, Robert, and Nancy Carnahan, Feb. 8, 1798.
McLandburg, John, and Margaret Young, Feb. 5, 1799.
Mitchel, Andrew, and Mary Ann McKeehan, Feb. 13, 1799.
Nicholdson, John, and Mary McElwain, July 29, 1794.
Patton, John, and Elizabeth McEntire, Aug. 18, 1789.
Patterson, Obediah, and Anne Patterson, May 5, 1791.
Porterfield, William, and Mary Shannon, April 21, 1795.

Patton, John, and Sarah Shannon, May 14, 1795.
Pennwell, Thomas, and Rachel Rodman, April 19, 1796.
Plunkett, Isaac, and Lydia Hanna, May 24, 1796.
Peebles, Robert, and Jane Kennedy, June 21, 1796.
Patton, Andrew, and Mary Patton, Oct. 18, 1796.
Patterson, Nathan, and Nancy Laughlin, Dec. 13, 1798.
Patterson, Robert, and ——— Armstrong, Sept. 27, 1792.
Patterson, John, and Jenny Neal, Oct. 11, 1792.
Quigley, James, and Grizelda McKinney, March 31, 1795.
Rainey, James, and Elizabeth Brownfield, April 23, 1795.
Roberts, John, and Nancy Gillespie, May 12, 1795.
Smith, Archibald, and Mary Anderson, Aug. 24, 1789.
Shannon, Isaac, and Jane Porter, Feb. 1, 1791.
Seelly, William, and ——— Morrow, Oct. 31, 1791.
Shannon, Leonard, and Jane Walker, Jan. 3, 1793.
Sterrett, James, and Margaret McClure, Dec. 9, 1793.
Sterrett, Benjamin, and Peggy Bell, March 27, 1794.
Scroggs, Allan, and Peggy Craig, Sept. 22, 1795.
Steel, Robert, and Letty Work, Oct. 27, 1795.
Scott, John, and Mary McFarlane, April 5, 1796.
Stephenson, James, and Elizabeth Sterrett, May 10, 1796.
Shannon, James, and Elizabeth Gees, March 16, 1797,
Sharp, David, and Isabella Orr, Aug. 14, 1798.
Thompson, Matthew, and Ruth Robinson, June 16, 1796.
Taylor, Andrew, and Mary Lightcap, Feb. 6, 1798.
Vanhorn, Joseph, and Martha Ewing, Nov. 22, 1792.
Vanderbelt, Cornelius, and Mary Steel.

Woodburn, Matthew, and Katharine Fulton, Feb. 12, 1799.
Wilson, Samuel, and Peggy Espey, June 11, 1789.
Wallace, Patrick, and Sally Officer, Sept. 20, 1791.
Wallace, Hugh, and Margaret Dearmon, July 2, 1792.
Woodburn, James, and Nancy Martin, Feb. 14, 1793.
Woodruff, Anthony, and Mary Chapman, March 5, 1793.
Young, John, and Sarah McCann, Sept. 18, 1798.

THE ADDRESS IN THE MARRIAGE CEREMONY USED BY REV. SAMUEL WILSON.

"Regular publication has been made of these persons intending to join in the near relation of husband and wife.

No objections have yet been made. I now call upon any person, who has any such to make, that he now speak, or forever hold his peace. We find no objections from without, but as it has been the custom of our church, in the solemnization of marriage, to put it seriously to the persons themselves, whether they know any cause, either by previous contract, or otherwise, why they may not be joined together in the near relation, that they declare it. It is true, such contracts do not bind in law, but it is as true, that they do bind conscience, and persons ought seriously to consider such matters before they violate them. Persons may consider such questions improper, as it is not likely that they came publicly to declare these things, but consider these are matters in which conscience alone is concerned, and if persons will injure themselves, it is no reason why those who are authorized to solemnize marriage should not faithfully discharge their duty. I then ask you sir, whether you know any lawful reason, why you may not be joined in marriage to this woman who stands on your left hand—do you know any reason? Do you know madam, any lawful reason, why you may not be joined in marriage to this man, who stands upon your right hand—Do you know any reason? Marriage is an early institution of God's own appointment; it took place between our first parents in a state of innocence, and therefore, is said to be honorable in all, and the bed undefiled, but whoremongers and adulterers, God will judge. Marriage is to be between one man and one woman, and there are certain degrees of consanguinity, which have been generally forbidden. The equal proportion of the different sexes forbids polygamy, or having more wives than one; the males in every age being to the females, as thirteen to twelve, or twenty to nineteen, as though infinite wisdom had so ordered it, that overplus of males, should make their deficiency by war and other dangerous occupations.

Although the form of marriage has varied in every age and nation, yet the essential part of it appears to be the consent of the parties, declared before witnesses; private consent, of whatever kind or nature it may be, will never come higher than a contract, and in consequence will not bind in law.

The design of marriage is, that fornication may be avoided, and as our race is more dignified than the lower creations, so then, our passions should be regulated by reason and religion. It is likewise intended for producing a legitimate offspring, and a seed for the church. There are duties incumbent upon those who enter this relation, some of them are equally binding upon both parties, some upon one party, some upon the other. First, it is equally binding upon you both, to love each others' persons, to avoid freedom with all others, which formerly might have been excusable, to keep each others' lawful secrets, fidelity to the marriage bed, and if God shall give you an offspring, it will be mutually binding upon you both, to consult their spiritual, as well as their temporal concerns. Secondly, it will be particularly binding upon you, sir, who is to be the head of the family, to maintain the authority which God hath given you. In every society there must be a head, and in families, by divine authority, this is given to the man, but as woman was given to man for an helpmeet and a bosom companion, you are not to treat this woman in a tyranical manner, much less as a slave, but to love and kindly entreat her, as becomes you towards one so nearly allied to you. The relation is so near, that a man is said to leave father and mother and cleave to his wife, and the twain shall be one flesh, and to show that love is due to such, it is added, no man ever hated his own flesh, but nourisheth and cherisheth it. Lastly, it is incumbent upon you, madam, who is to be the wife, to acknowledge the authority of him who is to be your husband, and for this, you have the example of Sarah, who is commended for calling Abraham Lord.

It seems to be your privilege in matters in which you and he cannot agree, that you advise with him, endeavoring in an easy way, by persuasion, to gain him to your side; but if you cannot in this way gain your point, it is fit and proper that you submit in matters in which conscience is not concerned. It will be your duty in a particular manner, to use good economy in regard to those things which may be placed in your hands. In a word, you are to be industrious in your place and station."

THE PASTORATE OF REV. JOSHUA WILLIAMS, D. D.

After the death of Rev. Samuel Wilson, and before the settlement of Rev. Joshua Williams, we find the pulpit was supplied by the following clergymen: Revs. Robert Wilson, Thomas Greer, P. Davidson, Matthew Brown, Mr. Burck, William Wilson, Mr. Anderson, Mr. Linn, Mr. Herron, Samuel Waugh, Mr. Kennedy, Dr. Cooper, Mr. Williams, and Robert Logan. The preaching of the latter seems to have pleased the congregation, as a subscription paper was circulated in 1800, with a view of raising salary and giving him a call. Whether a call was extended or not, we have been unable to find. A call was extended to Rev. Joshua Williams, then pastor of the churches of Derry and Paxton, which was accepted. He was installed April 14, 1802. Dr. Williams' ministry of twenty-seven years, was one of uninterrupted harmony and kindly feeling, between pastor and people, as usually attends the ministrations of an able preacher and a faithful pastor. In this congregation, he married 360 couples. On the marriage of John Scouller and Jane Brown, April 4, 1809, the bans were published the last time in the Big Spring Church. He baptized six hundred and seventy-four children, and admitted four hundred and fifty-two persons to the communion of the church. During the latter part of his ministry, the use of tokens were dispensed with at communion. In 1817, the first Sabbath school was organized in the church as a union school. Its organization was largely due to the efforts of John Moor, who afterwards became superintendent, in which capacity he served for a number of years. For several years, during the ministry of Dr. Williams, James Work was clerk or leader of the singing. He acted as such, at least from 1817 to 1824, at a salary of twenty-five dollars per annum. At a later date, John Davidson was precentor. In 1829, Dr. Williams severed his connection as pastor of the church owing to failure of health.

MEMBERS RECEIVED INTO THE BIG SPRING CHURCH BY REV. JOSHUA WILLIAMS, D. D.

MAY 1, 1802.

Mary Duncan.
John Laughlin.
Andrew Thompson.
Abraham Dunbar.

OCTOBER, 1802.

William Glenn and wife.
Matthew Thompson and wife.
Matthew Adams and wife.
Jane Adams.
Samuel Williamson and wife.
William Davidson.
Jane Lindsy.
Mr. McBride.
Charles Shaw.
Mrs Clendenning.
Rachel Fox.

JUNE 12, 1803.

Jane McCracken.
Mrs. McBride.
Widow Ripet.
John Martin and wife.
Samuel McCracken.
John Clendenning.
Richard Adams and wife.
Rebecca Long.

Mrs. Clendenning. Mary Brown.

SEPT. 11, 1803.

Alexander McBeth and wife.
Samuel Sibbet and wife.
Charity Laughlin.
Martha Hamilton.
Polly Laughlin.
Selfridge and wife.

JUNE 4, 1804.

Elizabeth Flint. Henry James.
Lacy Davidson. Susan Davidson.
John McKeehan, jr.

OCT. 28, 1804.

James Mathers. Agnes Kingborough.
Mary Heden. James Fleming.

MAY 19, 1805.

Isabella Davidson. Frances Hays.
Robert Thompson. Widow Vanderbilt.
Ann Davidson. James Graham.

OCTOBER 14, 1805.

Mary Stephenson. Mary Morrow.
Mary Woods. Nathan Woods.

MAY 13, 1806.

Mrs. McEntire. Jane McFarlane.
Jane Stephenson.

OCTOBER 5, 1806.

James Sharp and wife. Nathan Means.
Katharine Elliott. Martha Montgomery.
Joseph Williams. Rachel Williams.
Ann Montgomery.

MAY 10, 1807.

William Green. Margaret Buchanan.
Martha Roberts.

OCTOBER 4, 1807.

Thomas Connelly. Jane Lindsay.
Mary Garnel. Benjamin Garnel.
Mary Connelly. Elizabeth Duncan.

MAY 8, 1808.

Mary Russel. Jane Boyd.
Nancy Harper. Martha Boyd.
William Boyd. Catharine Pollock.

OCTOBER 30, 1808.

Mary McGuffin. Martha Graham.
Cornelius Vanderbilt and Susana Graham.
  wife.

MAY 13, 1809.

Daniel Leckey. James McCord.
David Rine.

OCTOBER 22, 1809.

John Benson and wife. Susan Davidson.
Joseph Duncan and wife. Nancy Davidson.
John McWilliams and Joseph Baker.
  wife. John Williamson.

JUNE 2, 1810.

William Williams. Paul Pierce.
Sarah Leckey. Mary McGuffin.
Martha Sharp. George Leckey.
James Montgomery. Mary Sharp.
Sarah Leckey. Philip Warner.
Mary Williams. Thomas Wallace.
Mrs. Irvine and daughter.

OCTOBER 21, 1810.

Catharine Laughlin. Barton Gray.
Martha Donaldson. Hannah Laughlin.
Prudence Davidson. Robert McBride.

Rhoda Thompson.
Margaret Gray.
Elizabeth Pollock.
Jane Donaldson.
——— Thompson.
Eleanor Vanderbilt.

JUNE 18, 1811.

Robert Espey and wife.
James Irvine.
Nancy Gillespie.
Mrs. Knettle.
Eleanor Brown.
Jane James.
David Davidson.
Ann Wallace.
John McClellan.
Eleanor Dahr.
Rachel Glenn.
Ann Gillespie.
William Lindsay.
John Brown.

OCTOBER, 1811.

William Vandyke.
Maria Patton.
Ralph Ewing.
Samuel McKeehan.
John Sawyer.
——— Ewing.
Deborah McKeehan.
Martha McKeehan.

JUNE 1812.

Eliza McFarlane.
John Gourd.
John Means.
Susana McCormick.
Nancy Mickey.
Mary Gourd.
Catharine Dougherty.
Robert McElwain.
Eleanor Mickey.
Priscilla Carson.
Martha Lytle.
Jane McElwain.

OCTOBER 25, 1812.

Sally Blair.
Rosanna McCord.
George Davidson and wife.
John Ross.
Jane Davidson.
Andrew McCord.
John McBride.

JUNE 6, 1813.

William Bell.
Francis Fulton and wife.
John McCune and wife.

PRESBYTERIAN CHURCH. 63

OCTOBER 24, 1813.

Ezra Morrison.
Andrew Morrow and wife.
John Shields.
John McBride and wife.
William McFarlane.

MAY 1, 1814.

William Connelly.
Martha Cowen.
John Montgomery.
Joseph Hershaw and wife.
Elizabeth Lynch.
Jane Montgomery, wife of John.
Mary Green.
Elizabeth Montgomery.
Sarah Lowry.

MAY 14, 1815.

Mary Alexander.
Wm. Davidson and wife.
Wm. McCune and wife.
Maria Laughlin.

OCTOBER 1, 1815.

Eliza Geddes.
Mary Huston.
Joseph Brown.
Eliza Woods.
Jane Wilson.
Nancy Huston.
David Ross.
Eliza Fleming.
John Johnston.
James Laughlin, jr.
Rosanna McCoy.
Jane Johnston, wife of John.
John Brown.

MAY 12, 1816.

John Shannon and wife.
William Cooper and wife.
Margaret McFarlane.
Samuel Lindsay.
Jeddiah Hadden.
Sarah Harper.

OCTOBER 20, 1816.

Widow Brown.
Priscilla Leacock.
James Ray.
Alexander Laughlin and wife.
Eliza Ross.
Mary French.
Rachel Crawford.
Joseph Connelly.
John French.

MAY 1817.

Nancy Graham.
William Brattan.
Alexander Glenn.
Polly McClure.
Esther McWilliams.
John Mathers.
Thomas Walker.

OCTOBER, 1817.

Alexander Donaldson and wife.
Andrew McCandlish and wife.
Thomas McEntire and wife.
Mary Davidson.
John Gray and wife.
James Green.
Elizabeth Cowen.
Ann Leckey.
Elizabeth Kennedy.
William McBride.
Catharine Dougherty.
Mary Leckey.
Sarah McElwain.

MAY, 1818.

Elizabeth Thompson.
Mary McEntire.
Susanna McElwain.
Nancy Laughlin.
Elizabeth Buchanan.
Mary McKnight.
Elizabeth McEntire.
John Dickson.
Eliza Laughlin.
Margaret Huston.
Margaret McKnight.
William McElwain.
Samuel Culbertson.
Mary Buchanan.

OCTOBER, 1818.

Mary Dunbar.
Martha Peebles.
Josiah Hood.
James Oliver.
Elizabeth McClure.
Alexander Williamson.
Rosanna Dunbar.
Joseph Thompson.
Jane Fleming.
Eleanor Davidson.
Mrs. Crowel.
Isabella Dunbar.
Mary Thompson.
William Brittan.
Arthur Graham.
James Williamson.

PRESBYTERIAN CHURCH. 65

MAY 9, 1819.

Mrs. King.
Rebecca Pierce.
Joseph Jacob.
Lydia Jacob.
Ebenezer Campbell and wife.

OCTOBER 10, 1819.

Mary Wilson.
Eleanor Morrow.
Margaret Carnahan.
Elizabeth Kilgore.
Rebecca Murphy.
Elizabeth Mickey.
Mary Wallace.
Jane Cowen.
William Allen.
Mary Allen.
Elizabeth White.
Nancy Lindsay.
Moses Williamson.
John Laughlin.
Jane G. Williams.
Thomas Piper.
John Heagy.
Eliza Heagy.

MAY 21, 1820.

William Morrow.
Thomas Sibbet.
Hannah McCune.
James Barr.
Margaret Laughlin.
Sarah Buchanan.
Nancy Buchanan.
William Lusk.
Mary Lusk.
Gusilla Kelly.
Ann Laird.

OCTOBER 22, 1820.

Mrs. McKane and daughter.
Matthew Davidson.
Emily Davidson.
James Beatty, jr.
Harry Culbertson.

MAY, 1821.

William Davidson.
Thomas Leacock.
Mary Beatty.
Jane Ewing.
Ruth Harlan.
Jane McBride.

OCTOBER, 1821.

James Allen.
Jane Allen.
Nancy Graham.
Agnes Brown.

Samuel McCormick.
James Lindsay.
Margaret Shields.
Agnes Richie.
Isabel Leckey.
Emily Leckey.
Eleanor Brittan.
Mary Brittan.

JUNE 2, 1822.

Elizabath Boyd.
Elizabeth Fitzsimmons.
Lacy Ralston.
Mary Caldwell.
Eleanor Thompson.
Esther Thompson.
Rachel Sterrett.
Eliza McFarlane.
Elsey McElwain.
Mary McElwain.
Eliza Vanderbilt.
Susanna Holmes.
Eleanor Montgomery.
David Ralston.
William French.
James Ross.
Andrew Thompson.
James McElwain.
Peter Wilt.
Patrick Fitzsimons.
James Mitchel.
Jane Mitchel, wife of James.
James Davidson.
Eliza Wills.
Ann Davidson, wife of James.
Mary Morrow.

OCTOBER 13, 1822.

Samuel Graham.
Elizabeth Graham.
John Davidson.
Jacob Stough.
Margaret Stough.
Mary Williams.
Elizabeth Ewing.
Mary Gillespie.
William Laughlin.
Mariah McCormick.

JUNE 13, 1823.

Nancy York.
Nancy Thornton.
Joseph McKibben.
Tabitha McKibben.
Mary Donnelly.
Joseph McElheny.
Jane McElheny.
Ezra Morrison.
John McKeehan.
Tabitha McKeehan.
Elizabeth Davidson.

OCTOBER 5, 1823.

William Duncan.
Rev. David Sterrett.
Tabitha Reed.
Margaret McCune.
Mark McKeehan.
Eleanor Wilt.
Esther Wilt.
Susan Irvin.
Sarah Koontz.

MAY 30, 1824.

Eliza Sterrett.
Eliza McCormick.
Jude Carnahan.
William Carnahan.
Margaret Sibbet.
Nancy Kennedy.
Jane Lindsay.
Jane Koontz.
Samuel French.
John Wilt.
Benjamin Cooper.
Sarah Cooper.
Isabella Richie.
Joshua D. Williams.

OCTOBER 10, 1824.

Eliza Connel.
Mary Brown.
Isaac Koontz.
Isabella McKibben.
Mary Brown.
Isabella Johnson.
Sarah Geddes.
Lewis H. Williams.

MAY, 1825.

John Lee.
James Logan.

MAY 26, 1826.

Martha Weakley.
Margaret Geddes.
Rebecca Miller.
William Atchison.
Robert Kennedy.
John Ewing.
Isabel Kilgore.
Jane Buchanan.
Letitia Work.
Susanna Work.
Ellis Thompson.

JUNE 2, 1827.

Matthew Laird.
Susanna Laird, wife of Matthew.
Eliza E. Melroy.
Margaret Carnahan.
Hannah McCune.

Jane Phillips.
Jane Smith.
Mrs. Lindsy.

Sarah Patterson.
Catharine Leckey.

JUNE, 1828.

Jacob Fosnaught.
Mary Fosnaught, wife of Jacob.
William Brown.
Jane Brown, wife of William.
Samuel Miller.

Jane McBride.
James Fulton.
Isabella Fulton.
Robert Adams.
Ann Adams, wife of Robert.
James Devenport.

BAPTISMS BY REV. JOSHUA WILLIAMS, D. D.

The records of Dr. Williams do not give the names of children baptized until 1821, consequently this record is incomplete.

John Laughlin, son of William Davidson, born Nov. 10, 1816, baptized May 6, 1821.

William Miller, son of William Davidson, born Nov. 19, 1820, baptized May 6, 1821.

Robert, son of Isaac Koontz, born Jan. 2, 1819, baptized June 4, 1821.

Isaac, son of Isaac Koontz, born Sept. 27, 1820, baptized June 4, 1821.

Mary A., daughter of John McWilliams, born June 12, 1809, baptized June 4, 1821.

James, son of John McWilliams, born Feb. 21, 1812, baptized June 4, 1821.

Eliza, daughter of John McWilliams, born Dec. 8, 1816, baptized June 4, 1821.

Hetty G., daughter of John McWilliams, born June 1, 1820, baptized June 4, 1821.

Theressa J., daughter of George Espy, born Feb. 14, 1814, baptized June 4, 1821.
Augustus A., son of George Espy, born June 16, 1816, baptized June 4, 1821.
Addah L., daughter of George Espy, born May 19, 1817, baptized June 4, 1821.
Mills B., son of George Espy, born Oct. 19, 1820, baptized June 4, 1821.
Mary Jane, daughter of Josiah Hood, born June 20, 1818, baptized June 4, 1821.
Margaret A., daughter of Josiah Hood, born Feb. 9, 1820, baptized June 4, 1821.
Ruth Harlan, aged 27 years, baptized June 4. 1821.
John M., son of Ruth Harlan, baptized 1821.
Secustus, son of Jane McBride, born Nov. 2, 1820, baptized June 4, 1821.
David, son of Robert McBride, born Sept. 15, 1801, baptized June 4, 1821.
Margaret, daughter of John Gourd, born Feb. 1, 1812.
William, son of John Gourd, born Sept. 14, 1814.
Joseph D., son of John Gourd, born April 19, 1818.
Nancy, daughter of Francis Fulton, born Feb. 16, 1802.
F. Huston, son of Francis Fulton, born April 16, 1805.
Isabel, daughter of Francis Fulton, born April 17, 1807.
Kezia, daughter of Francis Fulton, born Nov. 5, 1810.
Matilda, daughter of Francis Fulton, born Oct. 15, 1812.
William Harper Wallace, born May 15, 1819, baptized Oct. 18. 1819.
Elizabeth Ralston Jacob, born July 9, 1818.
Eleanor Jacob, born May 16, 1816.
John, son of Henry Drudge.
Jane, daughter of Henry Drudge.

Sarah, daughter of Henry Drudge.
Wilson, son of Henry Drudge.
Mary, daughter of Henry Drudge.
Elizabeth, daughter of Henry Drudge.
Cassendannah, daughter of Henry Drudge.
Rosanna, daughter of Henry Drudge.
Mary Ellen, daughter of Henry Drudge.
Mary Nicholdson, daughter of Richard and Rosanna McElvain, born Oct. 13, 1808.
Andrew Thompson, son of Richard and Rosanna McElvain, born June 18, 1811.
Elizabeth Bell, daughter of Richard and Rosanna McElvain, born March, 1813.
Mary Jane, daughter of Richard and Rosanna McElvain, born March, 18, 1816.
James, son of Richard and Rosanna McElvain, born March 12, 1819.
Marjory Ellen, daughter of Richard and Rosanna McElvain, born Sept. 4, 1822.
Ruth Rosanna, daughter of Richard and Rosanna McElvain, born Nov. 13, 1825.
Margaret Bell, daughter of James and Alice McElvain, born Nov. 20, 1824.
Andrew McKinney, son of James and Alice McElvain, born April 11, 1827.
Jane, daughter of James and Alice McElvain, born March 18, 1823.
William S., son of James and Alice McElvain, born Dec. 30, 1829.

MARRIAGES BY THE REV. JOSHUA WILLIAMS, D. D.

Applegate, John and Mary Rightmyer, May 13, 1802.

Adams, Henry and Mary McKeehan, July 22, 1802.
Asper, John and ——— McKinney, May 20, 1813.
Armor, Samuel and Hannah Davis, Aug. 7, 1821.
Alter, Benjamin and Nancy Lindsay, Mar. 20, 1823.
Adams, Thomas and Jane Eliza Adams, Nov. 19, 1835.
Basler, Thomas and Maria Wynkoop, Oct. 27, 1836.
Bigler, Jacob and Susanna Duck, July 11, 1803. Parents of Governor John Bigler, of California and Governor William Bigler of Pennsylvania.
Brady, Joseph and Barbara Rheme (?), Mar. 12, 1807.
Brown, John and Eleanor Gillespie, Mar. 17, 1807.
Benson, John and Elizabeth Gray, Dec. 10, 1807.
Baker, Samuel and Jane McElwain, Dec. 1, 1808.
Bell, George and Mary Willis, Apr. 26, 1810.
Butler, John and Nancy Hunter, Mar. 28, 1811.
Ballentine, George and Letitia Martin, Apr. 9, 1811.
Brackenridge, Andrew and Martha Sharp, Apr. 7, 1812.
Berkley, Robert and Elizabeth Martin, Apr. 6, 1813.
Blain, Thomas and Mary Sharp, Apr. 14, 1813.
Baker, Jacob and Mary Kincade, Nov. 23, 1815.
Blain, John and Elizabeth Kilgore, Mar. 25, 1819.
Brown, Joseph and Nancy Richie, July 25, 1821.
Benner, Joseph and Elizabeth Cook, Oct. 2, 1823.
Brown, John and Mary Richie, Mar. 30, 1824.
Barr, William and Sarah Geddes, July 27, 1825.
Carnahan, Adam and Ruth McElwain, Feb. 25, 1802.
Craighead, George and Polly Gillespie, Apr. 1, 1802.
Connelly, William and Rachel Scroggs, Apr. 20, 1802.
Clemmons. James and Nancy Hanna, Aug. 16, 1803.
Carson, Andrew and Mary Fortner, Apr. 8, 1806.
Charlton, Robert and Phebe Holt, July 2, 1807.
Campbell, James and Elizabeth French, Oct. 3, 1809.

Campbell, David and Sarah Cooper, Jan. 30, 1812.
Crow, John and Sally ———, July 1, 1813.
Carothers, Andrew and Mary Hays, Dec. 8, 1814.
Coulter, Joseph and Mary Wilson, Sept. 24, 1816.
Connelly, Joseph and Jane Carothers, Apr. 24, 1817.
Carson, John E., and Jane Peeple (?), June 18, 1818.
Clark, Jacob and Margaret ———, Sept. 22, 1818.
Carnahan, William and Mary Huston, Oct. 13, 1818.
Carothers, John R. and Margaret McBride, Nov. 12, 1818.
Clendennin, James and Elizabeth Barr, May, 27, 1819.
Culbertson, Samuel and Mary Ury, May 23, 1820.
Cope, Philip and Elizabeth Oxor, Nov. 30, 1820.
Carothers, Josiah and Mary McNair, Oct. 4, 1821.
Cook, Thomas and Sarah Scroggs, Mar. 5, 1822.
Crowell, James and Mary Leckey, Mar. 18, 1824.
Carnahan, William and Margaret Cooper, May 27, 1825.
Carothers, James and Mary C. Carothers, Apr. 24, 1827.
Carothers, Martin and Ellen Duffy, Oct. 12, 1827.
Clark, Peter and Hester Ward, Nov. 26, 1834.
Cope, Benjamin and Sarah McDowell, Apr. 25, 1822.
Duncan, William and Mary Mitchel, Dec. 1, 1801.
Dowds, Robert and Rachel Willis, Apr. 10, 1806.
Davidson, James and Jane McFarlane, June 23, 1807.
Davidson, George and Jennie McKeehan, Mar. 23, 1807.
Davidson, Patrick and Nancy Randolph, May 18, 1809.
Dahr, Joseph and Eleanor Vanderbilt, Nov. 6, 1810.
Douglas, George and Grissy McKeehan, Feb. 12, 1811.
Douglas, William and Eleanor Brown, Apr. 20, 1812.
Dearmond, William and Martha Gourd, Apr. 23, 1812.
Davidson, Alexander and Jane Woodburn, Oct. 14, 1813.

Davidson, William and Mary Miller, Nov. 3, 1814.
Davidson, Matthew and Emily Woodburn, Oct. 28, 1819.
Duncan, William and Isabella McCune, Oct. 5, 1820.
Davidson, John and Margaret Walker, Dec. 11, 1823.
Duncan, William and Nancy Fulton, Mar. 30, 1824.
Duncan, Joseph and Jane McNickle, Dec. 30, 1824.
Donaldson, Thomas and Eleanor Turner, Feb. 10, 1825.
Davidson, John and Eleanor Thompson, June 9, 1825.
Duffy, John and Sarah Longwell, Aug. 2, 1827.
Davidson, William and Ann Leckey, May 1, 1828.
Davidson, Samuel and Catharine Leckey, Oct. 19, 1830.
Davidson, James and Ann Logan, Apr. 5, 1831.
Dickson, John and Jane McKnight, June 20, 1822.
Endsly, James and Elizabeth Walker, Mar. 12, 1805.
Ewing, James and Eleanor Gillespie, Apr. 25, 1809.
Espy, Robert and Elizabeth Carson, Mar. 14, 1810.
Espy, George and Rebecca Glenn, Feb. 4, 1813.
Ewing, James and Elizabeth Gillespie, Oct. 21, 1813.
Ege, Joseph and Jane Woodburn, Oct. 7, 1829.
Fuhrhob, Godlieb and Eva Smith, Dec. 10, 1807.
Fulton, John and Sally Wills, Feb. 29, 1816.
Fenton, John and Elizabeth Carson, Jan. 28, 1819.
Fulton, James and Mary McKinnie (?), Apr. 29, 1819.
Farrier, David and Jane Ryan, Mar. 25, 1824.
French, James and Jane Cowen, Apr. 5, 1826.
Graham, Thomas and Mary McKeehan, Mar. 16, 1802.
Glenn, William and Rosanna Thompson, Apr. 15, 1802.
Grier, James and Amy Espy, Feb. 12, 1805.
Glenn, James and Mary Reid, May 8, 1806.
Greenwood, John and Catharine Ferguson, Sept. 17, 1807.
Gray, Barton and Margaret Mickey, Feb. 23, 1810.

Giffin, Robert and Catharine McCrea, May 9, 1811.
Glenn, David and Jane McKeehan, Feb. 11, 1812.
Geese, Christian and Elizabeth Mahon, July 1, 1813.
Greenfield, Hugh and Nancy Thompson, Mar. 9, 1815.
Graham, Rev. James and Rachel Glenn, Nov. 26, 1815.
Glenn, Alexander and Maria Laughlin, Mar. 5, 1816.
Graham, Robert and Elizabeth McFarlane, Feb. 10, 1824.
Graham, George and Elizabeth Alter, Feb. 3, 1830.
Greason, Samuel Carothers and Mary Davidson, Nov. 23 1837.
Hays, William T. and Polly McKibbin, Apr. 24, 1804.
Hard, John W. and Ann Brown, Nov. 4, 1806.
Herron, Thomas and Margaret Drudge, Nov. 26, 1807.
Hudson, George and Catharine Pollock, Feb. 9, 1809.
Huston, James and Rachel Crowel, Aug. 31, 1809.
Hamil, William and Mary Allen, Jan. 25, 1810.
Hays, Patrick and Margaret Mickey, Jan. 30, 1810.
Huston, Jonathan and Nancy Mickey, Jan. 4, 1810.
Hudson, James and Mary Pollock, 1810.
Hutton, John and Harriett Heigle, Feb. 18, 1813.
Huston, James and Sally McCullough, Mar. 17, 1814.
Hamilton, John and Lydia McKeehan, Mar. 12, 1816.
Haden, Jedediah and Mary Painter, May 30, 1816.
Hume, James and Mary McWilliams, Apr. 9, 1818.
Heagy, David and Mary A. Young, July 9, 1821.
Holms, John and Elizabeth Albert, Mar. 25, 1824.
Herron, James and Isabella Johnson, Sept. 15, 1815.
Huston, Samuel and Ann Fulton, Dec. 22, 1825.
Irvin, James and Prudence Leckey, Mar. 8, 1808.
Irvine, Samuel and Rosanna Dunbar, Apr. 14, 1829.
Jacob, Thomas and Jane Pierce, May 20, 1810.

Jacob, Thomas and Catharine McDonald, 1810.
Johnston, John and Jane Huston, Jan, 26, 1815.
Jackson, John and Elizabeth Rouse (?), Mar. 2, 1820.
Jacob, David and Eleanor Davidson, Mar. 8, 1821.
Johnston, John and Elizabeth Pollock, Nov. 8, 1821.
-Kelly, Robert and Sarah Norton, Dec. 31, 1807.
Kean, John and Jane Adams, Mar. 14, 1805.
Kinkaide, James and Dianna Lee, Nov. 9, 1809.
Kerr, Alexander and Sarah Galbraith, Mar. 3, 1814.
Kilgore, Samuel and Susan Thompson, Mar. 14, 1816.
Kinkaide, William and Elizabeth Scoby, Apr. 1, 1817.
Koontz, Isaac and Jane Carnahan, Mar. 26, 1818.
Kennedy, Robert and Nancy Kilgore, May 13, 1820.
Kerr, William and Eliza Sterrett, June 15, 1824.
Kennedy, James and Maria Barr, May 3, 1825.
Kilgore, Ezekiel and Elizabeth Graham, Nov. 9, 1825.
Knettle, William and Lacy Lindsay, Jan. 3, 1828.
Kilgore, Jesse and Nancy Sharp, Aug. 13, 1828.
Kinsley, Jacob and Charlotte Roberts, Apr. 8, 1830.
Lightcap, Thomas and Widow Delany, Apr. 21, 1803.
Lemon, Hugh and Rachel Hays, Apr. 24, 1804.
Leckey, George and Sarah Crowel, Nov. 22, 1808.
Leckey, Daniel and Ann Davidson, Mar. 16, 1809.
Lee, George and Sally Latshaw, Mar. 28, 1811.
Lee, John and Elizabeth Fulton, Apr. 21, 1812.
Laughlin, John and Margaret Alexander, May 18, 1813.
Linn, Samuel and Catharine Laughlin, Dec. 2, 1813.
Laughlin, John and Margaret Jones, June 30, 1814.
Laughlin, John and Mary Williamson, Dec. 5, 1815.
Linn, William and Hannah Laughlin, Apr. 2, 1816.
Lindsay, Samuel and Elizabeth Atchison, Oct. 23, 1817.
Lytle, George and Barbara Campbell, Feb. 26, 1818.

Leacock, Thomas and Elizabeth Fleming, Aug. 5, 1818.
Lowery, Isaac and Hannah Martin, Dec. 25, 1821.
Linn, John and Mary McClure, Mar. 11, 1814.
Logan, James and Ann Laird, Mar. 23, 1824.
Leckey, George and Nancy Davidson, July 28, 1825.
Leburn, Robert and Nancy Bell, Feb. 14, 1826. (Colored.)
Lefevre, David Alter and Mary H. Wilt, Mar. 20, 1827.
Logan, George and Nancy Huston, Oct. 4, 1827.
Lindsay, William and Mary Forbes, June 4, 1818.
Mason, Thomas and Nancy Kennedy, Mar. 30, 1802.
McGuire, Thomas and Rachel Purdy, Mar. 1, 1803.
McKinstry, Alexander and Sarah McDonald, Nov. 27, 1804.
McElrow, Hugh and Margaret Duncan, Apr. 29, 1806.
Morrow, James and Rachel Ingram, Dec. 31, 1807.
Maxwell, George and Mary Fulton, Feb. 2, 1808.
McCord, James and Susan Davidson, Feb. 11, 1808.
McKinney, Andrew and Sarah Young, Mar. 24, 1808.
McElwain, Robert and Jane Shannon, Apr. 12, 1808.
Martin, John and Ann Montgomery, Apr. 14, 1808.
McKeehan, Samuel and Deborah McBride, Nov. 3, 1808.
McWilliams, John and Sarah Dickson, Nov. 24, 1808.
McClelland, Elias and Mary McKinney, Dec. 22, 1808.
Martin, John and Rebecca Montgomery, Jan. 23, 1810.
McKeehan, Robert and Mary Trego, Feb. 23, 1810.
McFarlane, Robert and Eleanor Jacob, Apr. 26, 1803.
McKeehan, Samuel and Mary McKeehan, Mar. 26, 1812.
Montgomery, James and Margaret Walker, Apr. 7, 1812.
Montgomery, John and Jane Fulton, Sept. 9, 1812.
Milroy, William Rodman and Nancy Kingsborough, Oct. 13, 1812.

McCullough, William and Mary McGuffin, Nov. 2, 1813.
McCord, Robert and Lacy Davidson, Feb. 3, 1814.
McKibben, John and Isabella Mitchell, Mar. 3, 1814.
Mateer, Andrew and Ann Huston, Mar. 24, 1814.
Martin, Joshua and Eliza Williamson, Nov. 9, 1815.
Mathers, Robert and Mary Ingram, Feb. 1, 1816.
Mathers, John and Nancy Huston, Feb. 15, 1816.
McLane, William and Hannah McPherson, Feb. 29, 1816.
Moore, John and Rachel McCullough, Mar. 11, 1816.
McFarlane, Robert and Jane Kilgore, May 2, 1816.
Macfee, William and Elizabeth Sensebaugh, May 27, 1816.
Montgomery, William and Sally Barr, Nov. 24, 1816.
McElhenny, Robert and Margaret Carnahan, Mar. 28, 1817.
McBride, Robert and Jane Scroggs, May 15, 1817.
McDowell, John and Mary Laird, Mar. 12, 1818.
Morrow, William and Catharine Dougherty, Mar. 25, 1819.
McCord, James and Jane Sturges, July 1, 1819.
Maxwell, John and Jane Buchanan, Aug. 12, 1819.
McDermond, Joseph and Nancy ———, Nov. 30, 1819.
McKibben, Chambers and Jane Bell, Feb. 10, 1820.
McCullough, William and Jane Morrow (?), Mar, 2, 1820.
Mathers, John and Martha Peebles, Mar. 30, 1820.
McDonald, John and Elizabeth Moore, Oct. 5, 1820.
McKeehan, Mark and Elizabeth Vanderbilt, Dec. 7, 1820.
McDonald, Daniel and Elizabeth Kennedy, Oct. 18, 1821.
McClelland, John and Eleanor Morrow, Mar. 27, 1821.
McNeil, Samuel and Ann Irwin, Feb. 7, 1822.
McKeehan, John and Tabitha McBride, May 7, 1822.
McFarlane, James and Sarah Shannon, Mar. 12, 1822.

Moore, John and Molly Wilson, Mar. 14, 1822.
McKibben, Joseph and Tabitha McCulloch, Apr. 11, 1822.
McCune, Thomas and Sarah Fulton, Oct. 7, 1822.
Myers, Jacob and Nancy McBride, Feb. 27, 1823.
McCandlish, John and Maria McCormick, Mar. 13, 1823.
McClelland, William and Sarah Wilson, Mar. 27, 1823.
McCulloch, Thomas and Isabella Blean, Apr. 3, 1823.
Mitchel, William and Mary Stephenson, July 3, 1823.
McCune, Joseph and Mary Davidson, Apr. 27, 1824.
McCullough, John and Elizabeth Cowen (?), Sept. 28, 1824.
McCormick, Samuel and Susanna Alter, Mar. 3, 1825.
McCaleb, J. and Sarah Uhler, Mar. 24, 1825.
McCord, Robert and Margaret Woodburn, Oct. 25, 1825.
McCormick, Thomas and Jane Harper, Dec. 13, 1825.
McFarlane, Alexander and Rosanna McCanon, July 7, 1826.
McFarlane, Clemens and Lydia Miller, Mar. 8, 1826.
Miller, Samuel and Rachel Thompson, Jan. 18, 1827.
McKinstry, James and Margaret Hays, Dec. 3, 1828.
McKee, James and Isabella Fulton, Jan. 8, 1829.
Murdock, John and Sarah Saunders, Feb. 27, 1834.
McCachran, Rev. Robert and Jane Laughlin, Nov. 11, 1834.
McCulloch, John and Jane Dunbar, Aug. 12, 1835.
Miller, Thomas and Margaret Meradith, Nov. 5, 1835.
Montgomery, James Ramsey and Nancy Kilgore, Nov. 25, 1823.
Niven, John and Martha McCracken, May 11, 1802.
Norton, Thomas and Fanny Gray, Jan. 28, 1802.
Niven, David and Mary ———, Feb. 1, 1810.

Nelson, John and Elizabeth Ewing, Dec. 7, 1815.
Nisbit, Fisher and J. Adams, Mar. 4, 1824.
Noble, Daniel and Rachel George, Mar. 16, 1826.
Nickle, William and Catharine ———, Mar. 13, 1827.
Orr, John and Eleanor Moore, Dec. 24, 1807.
Oliver, John and Susan Sheldon, Jan. 19, 1815.
Oxor, John and Elizabeth Roberts, Nov. 4, 1817.
Oxor, George and Elizabeth Stewart, Oct. 7, 1819.
Patterson, Samuel and Mary Stuart, Apr. 1, 1802.
Patterson, James and Betsy Williamson, Apr. 18, 1805.
Piper, James and Catharine Irvine, Mar. 6, 1812.
Palm, Adam and Nancy Asken, Dec. 17, 1813.
Pierce, Andrew and Rebecca McKibben, Dec. 3, 1813.
Patton, Morgan and Elizabeth Campbell, Mar. 21, 1822.
Richy, James and Mary McElwain, Feb. 4, 1802.
Russel, William and Mary Elliott, May 31, 1803.
Rees, John and Margaret Brown, Oct. 3, 1805.
Ripton, John and Isabella Mathers, June 18, 1807.
Ross, Simon and Isabella Beaty, Mar. 14, 1810.
Robertson, Thomas and Elizabeth Shannon, June 18, 1812.
Ross, Joseph and Catharine ———, Mar. 25, 1813.
Reynolds, David and Eleanor Orr, Nov. 9, 1813.
Richie, William and Elizabeth Gourd, Dec. 26, 1816.
Ralston, David and Leacy McAlister, Mar. 6, 1821.
Roberts, Robert and Isabella Grimes, May 31, 1821.
Riley, John and Mary Duffy, Sept. 1821.
Randolph, John and Mary Knettle, Jan. 3, 1822.
Ripton, Peter and Louisa Ross, Apr. 22, 1824.
Ray, William and Anne McDonald, Aug. 12, 1824.
Ross, John and Esther McWilliams, Jan. 24, 1825.
Roberts, Andrew and Catharine Crotzer, Mar. 16, 1829.

Randolph, Paul and Betsy E. Leckey, June 9, 1829.
Shulenberger, Henry and Betsy Rightmier, Apr. 30, 1805.
Stevenson, James and Mary Morrow, Oct. 24, 1805.
Steel, John and Anna Weaver, Dec. 4, 1806.
Stuart, James and Jane McElwain, May 29, 1807.
Scroggs, Moses and Peggy Thompson, Dec. 10, 1807.
Stow, John and Mary A. Geese, Nov. 24, 1808.
Scouller, John and Jane Brown, Apr. 4, 1809.
Shannon, Hugh and Ruhanna McElwain, Aug. 3, 1811.
Spangler, Samuel and Rebecca Fager, Oct. 15, 1812.
Shields, James and Nancy Martin, June 15, 1813.
Sharp, John and Martha Huston, Dec. 13, 1814.
Sharp, John and Jane McCune, Mar. 19, 1815.
Stevenson, ——— and Sally Hays, Mar. 28, 1816.
Smith, George W. and Margaret Weakly, July 29, 1817.
Sharp, William and Jane Wilson, June 5, 1821.
Skiles, Davis and Elizabeth Moor, Oct. 18, 1821.
Skelly, David and Jane Dougherty, Mar. 28, 1822.
Skelly, Robert and —— Wilson, Dec. 12, 1822.
Sturm, David and Elizabeth Wolf, Feb. 10, 1824.
Shannon, James and Martha Mathers, June 10, 1824.
Shaw, John and Hetty Wilt, Mar. 30, 1826.
Smith, Joseph and Eliza McCormick, June 28, 1827.
Smith, William and Maria Dougherty, Jan. 31, 1828.
Stough, Samuel and Mary Peeples, Apr. 15, 1829.
Smith, John and Jane Cooper, June, 23, 1834.
Snyder, Jonathan and Catharine Lehmon, Oct. 2, 1834.
Stephens, William L. and Margaret Elliott, June 2, 1835.
Sterrett, Wilson and Ezemiah Hays, Mar. 1, 1835.

PRESBYTERIAN CHURCH. 81

Thompson, John and Elizabeth King, Nov. 19, 1807.
Thompson, Hugh and Elizabeth Scroggs, Jan. 19, 1815.
Turner, Joseph and Rosanna Abernethy, Apr. 4, 1820.
Underwood, John and Priscilla Leacock, Mar. 18, 1824.
Vandyke, William and Nancy Duncan, Apr. 1, 1813.
Wilt, John and Elizabeth Ripton, Dec. 22, 1801.
Wilson, Robert and Dorcus Hays, Mar. 9, 1802.
Woods, Matthew and Jane Galbraith, Dec. 23, 1802.
Weakley, Isaac and Martha Brittain, Mar. 10, 1803.
Walker, Robert and Jane Long, Dec. 25, 1805.
Wallace, Samuel and Eleanor Gillespie, Sept. 15, 1807.
Williams, William and Mary ———, Oct. 27, 1809.
Walker, Alexander and Sarah Martin, Mar. 26, 1812.
Withrow, Samuel and Mary Laughlin, Feb. 16, 1813.
Walker, David and Maria Patton, Dec. 17, 1813.
Woodburn, James and Eliza Jacob, Jan. 20, 1814.
Withrow, William and Elizabeth McKibben, Feb. 12, 1818.
Wallace, Thomas and Mary Harper, Apr. 7, 1818.
Weakley, James and Eliza Geddes, Feb. 23, 1819.
Wigly, Joseph and Elizabeth ———, Aug. 23, 1821.
Woodburn, Skiles and Margaret McKeehan, Dec. 20, 1821.
Wills, Dr. David and Elizabeth Peebles, Feb. 14, 1822.
Workman, William and Elizabeth Carothers, Dec. 5, 1822.
Wightman, William and Mary Dunfee, Feb. 19, 1824.
Woodburn, William and Margaret Geddes, Jan. 22, 1828.
Williams, Lewis H. and Tabitha McKeehan, Feb. 15, 1831.
Wilson, Robert and Martha J. Beatty, Oct. 25, 1832.
Woodburn, George and Mary C. Williams, Dec. 11, 1833.

MEMBERS OF THE FEMALE BIBLE CLASS, JUNE 11, 1817.

Deborah McKeehan,
Ann Brittain,
Nancy Laughlin,
Eliza Laughlin,
Eleanor Davidson,
Jane Wilson,
Elizabeth Pollock,
Elizabeth McKain,
Mary Brattan,
Elizabeth Atchison,
Margaret McKnight,
Jane McKnight,
Mary Davidson,
Isabel Johnston,
Jane Laughlin,
Sarah Leckey,
Mary Leckey,
Ann Leckey,
Jemima Crowell,
Sarah Shannon,
Margaret Carson,
Rachel Crawford,
Rebecca McCracken,
Margaret Woodburn,
Martha Peebles,
Nancy Gillespie,
Ann Gillespie,
Nancy Graham,
Mary McKnight,
Nancy Buchanan,
Priscilla Carson,
Nancy Lindsay,
Alice Thompson,
Margaret McBride,
Catharine Dougherty,
Sarah Geddes,
Lucy Walker,
Rosanna Dunbar,
Eliza Geddes,
Eliza Peebles,
Jane G. Williams,
Ann Wallace,
Keziah McKibben,
Margaret Adams,
Margaret McCandlish,
Jane McCullough,
Eleanor Brattan,
Mary Thompson,
Elizabeth Piper,
Priscilla Leacock,
Ruth Roan,

MEMBERS OF THE MALE BIBLE CLASS, JUNE 11, 1817.

Paul Pierce,
Samuel Lindsay,
George McCarron,
Chambers McKibben,
William Barr,
Thompson Glenn,

PRESBYTERIAN CHURCH.   83

James C. Williams,
James Laughlin, jr.,
Samuel Davidson,
John Shannon,
William Crawford,
Joseph McKibben,
James Davidson,
Andrew Pierce,
William McCulloch,
Joseph Brown,
Dr. John P. Geddes,
William Lindsay,
John Mathers,
Samuel Culbertson,
James Fenton,
Ezekiel Kilgore,
John McCulloch,
Ralph Ewing,
John Davidson,
James Shannon,
Rev. Alexander Sharp,
James Weakley,
Thomas Wallace,
George W. Woodburn,
Andrew Cooper,
Samuel Graham.

DISTRICTS, ELDERS, HEADS OF FAMILIES AND NUMBER OF PERSONS IN EACH FAMILY IN 1808.

William Stephenson's District, Upper Mifflin.

William Stephenson	6,	Walter Bell	4,
Joseph McElhenny	4,	John Gorrel,	
William Brown	5,	John Allen,	
James Shelly	6,	John Shannon	4,
John Martin	5,	John Morrow	8,
David Sterrett	5,	James McElwain	4,
Thomas Martin,		Paul Martin	6,
James Stephenson,		David Montgomery	6,
Hugh McElhenny	9,	Robert Barr,	
Andrew McElwain	4,	Thomas Martin,	
Andrew Patterson	8,		

Thomas McCormick's District, Lower Mifflin.

Thomas McCormick	5,	Mrs. Mitchel	4,

THE BIG SPRING

James Fenton,		Nathaniel Gillespie	5,
Henry Knettle	4,	Widow Walker	5,
Widow McClintock	6,	Robert Gillespie	5,
John McFarlane	5,	William Mathews	2,
Joseph McCormick	7,	Andrew Thompson	8,
Alexander Elliott	7,	James Purdy	4,
Robert Fenton,		James McFarlane	5,

James Brown's District, Newton Township.

James Brown	7,	Lewis Rightmyer	11,
James Beatty	11,	Robert Peebles	5,
James Irvine	6,	Cornelius Vanderbilt	6,
Robert Mickey	7,	William Mathers	7,

James Laird's District, North Frankford.

James Laird,	Widow Dickson,
George Dougherty,	Robert Gillespie,
Thomas Officer,	Alexander Leckey,
Widow Gillespie,	James Sharp,
Colonel Crawford,	James Clemmons,
Thomas Espy,	Joseph Hunter,
Matthew Wilson,	

William Lindsay's District, South Frankford and part of West Pennsboro township.

William Lindsay	6,	James McFarlane	12,
Isaiah Graham	7,	William Connelly	3,
Robert McFarlane	2,	Jared Graham	12,
James Johnson	4,	Thomas Graham	3,
James Graham	2,	Robert Lindsay	5,
Arthur Graham	6,	Joseph Connelly	3,

PRESBYTERIAN CHURCH. 85

Alexander Thompson's District—Succeeded Hugh Laughlin—Upper Mifflin and North Newton Township.

Alexander Thompson	3,	Robert McCune	3,
Matthew Thompson	6,	Hugh McCune,	
Samuel Morrow	3,	Jesse Kilgore,	
William Morrow	8,	David Mickey,	
James Nicholdson	2,	William Thompson	12,
James Work	3,	John Cooper	9,
Mary McCune,		Robert Carnahan	9,
John McCune,		David Williamson	12,
James Mickey,		John Laughlin	3,
Hugh Thompson	3,	Jonathan Martin	3,
James McGuffin	3,	Samuel McCune,	
David Morrow	9,	William Kilgore,	
Samuel Williamson	4,	John Long	2,
Alexander Laughlin	8,		

Thomas Jacob's District, South Mifflin Township and Newville.

Thomas Jacob	5,	Andrew Thompson	3,
David George	2,	Mrs. Glenn	5,
John Fox	4,	William Walker	7,
William Bell	5,	John Roberts	6,
John Patton	4,	John Michel	4,
Jeremiah McKibben	8,	John Carson	5,
James Ross	5,	James Woodburn	4,
Thomas Kennedy	7,	John Davidson	7,
John Davidson	12,	David Ralston	6,
Adam Bratton	8,	Letitia Wilson	2,
William Russel	2,	Stephen Rhine	2,
James McFarlane	2,	Dr. John Geddes	5,
James Brown	7,	Thomas Clark	2,

John Dunbar	4,	William Glenn	2,
James Reed	4,	Leonard Shuman	6,
Mr. Wilson	3,	Philip Murphy	5,
John Walker	4,	Rosanna McFarlane	3,
James Kirkpatrick	4,	Elisha Carson	9,
Gilbert Moon	3,		

Atchisons Laughlin's District.

Atchison Laughlin	11,	Widow Ripton	4,
Samuel Hays	3,	Matthew Adams	3,
Samuel Sibbet	7,	William Duncan	6,
David Glenn	9,	William Pipet	6,
Samuel Gourd	6,	John Brown	5,
John Boyd	6,	Richard Adams	2,
David Ralston	3,	William McDannel, Esq.	2,
Alexander McBeth	10,	Thomas Adams	9,
Jas. and Wm. Laughlin	7,	Joseph Shaw	3,
William Bell	6,	Samuel Mathers	8,
Nathaniel Eccles	7,	Joseph Mathers	8,
Robert McBride	7,	Thomas Johnson	5,

John McKeehan's District, West Pennsboro Township.

John McKeehan	5,	William Miller	8,
George McKeehan,		John Davidson, Esq.	9,
John Smith	7,	Richard Woods	2,
Matthew Davidson	8,	Benjamin McKeehan	9,
Lewis Williams (Pastor's father)	7,	William Ferguson	7,
		John Miller	9,
William McFarlane	5,	John Gray	8,
James McKeehan	5,	Alexander Weakley	4,
James Huston	8,		

Nathan Ramsey's District.

Nathan Ramsey,
Thomas Norton,
Nathan Means,
John Gray,
William Ewing,
Eliza Ramsey,
Sarah Norton,
Mrs. Adams,
Joseph Gourd,
Nathan Woods,
Mrs. Gray,
Thomas Adams,
Mrs. McKinstry,
Mrs. Ewing,
Margaret Ramsey,
Ann Patterson,
James McKinstry,
Mrs. Gourd,
Jane Woods,
Elizabeth Glenn,
Alexander McBride,

THE PASTORATE OF REV. ROBERT McCACHRAN.

After the resignation of Dr. Williams the congregation became divided in an attempt to call a pastor. A portion favoring Rev. John W. Nevin, and others Rev. John Kennedy, who was afterwards professor of mathematics in Jefferson College, Pa. They however finally united on the Rev. Robert McCachran, and in the fall of 1830, sent a commissioner to prosecute the call before the Presbytery of New Castle, of which he was a member. The call was accepted and Mr. McCachran was installed pastor April 13, 1831. The diligent, faithful and conscientious pastoral work performed by Mr. McCachran is shown by the large accessions to the church during his ministry. There were received into its communion, five hundred and seventy-five members. Four hundred and eighty-five of these were received on profession of faith and ninety on certificate. *"In the years 1832, 1833 and 1834 there seems to have been almost a continuous revival of religion in the church, resulting during that time in an accession of over one hundred and forty members on confession of faith. As an evidence of the deep interest in spiritual things which at that time existed, a prayer meeting was instituted and sustained for a period, at day light in the morning." He baptized three hundred and ninety-eight children, and married two hundred and eight couples. After the first year or two of Mr. McCachran's ministry, the exclusive use of psalms in public worship was abandoned. He resigned the pastoral charge of the Big Spring Church October 8, 1851.

* Memorial Presbytery, Carlisle.

PRESBYTERIAN CHURCH.

MARRIAGES BY THE REV. ROBERT M'CACHRAN.

Adams, Ephriam and Elizabeth Barr, Nov. 16, 1840.
Albert, John and Catharine McDannell, Nov. 12, 1846.
Bratton, George and Jane Sharp, Jan. 7, 1832.
Barr, Samuel and Eliza McCune, Feb. 5, 1835.
Boyd, James and Jane McCune, Dec. 17, 1835.
Black, Philip and Mary Murray, June 13, 1837.
Brown, Joseph and Mary J. Davidson, Feb. 13, 1838.
Bessor, William and Eliza Grip, Feb. 22, 1841.
Blankney, George and Margaret Denny, Apr, 7, 1842.
Belt, Burt and Elizabeth Harris, Aug. 6, 1846.
Butler, John and Sarah Hart, Sept. 28, 1847.
Blean, Jesse and Agnes Brown.
Barr, John and Jane Barr, Sept. 3, 1850.
Bartnett, John M. and Lavina Conner, May 22, 1857.
Brown, Thomas and Susanna Creamer, Aug. 3, 1854.
Bush, John and Sarah J. McCune, Nov. 23, 1854.
Bowers, John and Nancy Landis, Feb. 29, 1860.
Boyles, Alexander and Jane Blean, Sept. 23, 1869.
Claudy, George and Catherine Rodgers, Mar. 26, 1833.
Connelly, Joseph and Eliza Connelly, Jan. 29, 1835.
Cope, ——— and Eliza Stough, May 31, 1836.
Cook, Fenix and Elizabeth McDannel, Sept. 21, 1837.
Casey, John and Martha Hye, Mar. 3, 1842.
Cremer, Theodore H. and Martha J. Graham, June 15, 1843.
Cobean, William and Mary McFarlane, Nov. 2 1848.
Carothers, Andrew and Louisa Bender, June 28, 1849.
Crain, ——— and Sarah G. Adams, April 12, 1857.
Cochran, Stephen and Margaret Griffin, Dec. 4, 1857.
Cooper, James and Eliza Morrow, Dec. 9, 1857.
Cole, Samuel and Hetty Johnson, Mar. 28, 1867.

Carlisle, T. Calvin and Rebecca J. McCachran, Mar. 9, 1854.
Duffield, Robert E. and Miss Torbet, June 22, 1837.
Dunlap, Daniel and Eliza Heffleman, Mar. 14, 1838.
De Peyster, Robert and Virginia E. Shepherd, July 17, 1838.
Davidson, William and Rosanna McFarlane, Sept, 13, 1838.
Dunlap, William and Elizabeth Skiles, Nov. 26, 1840.
Davidson, John and Mary Randolph, Jan. 7, 1841.
Dallas, William and Elizabeth Boyd, Mar. 16, 1841.
Dunfee, John, and Sarah Talbert, Sept. 3, 1842.
Dunlap, James and Lucetta Hays, Feb. 26, 1846.
Davidson William and Hannah Hoover, Sept, 17, 1846.
Ervin, James B. and Isabella McElwain, Nov. 30, 1831.
Elliott, John and Dorothy Myers, Sept. 23, 1847.
Frank, Henry and Eliza Kellen, Nov. 15, 1836.
Filer, David and Sarah Keller, Oct. 11, 1838.
Finkenbinder, John and Jane Beaston, Dec. 9, 1841.
Filer, David and Esther Smith, Oct. 24, 1845.
Frazer, Wilson and Mary Mechey, Jan. 6, 1848.
Gaster, John and Sarah Jane Lee, Dec. 20, 1832.
Graham, William and Nancy Davidson, Jan. 19, 1837.
Geddes, Thomas M. and Lucy McCord, Mar, 16, 1837.
Gray, James and Mary A. McCune, July 3, 1840.
Gray, Thomas and Elizabeth Drudge, June 3, 1845.
Goodman, Alfred and Mary A. Singleton, Aug. 12, 1847.
Gayman, ——— and ——— Mercer, Jan, 1, 1852.
Garman, John and Emily McKeehan, Jan, 19, 1843.
Hudson, Jonathan and Widow Thompson, Jan. 21, 1836.

Hood, John and Sarah A. Wallace, Nov. 15, 1841.
Hackett, Robert and Margaret Thompson, Jan. 14, 1843.
Hume, William D. and Hetty McWilliams, Sept. 12, 1844.
Harris, —— and Susan Wilt, Sept. 4, 1845.
Holler, John and Sarah Ramp, Apr. 19, 1849.
Hamil, George and Margaret E. Johnson, May 24, 1849.
Hackett, Thomas and Ruth E. Davidson, July 30, 1850.
Hefflefinger, Thomas and Martha McElhenney, Oct. 19, 1869.
Irvine, Dr. James R. and Sarah Bella Davidson, June 27, 1839.
Irvine, Samuel and Isabella Kilgore, Mar. 15, 1838.
Irvine, Dr. James R. and Mary Johnson, May 17, 1842.
Irvine, Dr. James R. and Jane Morrow, Sept. 25, 1849.
Johnson, Andrew and Eliza J. Martin. Mar. 23, 1831.
Johnson, Henry and Kate Hawkins, Nov. 18, 1868.
Kelso, John and Matilda Fulton, Nov. 6, 1832.
Keans, John and Emily Ramp, Jan. 29, 1840.
Koons, Isaac and Harriet Kilgore, Jan. 29, 1846.
Kishler, Jacob and —— Whistler, Feb. 2, 1847.
Keeper, Augustus A. and Margaret A. Woods, Dec. 16, 1847.
Keizer, David and Mary A. Bender, Oct. 4, 1849.
Kelso, John and Mary Duncan, Dec. 5, 1850.
Kelley, Cornelius and —— Brown, 1860.
Lemon, —— and —— Royal, June, 19, 1836.
Lindsay, James and Jane Brown, Nov. 18, 1840.
Lindenburg, Charles and Susan Mauer, Nov. 30, 1848.
Landis, David and Mary A. Albert, Apr. 25, 1850.
Lenny, William and Catharine Elliott, May 27, 1857.

Mullin, William and Eliza Whitecap, Feb. 21, 1833.
McCoy, Joshua and Sarah McCarroll, Dec. 6, 1831.
McElvain, John S. and Jane Stephenson, Mar. 2, 1833.
McKibben, Joseph and Mary McCord, Sept. 3, 1834.
McCullough, James and Margaret McKeehan, Jan. 22, 1835.
McKeehan, Joseph and Mary J. Skiles, Dec. 1835.
McGinness, J. H. W. and Catharine A. Laughlin, Oct. 23, 1851.
Markward, Isaac and Jane Dougherty, Feb. 18, 1838.
McCune, William and Mary A. Hays. Apr. 5, 1838.
Miller, Joseph and Elizabeth Thompson, Mar. 14, 1839.
Myers, Jeremiah and ——— McKeehan, Feb. 23, 1840.
Moody, Joseph and Ezemiah Mickey, Feb. 27, 1840.
McKeehan, Robert and Rebecca C. Skiles, Mar. 5, 1840.
McCullough, Samuel and Mary J. McKeehan, Dec. 24, 1840.
McKee, Alexander and Francia Bowan, Nov. 15, 1841.
Middleton, Andrew and Nancy Elliott, Jan. 3, 1843.
McFarlane, Robert and Lydia B. McKinney, Feb. 9, 1843.
McLaughlin, Samuel and Maria Harper, Feb. 21, 1843.
McKeehan, Benjamin and ——— Kinkaid, Jan. 4, 1844.
Myers, Benjamin and Eliza Carothers, Feb. 10, 1845.
McCoy, Daniel and Mary E. McElvain, Sept. 4, 1845.
McCandlish, Thomas and Mary W. Coyle, Dec. 25, 1845.
McDannel, William and Mary Martin, Jan. 8, 1846.
McCullough, W. Linn, and Ann E. Glenn, Nov. 11, 1846.
McLaughlin, William and Eliza A. Moore, Jan. 21, 1847.

PRESBYTERIAN CHURCH.

Montgomery, Robert and Rachel Thompson, Jan. 28, 1847.
McCullough, James and Martha Brown, Feb. 4, 1847.
Myers, Henry and Mary A. Ramp, Feb. 17, 1848.
Matthews, Edward and Velotta Bush, Apr. 18, 1848.
McKinney, Thomas and Jane Rachel Glenn, May 11, 1848.
McCullough, William H. and Sarah Mickey, Jan. 18, 1849.
Miller, —— and Elizabeth Walker, Oct, 14, 1850.
McCullough, T. Henderson and Rebecca Herron, Feb. 13, 1851.
McCullough, Robert and Jane Duncan, Mar. 25, 1852.
McCune, S. Elder and Margaret J. Laughlin, Nov. 17, 1859.
Mart, Alexander G. and Sarah J. Miller.
McCachran, Robert and Mattie McCandlish, Dec. 16, 1874.
Nettle. George and —— Stewart, Jan. 27, 1835.
North, Andrew and Margaret Myers, Jan. 28, 1841.
Nave, George and Barbara French, June 17, 1841.
Noftsker, George W. and Susan Green, Jan. 25, 1848.
Oliver, James and Mary McCachran, May 15, 1872.
Patterson, James and Eliza Montgomery, Jan. 10, 1839.
Pilgrim, Henry and Maria Miller, June 13, 1850.
Patterson, —— and Margaret Martin, Oct. 14, 1850.
Peters, John and Alice Baxter, Sept. 10, 1862.
Richards, Robert and Susan Spear, Jan. 29, 1834.
Russel, Fauster and Mary Mateer, Feb. 12, 1835.
Reed, David L. and Mary Fitzsimmons, Apr. 5, 1836.
Reed, James and Elizabeth Elliott, Mar. 20, 1857.
Richardson, James and Isabella Vanlever, Apr. 15, 1866.

Richardson, William and Ann Wilson, Sept. 23, 1869.
Steel, James and Mary McElvain, Mar. 15, 1831.
Shaw, James and Catharine Goodhart, Mar. 13, 1834.
Stoneberger, William and Josephine Roberts, Dec. 12, 1835.
Stewart, Mitchel and —— Miller, June 23, 1836.
Sailor, Isaac and Lucetta Rutgers, Jan. 24, 1839.
Smith, John and —— Brown, Oct., 1840.
Scouller, William and Eleanor Jacob, Nov. 26, 1840.
Straw, William and Catharine Albert, Jan. 7, 1841.
Snodgrass. William and Nancy Fulwiler, Jan. 16, 1844.
Sharp, Samuel and Eliza A. McKeehan, Mar. 5, 1844.
Snodgrass, Benjamin and Nancy Buchanan, Mar. 26, 1844.
Steel, Robert and Mary McCandlish, Nov. 26, 1844.
Stevick, Jacob and —— Snoke, Aug. 12, 1847.
Shover, B. and —— McDonnel, Sept. 23, 1847.
Sanders, William and Eliza Layburn, Dec. 16, 1847.
Snyder, Jacob and Hannah M. Randolph, Sept. 9, 1850.
Stickfield, Michael and Dolly Wilkison, Nov. 24, 1833.
Spree, John and M. A. Runsher, Feb. 29, 1860.
Sprigs, David and Margaret A. W. Baxter, Sept. 10, 1862.
Stanton, William and Annie Kennedy, Mar. 8, 1866.
Shullenberger, Adam and Adaza Hefflefinger, Nov. 25, 1869.
Treat, William and Wilhemina Rudgers, Apr. 16, 1833.
Thompson, John and Sarah Peebles, Mar. 26, 1835.
Thompson, James and Isabella Kilgore, Nov. 19, 1835.
Thompson, Matthew and Elizabeth Jacob, Sept. 1, 1836.
Thompson, Hugh and Jane Kennedy, Apr. 1, 1841.
Tritt, Samuel and Julia Heagy, Oct. 17, 1844.
Torbet, Robert and Mary Mitten, Nov. 30, 1848.

Topley, Absalom H. and Sarah E. Gardner, Feb. 15, 1852.
Trego, James S. and Lizzie R. Nagle, Mar. 25, 1873.
Thompson, Charles and Savilla Johnson.
Woodrow, Enoch and Jane Vanderbilt, July 31, 1831.
Wilson, Irving and Ann Weaver, Aug. 7, 1832.
Weaver, John H. and Lucy McCord, Mar. 6, 1833.
Wallace, Thomas and Mrs. Wilson, Feb. 13, 1834.
Watson, George and Mrs. Eliza J. Johnson, July 24, 1834.
Weidner, James and Elizabeth Spear, May 26, 1836.
Woodburn, James and Jane Johnson, Jan. 10, 1837.
Whistler, Christopher and ——— Filer, June 7, 1838.
Wolff, George and Eliza Harper, Dec. 27, 1838.
White, Robert and Jane Ferguson. Feb. 18, 1841.
Wise, Michael and ——— Donnelly, Sept. 9, 1841.
Williams, Joseph C. and Sarah J. McKeehan, Jan. 12, 1843.
Wilson, Joseph and Esther Butler, Nov. 20, 1845.
Woodburn, Benjamin and Elizabeth A. Brown, Jan. 1, 1846.
Welcome, David and Margaret Elliott, Sept. 23, 1847.
Woods, John and Rachel Layburn, Nov. 22, 1849.
Whisler, Elijah and Mary Nyas, Jan. 10, 1850.
Watson, Christian and Elizabeth Duffy, Aug. 27, 1850.
Woodburn, John and Lucinda Stewart, Feb. 26, 1859.
Zeigler, John and Jane Russell, Nov. 28, 1833.
Zug, John and Margaretta A. Hood, July 28, 1841.

BAPTISMS BY REV. ROBERT M'CACHRAN.

Atchison, Andrew Mitchel, son of William and Nancy, Aug. 30, 1836.
Alexander, William, son of William and Anna, July

23, 1832.
Adams, Margaret J., daughter of Robert, May 10, 1834.
Adams, Jemima, daughter of Robert, July 30, 1836.
Adams, Susanna, daughter of Robert, Aug. 9, 1839.
Allen, Jesse K., son of James and Jane, Oct. 30, 1841.
Adams, Martha S., daughter of Ephriam and Elizabeth, Barr, Aug. 7, 1842.
Adams, Rebecca E., daughter of Robert, Oct. 13, 1842.
Adams Margaret Clark, daughter of Ephriam and Elizabeth, May 4, 1844.
Brown, Elizabeth, daughter of William and Jane, Aug. 14, 1831.
Brown, Margaretta, daughter of Joseph, Apr. 13, 1832.
*Brown, Elizabeth J., daughter of John, Oct. 21, 1832.
*Brown, Agnes R., daughter of John, Oct. 21, 1832.
Bales, Thomas J., son of Eliza, Nov. 25, 1832.
Barr Mary A., daughter of Hugh, May 11, 1833.
Bales, Jane McFarlane, daughter of Eliza. Nov. 25, 1832.
Brown, Joseph Thompson, son of William, July 7, 1833.
Brattan, James Sharp, son of George, Mar. 10, 1834.
Brown, Sarah I., daughter of Joseph, Sept. 7, 1834.
Barr, Robert Lusk, son of Hugh, June 10, 1835.
Barr, Alexander, son of William and Sarah, Dec. 5, 1835.
Barr, John Geddes, son of William and Sarah, Dec. 5, 1835.
Barr Margaret L., daughter of William and Sarah, Dec. 5, 1835.
Brown Caroline, daughter of Joseph, May 15, 1836.
*Twins.

PRESBYTERIAN CHURCH.

Barr, J. W., son of William, (apothecary) July 8, 1838.
Brown, Mary J., daughter of William, Aug. 24, 1838.
Barr, Esther Thompson, daughter of Hugh and Martha, Dec. 13, 1838.
Brown, Andrew McElwain, son of William, July.11,1841.
Boyd, Rebecca, daughter of James and Jane, Nov. 11, 1842.
Brown, Samuel A., son of John and Lacy, Aug. 6, 1843.
Barr, Hugh A., son of Hugh and Martha, Oct. 29, 1843.
Best, Frances, daughter of Henry, May 4, 1844.
Brown, John C., son of William, June 23, 1844.
Brown, Ellen D., daughter of Lacy, Aug. 10, 1844.
Best, Richard, son of Henry, Nov. 8. 1844.
Best, Robert, son of Henry, Aug. 8, 1846.
Best, Sarah E., daughter of Henry, May 12, 1849.
Best, James, son of Henry and Catharine, Nov. 8, 1850.
Coyle, William H., son of Scott and Nancy, Sept. 13, 1834.
Coyle, Robert Elliott, son of Andrew and Eliza, Dec. 22, 1833.
Carnahan, John McD., son of William, Mar. 29, 1835.
Coyle, Samuel McCord, son of John and Eliza, Sept. 6, 1835.
Coyle, Martha Linn, daughter of Scott and Nancy, May 1, 1836.
Claudy, William B., son of George and Catharine, May 15, 1836.
Coyle, David Linn, son of Andrew and Eliza, Dec. 31, 1837.
Claudy, Samuel R., son of George and Catharine, Jan. 20, 1838.
Cook, Hannah E., June 12, 1842.
Cook, Alfred Dewey, son of Samuel, Nov. 11, 1842.

Cook, Caroline, daughter of Samuel and Jane, Nov. 11, 1842.
Claudy, Margaret E., daughter of George and Catharine, Jan. 19, 1845.
Cook, George Grove, son of Felix and Elizabeth, Aug. 23, 1846.
Davidson, Alex. Leckey, son of Samuel and Catharine, Mar. 25, 1832.
Davidson, Sarah E., daughter of John, June 10, 1832.
Duncan, James Mitchel, son of John and Harriet, June 30, 1833.
Davidson, James Wilson, son of John and Eliza, Apr. 20, 1834.
Davidson, Isabella A., daughter of Matthew, Apr. 23, 1834.
Davidson, John Blair, son of Samuel, July 29, 1834.
Davidson, Rebecca E., daughter of Alex, and Jane, Nov. 22, 1834.
Davidson, Nancy E., daughter of John and Eliza, May 7, 1837.
Davidson, Marjory T., daughter of John and Eleanor, Apr. 27, 1838.
Davidson, Elizabeth A., daughter of Samuel and Catharine, May 19, 1839.
Davidson, John Young, son of William and Rosanna, Nov. 1, 1839.
Dunlap, William, son of Daniel and Eliza, Nov. 1, 1839.
Davidson, Robert McFarlane, son of William and Rosanna, Aug. 6, 1843.
Dunfee, John T., son of John and Sarah, Aug. 10, 1844.
Davidson, Mary Jane, daughter of John and Mary, May 10, 1845.

Davidson, Ellen Jacob, daughter of William and Rosanna, June 7, 1846.

Davidson, Arabella, daughter of George G. and Jane, June 7, 1846.

Dunfee, Mary E., daughter of John and Sarah, Feb. 5, 1847.

Dunlap, Addella, daughter of Daniel and Frances, June 16, 1847.

Dunlap, Mary, daughter of Daniel and Frances, June 16, 1847.

Dunlap, Virginia, daughter of Daniel and Frances, June 16, 1847.

Davidson, George E., son of George and Jane, Nov. 12, 1847.

Davidson, Samuel Rankin, son of William, Nov. 3, 1849.

Dunlap, Anna, daughter of Daniel and Frances, Feb. 3, 1850.

Dunfee, John Rankin, son of John and Sarah, Nov. 8, 1849.

Davidson, Sarah E., daughter of William, May 9, 1851.

Davidson, John H., son of George and Jane, Sept. 21, 1851.

Ege, Mary A., daughter of Joseph and Jane, Aug. 25, 1835.

Ege, Frances Hopkins, daughter of Joseph and Jane, May, 24, 1850.

Ege, Mary E., daughter of Joseph and Jane, May 24, 1850.

Fulton, Sarah, daughter of James, Oct. 7, 1832.

Fulton, Francis, son of James, Mar. 29, 1835.

Fulton, Elizabeth J., daughter of Houston and Jane, Apr. 16, 1836.

Fulton, David Blean, son of James and Grizzelda, Oct. 3, 1836.
Fulton, Samuel H., son of Houston and Sarah, Oct. 14, 1837.
Fulton, Mary E., daughter of Houston and Sarah, Apr, 24, 1841.
Fulton, Martha, daughter of James, Aug. 7, 1842.
Ferguson, David Morrow, son of William and Mary, July 20, 1845.
Fulton, James, son of James, Aug. 8, 1846.
Ferguson, Mary J., daughter of William and Mary, Sept. 6, 1845.
Fosnot, John C., son of Jacob, Feb. 16, 1832.
Glenn, Atchison L., son of Alexander and Maria, 1831.
Givler, Martha J., daughter of Benjamin and Isabella, Apr. 1, 1832.
Givler, Thomas McFarlane, son of Benjamin and Isabella, Apr. 1, 1832.
Geddes, William M., son of Dr. John P. and Catharine, July 2, 1832.
Gaster, John Henderson, son of James and Sarah, June 1, 1834.
Geddes, Charles King, son of Dr. John P. and Catharine, Apr. 16, 1836.
Gillespie, James Stewart, son of Samuel, May 14, 1837.
Geddes, Williamson Niven, son of Dr. John P., Aug. 9, 1837.
Gillespie, Alfred Ewing, son of Samuel, Nov. 1, 1839.
Graham, John Davidson, son of William and Nancy, Aug, 8, 1840.
Gilmore, David McKinney, son of James and Eleanor, Aug. 16, 1840.

PRESBYTERIAN CHURCH.

Gillespie, Sarah I., daughter of George and Lucinda, Apr. 22, 1842.
Graham, James McFarlane, son of William and Nancy, Aug. 14, 1842.
Gillespie, Thomas G., son of George and Lucinda, May 12, 1843.
Gillespie, Sarah E., daughter of Samuel, July, 16, 1843.
Green, Matilda I., daughter of Samuel and Mary, Feb. 8, 1844.
Gilmore, Nancy Jane, daughter of James and Eleanor, June 23, 1844.
Graham, William Finley, son of William and Nancy, July 21, 1844.
Green, Barbara I., daughter of Samuel and Mary, May 17, 1846.
Gillespie, John A., son of Samuel, May 24, 1846.
Gillespie, Albert Stewart, son of George and Lucinda, Nov. 8, 1846.
Gilmore, Lydia B., daughter of James and Eleanor, Nov. 8, 1846.
Graham, Arthur, son of William and Nancy, Oct. 10, 1847.
Green, Joseph E., son of Samuel and Mary, May 27, 1848.
Glenn, Anna M., daughter of William M. and Mary, Aug. 19, 1848.
Gillespie, Elizabeth J., daughter of George and Lucinda, May 11, 1849.
Gillespie, Samuel S., son of George and Lucinda, Nov. 3, 1849.
Glenn, Robert E., son of William M. and Mary, Aug. 9, 1850.

Graham, Alfred Mateer, son of William and Nancy, Sept. 8, 1850.
Green, John C., son of Samuel and Mary, Apr. 1, 1851.
Green, Mary G., daughter of Samuel and Mary, Apr. 1, 1851.
Harlan, Mary C., Aug. 14, 1831.
Harper, Sarah A., Sept. 24, 1831.
Hood, Jane S., Nov. 13, 1831.
Herron, Margaret Davidson, daughter of James, Jan. 15, 1832.
Harlan, Jacob W., Mar. 7, 1832.
Harlan, Catharine, Mar. 7, 1832.
Harlan, Samuel A., Mar. 7, 1832.
Herron, Mary, E., daughter of James, Aug. 25, 1833.
Harlan, Eliza J., Sept. 9, 1833.
Harlan, Caroline, daughter of George, Nov. 10, 1833.
Harper, Margaret, daughter of William, July 12, 1835.
Harlan, Jane E., daughter of George, Aug. 25, 1835.
Herron, James Johnson, son of James, July 30, 1836.
Herron, William, son of James, Sept. 3, 1838.
Hudson, Martha E., daughter of Jonathan, Aug. 24, 1838.
Hays, John Sharp, son of Robert and Hannah, May 13, 1843.
Hackett, Ross, son of Robert and Margaret, Aug. 17, 1845.
Hood, John Wallace, son of John and Sarah, May 18, 1846.
Humes, Emma M., daughter of William and Hetty, Aug. 8, 1846.
Hays, Edwin R., son of Robert and Hannah, Nov. 7, 1846.
Hackett, Mary E., daughter of Robert and Mary, Aug. 7, 1847.

Hume, James Davidson, son of William and Hetty, Aug. 19, 1848.
Hood, Margaret Harper, daughter of John and Sarah, Aug. 3, 1849.
Huston, John D. Line, son of James, Aug. 3, 1849.
Hume, John McWilliams, son of William and Hetty, Aug. 9, 1851.
Hood, Walter L., son of John and Sarah, Sept. 21, 1851.
Irvine, James B., son of James and Isabella, July 7, 1833.
Irvine, James Davidson, son of Dr. James R. and Sarah, Mar. 18, 1840.
Irvine, Susan M. S., daughter of Samuel and Margaret, May 24, 1848.
Jacob, Joseph A., son of Joseph, Sept. 24, 1831.
Johnson, John Bell, son of William B. and Ann, Aug. 25, 1839.
Johnson, Robert G., son of William B. and Ann, May 12, 1843.
Johnson, William Houston, son of William B. and Ann, Feb. 5, 1847.
Koons, Thomas, son of Isaac and Jane, Apr. 13, 1832.
Kelley, Mary A., daughter of Jane, Aug. 29, 1832.
Kelley, Alexander, son of Jane, Aug. 29, 1832.
Kelley, Emaline, daughter of Jane, Aug. 29, 1832.
Kelley, William, son of Jane, Aug. 29, 1832.
Kelley, Sarah J., daughter of Jane, Aug. 29, 1832.
Ker, David Sterrett, son of William and Eliza, Oct. 21, 1832.
Kennedy, Alexander Barr, son of James and Maria, Dec. 16, 1832.
Kennedy, Thomas, son of James and Maria, Dec. 16, 1832.

Kennedy, Robert, son of James and Maria, Dec. 16, 1832.
Kelley, Ann G., daughter of Grizelda, Aug. 2, 1833.
Kelley, Samuel Kennedy, son of Jane, Sept. 28, 1834.
Ker, Elizabeth J., daughter of William and Eliza, July 12, 1835.
Kennedy, John, son of James and Maria, Aug. 2, 1835.
Kilgore, Nancy J., daughter of Ezekiel and Elizabeth, Aug. 25, 1835.
Kilgore, Ezekiel J., son of Ezekiel and Elizabeth, Aug. 25, 1835.
Kilgore, William M., son of Ezekiel and Elizabeth, Aug. 25, 1835.
Kelso, Mary E., daughter of John and Matilda, Jan. 31, 1836.
Koons, James, son of Isaac, Apr. 16, 1836.
Kelley, Margaret, daughter of Jane, Apr. 16, 1836.
Kennedy, Margaret, daughter of James and Maria, Aug. 18, 1837.
Ker, Mary I., daughter of William and Eliza, May 20, 1838.
Kelley, John A., son of Jane, July 15, 1838.
Koons, Joseph, son of Isaac, Sept. 3, 1838.
Kilgore, Mary E., daughter of Jesse and Mary, Dec. 25, 1838.
Kinsley, George, son of Jacob and Charlotte, Jan. 15, 1839.
Kinsley, John R., son of Jacob and Charlotte, Jan. 15, 1839.
Kennedy, James McFarlane, son of James and Maria, Apr. 11, 1841.
Knettle, Hannah M., daughter of George, Oct. 30, 1841.
Kelley, Margaret, daughter of Grizelda, Sept. 18, 1842.

Kelley, George S., son of Grizelda, Sept. 18, 1842.
Knettle, James H., son of George, May 12, 1843.
Kennedy, William L., son of James and Maria, May 13, 1843.
Kennedy, John G., son of James and Maria, May 10, 1845.
Kennedy, Mary Barr, daughter of James and Maria, July 25, 1847.
Knettle, Lauretta, daughter of George, June 11, 1848.
Knettle, Jane E., daughter of George, July 14, 1851.
Lee, Samuel, Sept. 24, 1831.
Lindsey, Joseph H., Sept. 24, 1831.
Lefevre, Kitty A., May 10, 1834.
Lefevre, Isaac Lawrence, May 10, 1834.
Lefevre, Mary E., May 10, 1834.
Lefevre, Peter Wilt, son of David and Mary A., Mar. 29, 1835.
Lytle, Annie M., daughter of William, June 13, 1847.
Lyttle, Sarah E., daughter of William, June 13, 1847.
McKeehan, Mary, daughter ot John and Eleanor, Apr. 24, 1831.
McKeehan, Mary, daughter of Benjamin, Apr. 24, 1831.
McFarlane, Daniel Ligget, 1831.
McCune, Sarah J., daughter of John and Mary A., Apr. 1, 1832.
McKeehan, Margaret, daughter of John and Eleanor, Aug. 26, 1832.
McElvain, James R., son of James, Sept. 3, 1832.
Mathers, Susan, daughter of Thomas, Sept. 8, 1832.
Moore, Martha, daughter of Mary, Sept. 15, 1832.
Martin, Sarah E., daughter of John, Sept. 15, 1832.
McFarlane, Martha E., May 2, 1833,

McFarlane, Margaret, May 2, 1833.
McElhenny, Margaret J., daughter of James, June 23, 1833.
McElvain, Robert McCachran, son of Robert, July 7, 1833.
McElvain, Ellen, daughter of William and Susanna, May 11, 1833.
McGaw, Sarah M., daughter of Samuel and Elizabeth, July 24, 1833.
McGaw, James, son of Samuel and Elizabeth, July 24, 1833.
McGaw, Isabella, daughter of Samuel and Elizabeth, July 24, 1833.
McFarlane, Jane S., Sept. 7, 1833.
McWilliams, John, son of John and Sarah, Feb. 9, 1834.
McGaw, Jane E., daughter of Elizabeth, May 10, 1834.
Mickey, Hays, son of Lucetta, May 10, 1834.
McKeehan, David, son of John and Eleanor, May 10, 1834.
Miller, Mary, daughter of Samuel and Rachel, July 6, 1834.
McCune, Margaretta, daughter of John and Mary A., Sept. 12, 1834.
McFarlane, Robert, daughter of Clemens and Lydia, Sept. 13, 1834.
McFarlane, Jane M., daughter of Clemens and Lydia, Sept. 13, 1834.
McBride, David, son of Andrew and Hannah, Sept. 15, 1834.
McCune, Ellen, Culbertson, daughter of Hugh, Mar. 29, 1835.
McElhenny, James, son of James and Elizabeth, Mar. 29, 1835.

PRESBYTERIAN CHURCH.

Miller, Lewis, son of Joseph, Aug. 30, 1835.
McCachran, Robert, son of Rev. Robert and Jane, Apr. 16, 1836.
McKeehan, Benjamin, son of John and Eleanor, Dec. 11, 1836.
McCune, Rebecca, daughter of Hugh, Dec. 27, 1836.
McKibben, Susan M., daughter of Joseph and Nancy, Jan. 28, 1837.
McCachran, Mary C., daughter of Rev. Robert, Aug. 20, 1837.
McKeehan, Mary C., daughter of Joseph and Mary, Aug. 21, 1837.
Michels, James, son of Jane, Feb. 6, 1838.
Michels, Samuel, son of Jane, Feb. 6, 1838.
Michels, William, son of Jane, Feb. 6, 1838.
McGaw, Scott, son of Samuel and Elizabeth, Feb. 6, 1838.
McGaw, Mary, daughter of Samuel and Elizabeth, Feb. 6, 1838.
McElhenny, Robert, son of James and Elizabeth, Aug. 11, 1838.
McCune, Ezemiah, daughter of William and Mary A., Aug. 9, 1839.
Mickey, Margaret E., daughter of Benjamin and Eliza, Aug. 9, 1839.
McKeehan, John, son of John and Eleanor, Oct. 20, 1839.
McCune, Ann M., daughter of Hugh B., July 12, 1840.
Morrow, Jane, daughter of John S. and Rachel, Dec. 11, 1840.
Morrow, William Stevenson, son of John S. and Rachel, Dec. 11, 1840.

Morrow, Eliza, daughter of John S. and Rachel, Dec. 11, 1840.

Morrow, Rachel, daughter of John S. and Rachel, Dec. 11, 1840.

Morrow, John Benton, son of John S. and Rachel, Dec. 11, 1840.

Mickey, Rebecca S., daughter of Benjamin and Eliza, Aug. 18, 1841.

McCune, Hannah M., daughter of William and Mary A., Oct. 30, 1841.

McKeehan, Albert, son of John and Eleanor, Apr. 22, 1842.

McKeehan, Rebecca J., daughter of Joseph and Mary J., Apr. 25, 1842.

McCune, Samuel, son of Hugh, July 31, 1842.

McKeehan, Jane M., daughter of Robert and Caroline, Apr. 25, 1842.

McGaw, John, son of Samuel and Elizabeth, Oct. 13, 1842.

McGaw, George W., son of Samuel and Elizabeth, Oct. 13, 1842.

McLaughlin, Margaret A., daughter of Samuel and Maria, May 4, 1844.

McFarlane, Jane E., daughter of Robert and Lydia B., June, 23, 1844.

McKeehan, Ellen, daughter of John and Eleanor, Aug. 10, 1844.

Morrow, Emma, daughter of John S. and Rachel, Aug. 10, 1844.

McCune, William A., son of Hugh, Nov. 20, 1844.

Mickey, Benjamin J., son of Benjamin and Eliza, Nov. 20, 1844.

McKeehan, George, son of Robert and Caroline, Mar. 12, 1845.
McLaughlin, Daniel Harper, son of Samuel and Maria, Nov. 8, 1845.
McLaughlin, Robert, Apr. 20, 1846.
McLaughlin, Susan, wife of Robert, Apr. 20, 1846.
McLaughlin, Lavina, daughter of Robert and Susan, Apr. 20, 1846.
McLaughlin, Eliza E., daughter of Robert and Susan, Apr. 20, 1846.
McLaughlin, Emaline, daughter of Robert and Susan, Apr. 20, 1846.
McLaughlin, Zachariah, son of Robert and Susan, Apr. 20, 1846.
McLaughlin, Robert J., son of Robert and Susan, Apr. 20, 1846.
McFarlane, John Finley, son of I. G. and Margaret, May 18, 1846.
McWilliams, Albert, son of Jane, Aug. 8, 1846.
McCune, Samuel Brady, son of William and Mary A., Nov. 7, 1846.
McCoy, William A. Shannon, son of Daniel and Margaret, Feb. 5, 1847.
McKeehan, Robert M., son of Robert and Caroline, Nov. 12, 1847.
McFarlane, Anna M., daughter of I. G. and Margaret, Nov. 12, 1847.
Mickey, Sarah Belle, daughter of Robert and Elizabeth, Nov. 15, 1847.
McDannel, John Martin, son of William and Mary, June, 11, 1848.
McLaughlin, Samuel J., son of Samuel and Maria, Aug.

19, 1848.

McKinney, Maria, daughter of Thomas and Rachel, May 12, 1849.

McFarlane, James Graham, son of J. G. and Margaret, July 8, 1849.

McCune, Cyrus, son of Hugh, July 22, 1849.

Mickey, John E., son of Robert and Elizabeth, Aug. 3, 1849.

Montgomery, Hannah E., daughter of Robert and Rachel, Feb. 3, 1850.

McDannel, Jane A., daughter of William and Mary, Feb. 3, 1850.

McKeehan, Emma, daughter of Robert and Mary, Aug. 10, 1850.

McKinney, David A., son of Thomas and Rachel, Feb. 7, 1851.

Mickey, Laura A., daughter of Robert and Elizabeth, Feb. 7, 1851.

Morrow, Ada, daughter of John S. and Rachel, July 14, 1851.

Owens, Benjamin, F., son of Albert and Hannah, Aug. 10, 1850.

Piper, Maria E., daughter of Elder and Elizabeth, Nov. 9, 1850.

Piper, John A., son of Andrew and Eliza, June 10, 1832.

Philips, Nancy I., daughter of Edward, Oct. 21, 1832.

Pierce, William, son of Andrew and Rebecca, Mar. 31, 1833.

Piper, James, son of Andrew, May 11, 1833.

Philips, John G., son of Edward, Oct. 16, 1836.

Patterson, William O., son of Samuel H., Feb. 6, 1838.

Richie, Elizabeth, daughter of William and Elizabeth.

PRESBYTERIAN CHURCH.

Nov. 6, 1831.

Rea, John McKeehan, son of Joseph and Adaline, Nov. 27, 1831.

Ralston, Mary E., daughter David and Ellen, Sept. 15, 1832.

Richards, Andrew T., son of Robert and Susan, Aug. 12, 1837.

Roberts, John, son of Andrew and Catharine, Jan. 9, 1839.

Roberts, William H., son of Andrew and Catharine, Jan. 9, 1839.

Roberts, Elizabeth, daughter of Andrew and Catharine, Jan. 9, 1839.

Roberts, Robert Gillespie, son of Andrew and Catharine, Apr. 24, 1841.

Rankin, William F., son of Dr. A. and Mary J., Mar. 29, 1846.

Ross, Alexander, McWilliams, son of John and Hetty, Sept. 6, 1835.

Randolph, Alexander L., son of Paul and Amelia, Dec. 27, 1838.

Smith, Lacy J., Sept. 24, 1831.

Skelly, Robert M., Mar. 4, 1832.

Sponseler, Jane, daughter of Widow, Apr. 14, 1832.

Skelly, Margaret J., daughter of Jane, Sept. 3, 1832.

Sharp, Alexander McNitt, son of Samuel H. and Elizabeth, Sept. 13, 1834.

Sterritt, Isabella E., daughter of David and Rebecca, Aug. 25, 1835.

Shaw, Peter Wilt, son of John F., Sept. 2, 1835.

Swiler, William Davidson, son of James, Jan. 16, 1836.

Swiler, Christopher Hume, son of James, Apr. 1, 1838.

Sailor, William J., son of Isaac and Lucetta, Apr. 25, 1840.
Stewart, Jane A., daughter of John and Rebecca, Apr. 24, 1841.
Seitz, John Wilson, son of Abraham, July 11, 1841.
Smith, Margaret J., daughter of James and Matilda, May 17, 1841.
Stewart, Susan E., daughter of John and Rebecca A., Aug. 7, 1842.
Smith, Sarah I., daughter of James, May 13, 1843.
Swiler, Sarah E., daughter of James, May 13, 1843.
Saylor, Rebecca J., daughter of Isaac and Lucetta, Nov. 26, 1843.
Stewart, John M., son of John and Rebecca, Aug. 10, 1844.
Stewart, Mary E., daughter of John and Rebecca, May 26, 1846.
Stewart, Caroline E., daughter of John and Rebecca, June 11, 1848.
Smith, James Houston, son of James, May 12, 1849.
Thompson, Margaret A., July 7, 1833.
Thompson, Robert Houston, Sept. 22, 1833.
Thompson, Alexander, son of Alexander, Dec. 19, 1834.
Tritt, Samuel R., son of William and Wilhemina, Dec. 19, 1834.
Thompson, Alexander, son of John and Sarah, July 30, 1836.
Tritt, Elizabeth A., son of Maj. Samuel, Sept. 4, 1836.
Tritt, Sarah E., daughter of William and Wilhemina, Aug. 27, 1837.
Thompson, Ellen S., daughter of Matthew and Elizabeth, Aug. 11, 1838.

Tritt, Jane M., daughter of Samuel, Apr. 24, 1841.
Torbet, Joseph Wallace, son of George and Tabitha, June 30, 1841.
Trego, Mary E., daughter of Joseph and Margaret, Mar. 12, 1845.
Trego, Margaret D., daughter of Joseph and Margaret, Mar. 12, 1845.
Tritt, Martha E., daughter of Samuel and Julia, June, 7, 1846.
Trego, Rachel R., daughter of Joseph and Margaret, Oct. 10, 1847.
Tritt, George W., son of Samuel and Julia, Nov. 12, 1847.
Underwood, William E., Sept. 24, 1831.
Underwood, Jane E., Sept. 24, 1831.
Vanderbilt, Jane E., daughter of Cornelius, May 17, 1840.
Vanard, Letitia, Peter Wilt guardian, July 29, 1840.
Vanard, Wilson, Peter Wilt guardian, July 29, 1840.
Vanderbilt, Enoch, son of John and Jane, May 10, 1845.
Vanderbilt, William A., son of Cornelius and Mahala, Aug. 8, 1848.
Vanbeaver, Mary E., daughter of Joseph and Rebecca, Oct. 14, 1846.
Vanbeaver, Isabella Oliver, daughter of Joseph and Rebecca, Oct. 14, 1846.
Vanderbilt, Jane E., daughter of John and Jane, Mar. 18, 1849.
Wilt, John, son of William and Mary, Apr. 14, 1832.
Wilt, Jane Mary, daughter of William and Mary, Apr. 14, 1832.
Woods, Samuel, son of William, July, 22, 1832.

Wilson, John S., son of Mary, Aug. 26, 1832.
Wilt, Eliza J., daughter of Hannah, Oct. 7, 1832.
Wilt, Catharine S., daughter of Hanna, Oct. 7, 1832.
Wilt, Rachel A. M., daughter of Hanna, Oct. 7, 1832.
Woods, Dorcas J., daughter of William, Apr. 12, 1834.
Woods, Martha I., daughter of William, June 7, 1835.
Williams, Jane Whiteside, daughter of Louis H. and Tabitha, Jan. 28, 1837.
Woodburn, James H., son of George and Mary, Jan. 17, 1838.
Woodburn, John J., son of James and Jane, Apr. 27, 1838.
Wallace, Samuel Gowdy, son of Thomas, Apr. 28, 1838.
Wallace, William Laird, son of Thomas, Apr. 28, 1838.
Woods, William, son of William and Margaret, July 1, 1838.
Watson, John M., son of George and Eliza J., Aug. 11, 1838.
Work, James Scott, son of James and Margaret, Jan. 25, 1840.
Watson, William E., son of George and Eliza J., Dec. 7, 1840.
Work, Thomas McFarlane, son of John and Margaret, June 18, 1843.
Watson, Beaty, son of George and Sarah, May 10, 1845.
Woodburn, Joseph A., son of John and Ann, Aug. 8, 1846.
Woodburn, Laura, daughter of John and Ann, Aug. 8, 1846.
Williams, Samuel M., son of Joseph H. and Sarah I., Feb. 5, 1847.
Watson, Martha J., daughter of George, Nov. 12, 1847.

Woods, William, son of Paxton and Jane, Aug. 9, 1851.
Woods, James Woodburn, son of Paxton and Jane, Dec. 22, 1850.
Woods, Thomas Jacob, son of Paxton and Jane, Dec. 22, 1850.
Woods, Elizabeth J., daughter of Paxton and Jane, Dec. 22, 1850.
Woods, Margaret A., daughter of Paxton and Jane, Dec. 22, 1850.
Woods, Samuel A., son of Paxton and Jane, Aug. 9, 1851.
Watson, Anna M., daughter of George and Sarah, Aug, 17, 1851.
Zeigler, Nancy Herron, daughter of Dr. and Sarah, Aug. 19, 1850.

PASTORATE OF REV. JAMES S. H. HENDERSON.

At a congregational meeting held April 19, 1851, a unanimous call was extended to Rev. Robert Johnson, which call was not accepted. On the 26th of the following July the congregation elected Rev. J. S. H. Henderson, pastor of the Big Spring Church. Mr. Henderson accepted the call and soon after entered upon his pastoral duties. During the ministry of Mr. Henderson very serious difficulties arose between the pastor and members of the congregation, which resulted in many leaving the church. The trouble was taken to Presbytery and that body found nothing to censure in Mr. Henderson. In October, 1862, the pastoral relation existing between the Big Spring congregation and Mr. Henderson was dissolved. The congregation expressed their confidence in Mr. Henderson by passing the following resolution: "Resolved, that we regret the necessity which impelled Mr. Henderson to ask for the dissolution of the pastoral relation; that we cordially bear testimony to the faithfulness of our beloved pastor during the time he was with us, and still have unwavering confidence in him as a servant of Jesus Christ, and a faithful messenger of the Church of God; that in going from us he bears with him our prayers for his success and happiness, and we cordially commend him to the love and care of the Christain community where his lot may be cast." Mr. Henderson received into the church two hundred and fifteen members; baptized one hundred and sixty children, and married ninety-seven couples.

PASTORATE OF REV. PHILIP H. MOWRY, D. D.

Rev. P. H. Mowry was elected pastor of the Big Spring Church October 17, 1863, and entered upon his pastoral duties the following December. He was installed June, 1864.

The short ministry of Dr. Mowry was marked by advancement in temporal and spiritual things. Unkind feelings of former years were, to a great extent, healed. A deep religious feeling pervaded the congregation, particularly was this the case during the months of April and May, 1866. Special services were held by the pastor which resulted in large accessions to the church. The church edifice was remodeled, and the pipe organ now in use was purchased. The use of tables in the administration of the communion were dispensed with by resolution of the session, September 9, 1864. In October, 1868, the pastoral relation was severed. The efficient work performed by Dr. Mowry and the high esteem in which he was held by the congregation is best expressed by an extract from resolutions passed by the congregation at the time of his resignation. "Resolved, that the pastoral relation existing between this congregation and Rev. P. H. Mowry, has been marked by uninterrupted harmony and good feeling; that we have every reason to be thankful for the signal manner in which his labors in our midst have been blest, and that he carries with him our highest esteem and warmest affection." One hundred and thirty-six members were added to the church during this pastorate.

PASTORATE OF REV. EBENEZER ERSKINE, D. D.

On the 17th of August, 1869, the congregation elected Rev. Dr. Erskine pastor. He accepted the call and entered his ministerial duties October 9, 1869. During the ministry of Dr. Erskine, pastor and people have done aggressive church work. Special series of services were introduced from time to time, resulting in several revivals of religion. The most note worthy of which was the revival of 1876. In the last week of December, 1875, Rev. Edward P. Hammond preached for a couple of days which was followed by union services by the different pastors of the town in their respective churches, for six weeks. These services produced a profound impression upon the community and resulted in much good. Business in the town was almost suspended for a time, people giving themselves up to church going and conversation on matters of religion. Many accessions were made to all the churches, the Presbyterian receiving one hundred and two members. The next largest in gathering followed the special union services held in the different churches of Newville by Rev. Francis E. Smiley in 1892. At that time thirty-three persons united with the Big Spring Church.

The congregation led by the pastor has taken advanced grounds on the moral questions of the day, especially in temperance lines. Five Missionary societies and a Christian Endeavor Society have been organized during Dr. Erskine's ministry. Notwithstanding the frequent demands upon his time by the church at large, rarely a Sunday passes without finding Dr. Erskine in his pulpit faithfully presenting the offers of salvation to the impenitent, and strengthening christians in their most holy faith. Five hundred and seventeen persons have been added to the church during the ministry of Dr. Erskine. We take from the last report of Dr. Erskine to the Presbytery on the State of Religion in the congregation, the following: "Number of members of the church, three hundred and thirty-nine. Four services are held on the Sabbath and one during the week the greater part of the year. The attendance has been generally good. The catechism is taught in the Sabbath School. The woman's and young people's missionary societies are well attended, and are active and liberal in support of the work. The spirituality of the church has been much quickened during the past winter by a series of special religious services. Five hundred and ninety-six dollars were contributed during the year for Home and Foreign Missions. The cause of temperance has been strengthened and advanced during the year. The gospel, however, is our chief dependence in the moral elevation of the community when faithfully preached, attended by the demonstration of the Holy Spirit, which makes it the power of God unto salvation to all true believers."

CHURCH BUILDINGS.

The first church building was erected in 1737 or 1738, shortly after the organization of the congregation. It was a log structure and stood in the present grave yard until 1790. We have nothing descriptive of its appearance or arrangement. In 1790 the congregation built a large stone church in the style then prevailing. It is said the plan was furnished by Rev. Robert Davidson, then pastor of the Presbyterian Church of Carlisle, and afterwards president of Dickinson College. The two back pews along the south wall in every tier from east to west wall were raised above the floor; the one next the wall about sixteen inches. The one in front of it about eight inches. The same was true of the elevation of the back pews in the tiers on the east and west of the pulpit. Every pew in the church had its price marked on it in shillings and pence, varying from sixty shillings the highest to twenty shillings the lowest. The raised pews at the back walls were about eight shillings higher than those before them. The church was heated by three stoves placed in the three aisles leading from the front doors. The pulpit was placed high against the north wall and was reached by a flight of steps on each side. The pews had high straight backs.

In 1832 the propriety of building a new church or remodeling the old one was agitated, and in February of that year the congregation resolved to build a new church and voted three thousand dollars for the purpose. The records of the church show considerable confliction of opinion in the matter and, although it was frequently brought before the congregation and board of trustees, nothing was accomplished for several years.

Some of the members were in favor of using the "funds of the church" which were the quit rents and the sale of quit rents, others opposed this vigorously. Finally more decisive action was taken. On January 25, 1840, the congregation instructed the trustees to raise funds and proceed to the repairing of the church, and at a meeting held the fifteenth of the following February the congregation "resolved that the trustees are hereby authorized and required to appropriate three years interest accruing from the monies and bank stock, together with three years quit rents, accruing from the lots in the borough of Newville, to the repairing and remodeling of this house, provided the sum does not exceed seven hundred dollars. "From this time the work of remodeling proceeded without interruption until completion. The trustees in conjunction with the congregation decided on making the following changes in the church edifice: The pulpit was to be placed in the east end of the church, and a lobby of nine and a half feet was to be taken from the west end of the church and over the lobby a gallery was to be made. The two principal aisles were to be six feet wide, and to run east and west. The aisle in front of the pulpit was to be seven and a half feet wide. The pews on the right and left of the pulpit were to be eight feet in length, and the two last pews in the west end were to be raised across the whole range, and all pews to have panel doors. There were to be four windows on each side of the building and two at each end, lowered to the standard of making windows in modern churches, each window to contain twenty-four panes of glass, twelve by fourteen. There were to be two doors opposite the aisle running north and south; two doors from the west end from the lobby into the church, and a large door from the west end to enter the lobby, with circular top and glass above. Three center pieces were to be placed on the ceiling. A new floor was to be laid. A cupola was to be placed on the west end in which a bell was directed to be hung. The bell, however, was not bought until 1854. All of these changes seem to have been made and the work completed by the fall of 1841, for on the second of November of that year at a meeting of the trustees a committee was appointed to settle with the contractor, Jacob Zeigler. The report made of the expense of remodeling the church shows an expenditure of two thousand three hundred and thirty-nine dollars and thirty-five cents. Prior to 1853 the cupola appears to have become damaged by some means, and in the fall and winter of 1853 it was taken down and replaced by another. About this time the two small rooms in the lobby were removed and stairs to the gallery placed at each end of the lobby. A bell was purchased and placed in the new cupola at an expense of one hundred and seventy-five dollars, and was reported as being paid for at a meeting of the congregation February 12, 1854. In 1865 the gallery of the church was taken down and a platform erected in its place for the use of the choir and the accommodation of the pipe organ which was purchased at that time. The pulpit was lowered and a new carpet was laid. At a a congregational meeting held November 23, 1880, it was resolved to remodel the old church building. This was done during the year 1881, and the remodeled edifice was reopened for worship.

The improvements consisted of erecting a spacious and

well appointed lecture room at the east end of the church, the same being divided into two apartments for Sabbath School purposes; the erection of a square tower with belfry on the south side of the church; the enlarging of the audience room by adding a recess to the east end for the pulpit; erecting a porch at the west end serving the purpose of a vestibule, and adding a recess at the north and south sides in which the stoves are placed. The audience room was changed by a broad central aisle running east and west, and side aisles along the south and north walls. The church was furnished with handsome gothic pews in walnut and chestnut; gothic pulpit, furniture in walnut, and crimson carpet. The ceiling was raised in gothic shape to the rafters and ornamented in stucco work, finished in white. The organ was placed to the left of the pulpit on a raised platform. The old square windows were changed to gothic, memorials to the families of James McFarlane, Daniel McDannel, Andrew Ralston, Robert Mickey, Samuel and Deborah McKeehan, James and Susan McCord, Rev. Samuel Wilson, Rev. Joshua Williams, D. D., Daniel Leckey and David McKinney.

When the church was remodeled in 1841 the exterior was rough coated, after a few years this coating fell off in patches and gave the walls a very unsightly appearance. It was again coated in 1881. In 1894 it was all removed showing the solid stone masonry erected by the fathers over a century ago.

In the summer and fall of 1896 the interior of the Church was greatly beautified, largely due to the exertions of the ladies of the congregation. The walls were handsomely frescoed; a brussels carpet in green was laid; the pews cushioned throughout; an artistic brass rail was placed around the organ loft, from which was hung curtains of green velour; all presenting a harmonious and pleasing effect. The amount expended on these improvements, was seventeen hundred and sixty-four dollars.

Tradition says, that a log study or session house was built near the first church, but we have no records showing the fact. In 1796, a stone building was erected at the north side of the church, at a cost of about $500. Archibald McCoy, was the contractor. This building was called by some, a study house, by others, a session house, and was also known as the school house from the fact that a Latin school was taught there for a number of years. This building stood until about 1840, when it was taken down and a brick building erected at the east end of the church. This building served for school and sessional purposes until the erection of the present lecture room in the rear of the church in 1881.

OCCUPANTS OF PEWS IN 1790.

NO.
1. Rev. Samuel Wilson.
2. John Davidson, Andrew Patterson.
3. Robert Patterson, Andrew Patterson.
4. James Graham, Jared Graham.
5. Samuel Woods, William Woods, Joseph Pollock.
6. John Lemond, Thos. Glenn, W. Woods.
7. John McKeehan, James Huston.
8. Alexander Officer, William Douglas.
9. Matthew Davidson.
10. Samuel Blair, William Mitten.

PRESBYTERIAN CHURCH.

Ground plot of the Church as it was in 1790, showing numbered pews arranged around the Small West Entry, Middle or Great Entry, Small East Entry, and the Great or Long Entry, with the Pulpit on the east side and doors on the west, south (two), and east.

11. William Clark.
12. Benjamin McKeehan, George McKeehan.
13. William Given, William Wilson.
14. Thomas Johnson, John Boyd.
15. Joseph Connelly, John Connelly, William French.
16. John McDonald, John Davidson, A. Leckey.
17. James McCune, William Auld, John Monroe.
18. Thomas Espey, James Johnson.
19. William Brattan, John Brattan.
20. John Ewing, William Ewing.
21. James McFalane, Widow McFarlane.
22. William McFarlane, Alex. Buchanan, Alex. Boyle.
23. James Laughlin, William Laughlin.
24. John Hays, James Woodburn.
25. James Graham, Samuel Lindsay.
26. George Lefevre.
27. Samuel Reauge, Mary Reauge, R. Beard, D. Crawford.
28. John Espey, George Espey, John McDowell.
29. John Beale, James Johnson.
30. John Rippet, John Shannon.
31. Widow Cummins, James Kirkpatrick.
32. Richard Woods, Gabriel Glenn.
33. David Stevick, James Nicholson.
34. James Irwin, Matthew Ramsey.
35. Thomas Jacobs, David Ralston.
36. Paul Martin, Thomas McGuffin, I. Dearborough.
37. Robert Hutchinson, John Patton.
38. James Turner, John Turner.
39. Samuel Mathers, Joseph Mathers.
40. John Reid, W. Hunter, A. Brown, D. Gallespie.
41. James McKeehan, Jarman Jacobs.

42. William Lusk, John Caldwell.
43. Matthew Walker, Samuel Finley.
44. Jere McKibben, Benjamin Stewart, James Brown.
45. John Brown, James McCulloch.
46. Robert McClure, James Laird, Matthew Wilson.
47. John Huston, Thomas Norton, Alexander McBride.
48. William Bryson, Hugh Allen.
49. John Carson, Samuel Emmett, Joseph Parks.
50. John McCune, Samuel Wier.
51. Hugh Laughlin, Alexander Laughlin.
52. Robert McFarlane, William Thompson.
53. Samuel Morrow, Samuel McCormick.
54. Robert Mickey, James Jack.
55. Robert Shannon, William Stevens.
56. Solomon Lightcap, Daniel McLaughlin.
57. Robert Walker, James Walker, Samuel Wilson.
58. James McGuffog, William McGuffog, John Robinson.
59. John Work.
60. Nathaniel Roberts, ——— Gillespie.
61. Alexander McClintock, Adam Carnahan.
62. John Morain, Dr. Laughlin.
63. Adam Bratton, George Gillespie, Thomas Gillespie.
64. Robert Mickey, Andrew Mickey, ——— Carnahan.
65. Thomas McDonald, William McDonald, William Hunter.
66. James Mickey, William Kilgore.
67. Joseph Vanhorn, John Kelley, Joseph Kelley.
68. William Duncan, John Doyle, Henry Clark.
69. Alexander Elliott, Thomas Mathers.

70. Samuel Walker, ——— McCune.
71. Wm. Walker, Andrew Walker, D. Walker, Robert Officer.
72. Thomas Kennedy, John Bratton.
73. Samuel McElhenny and sons, John Morrow.
74. Joseph Wilson, Jesse Kilgore, Robert Kilgore.
75. Andrew McElwain, John Bell.
76. John Purdy, David Ramsey, John Walker.
77. John Brown, Widow Walker.
78. John McFarlane, John Mitchell, Samuel Mitchell.
79. Alexander Thompson, William Thompson.
80. James W. Appleby, James McCurdy.
81. Robert McElwain, Nellie Stewart.
82. David Williamson, Andrew Thompson.
83. Robert Beale, Andrew Beale.
84. James Hamilton, Robert Lusk.

THE GLEBE.

The Glebe or land belonging to the church, consisted of eighty-nine acres and some perches. A warrant for this tract was issued from the Land Office of the Provence, March 2, 1744, to William Lemond, James Walker, Alexander McClintock and David Killough, for the use of and in tract for the Presbyterian congregation of Big Spring. This trust was called "Reliance" and was held under the original warrant until the 23rd of September, 1794, when it was patented by the State authorities. The congregation built a stone parsonage on the glebe on the high ground on the north side of Main street near the Big Spring, the ruins of which stood until a few years ago. The parsonage was occupied by the pastor until some time after the settlement of Mr. Wilson. He bought a farm on the north side of the Conodoguinet where he built a stone house. The farm is now owned by his great grand son, James W. Sharp. During Mr. Wilson's residence over the creek the parsonage was rented. On Jan. 10th, 1797, the parsonage property was offered at public sale. Rev. Samuel Wilson purchased it at £35 8d. per acre for about five acres.

The propriety of laying out a town on the glebe land had been discussed several years before it was accomplished. The first record of a meeting of the trustees or congregation when the expediency of laying out a town was considered, is taken from the trustees minute book of 1788; the first book used after the church was incorporated. The church was incorporated February 27, 1785, under the style and title of "The First Presbyterian Church in Newton township in the County of Cumberland. The resolutions taken from that book are as follows:

"Aug. 16, 1790.—It was moved and agreed that the time for laying off the town upon the glebe be deferred until the next meeting."

"Friday, Aug. 20. The trustees met for laying off the town upon the glebe land, agreeable to instructions from the congregation, and their own resolutions of the last meeting, but on Rev. Mr. Wilson's opposition thereto, the trustees agreed to postpone the prosecution of the business until they had further instructions from the congregation."

"Sept. 9, 1790.—The trustees met and laid off sixty lots of ground, sixty feet front and one hundred feet back; after which they directed Mr. Vanhorn to make a drawing of the same, and appointed the president, Mr. Mathias, Mr. Vanhorn and the secretary, a committee to meet the following Tuesday at the office of the secretary for the purpose of making a plan, &c., for the disposition of lots." The plan drawn consisted of one street, Main street, to run from the spring to the west, with Glebe alley running parallel on its south, and Cove alley on its north; to be crossed by the streets Corporation, High and West; the former two to extend north to the boundary of the glebe. Building lots were laid out on these streets, and all the remaining land of the tract was divided into parcels of from two to five acres for pasture and tillage.

"Sept. 16.—The trustees met. The committee submitting the plan of the town and the conditions of sale to them; it was agreed as follows: That the town shall be called Newville, that the lots already laid off be disposed of by lottery, at a rate of six dollars a ticket reserving one and forty-four, which shall be sold at public vendue. That all the lots fronting on Main street be subject to a ground rent of ten shillings. No. 1 of the reserved lots to be subject to a ground rent of twelve shillings, and No. 44 to sixteen shillings and eight pence. That adventures pay one-third of the price of their tickets in hand, and give their obligation for the balance, payable in three months."

Oct. 28.—The day appointed for the sale of reserved lots, and likewise for the drawing of the lottery. The sale and drawing was postponed until Thursday of November.

Nov. 4.—The trustees proceeded to the sale of lot No. 1, which was duly purchased by William Laughlin, sen., for the sum of eighty pounds currency, and lot 44, by George McKeehan, for the sum of eighteen pounds, twelve shillings. The sale being over, they proceeded to the drawing of the lottery. The following scale of drawing was the result:

Sixty lots were drawn at about three pounds each. On the 12th of December, six were sold for six dollars the lot. The balance of the lots were not drawn but were sold at private sale. The pasture lots were sold at from $24 to $27 per acre. About eight acres of the north-east corner, was reserved for parsonage use, and subsequently sold to the Rev. S. Wilson. The reason lots Nos. 1 and 44 were considered more valuable, was their water privileges, they bordering on the spring. All of the lots were deeded in limited fee with a reserved incumbrance, which was to yield an annual six per cent rent to the church. The incumbrance on the front lots, as given in the foregoing resolutions, was

$22.22, each making an annual quit rent of $1.33; on the back lots, $17.90 each, with a quit rent of $1.07; and upon the out lots, $13.33 per acre, with a quit rent of eighty cents.

The collection of these rents as well as the other revenues of the church, was always annoying, and the records abound in different methods that were employed for their collection. Some were of a rather severe character and would hardly be tolerated in this day. On one occasion, we find that "Pews will be declared vacant and given to others if rent is not paid at the end of the year." On another, "Resolved that all persons who are indebted to the congregation, be notified to pay in six weeks, or suit will be instituted for recovery of the same. Provided that in no case, suit be brought against any desolate or indigent female, or any other individual whom the trustees may consider from sickness, poverty, or like cause, to be unable to pay at present." For many years the collectors of the church funds were given five per cent of their collections for their trouble and to stimulate them to greater activity. The trustees of the church in 1836, resolved to abolish the quit rents by collecting the incumbrance and giving the owner of the property a deed in fee simple. Many persons took advantage of the offer, but some of the quit rents were held by the church as late as 1884. Happily for all parties, the contentions which existed for so many years between the church and the town over the right of the congregation to collect the ground rents, have passed away, and now all things move along smoothly. It is thought by many, that those early difficulties over the ground rent, served to retard the growth of the town.

PRESBYTERIAN CHURCH. 133

The original purchasers of lots from the trustees were Ludwig Andrews, David Auld, Wm. Auld, Henry Aughinbaugh, Philip Beck, Isaiah Blair, John Boyd, James Boyd, John Bratton, Wm. Cowden, George Carmer, Samuel Crowel, John Clark, Joseph Crawford, John Davidson, John Dunbar, Samuel Finley, Thomas George, James Graham, Patrick Greer, Andrew Harvey, Abraham Hildebrand, Hugh Holmes, John Jacob, Isaac Jamison, George Keiser, William Leiper, William Laughlin, Felix Scott, Martha Lusk, Robert Lusk, Thomas Lusk, David McClintock, Samuel McCulloch, Archy McCoy, Henry McDermond, Samuel McIlheny, William McElwain, Jere. McKibben, Daniel McQuire, Ezra McCall, George McKeehan, William McFarlane, William McGonegal, Isaac Mason, John Mason, Titus Miller, John Moore, Samuel Morrow, John Nickle, James Nicholson, David Ogler, Robert Officer, James Patrick, William Porterfield, William Patton, Samuel Silver, Leonard Shannon, Daniel Sourpike, Brice Sterrett, Matthew Thompson, John Turner, J. D. Waltenberger, John Weily, Samuel Wilson, Hugh Wallace, David Williamson, Thomas Wilson, James Woodburn, Alexander Work.

The following is a copy of one of the first deeds granted by the Big Spring Church, dated Aug. 25, 1797:

"This Indenture Witnesseth, That John Carson, George McKeehan, Samuel Matthias, Thomas Jacobs, John Davidson, Jr., Alex. Thompson, John Geddes, Esqs., the present trustees of the incorporated congregation of Big Spring, in Cumberland County, and State of Pennsylvania, have in virtue of the trust reposed in us by the said congregation, and in consideration of the sum of two pounds, two shillings and two pence in full, have bargained, &c., to ———, of Newville, Newton township (here follows a description of the lot); being the same lot drawn at the lottery of the said town lots, on the 4th of March, 1790; and it is part of a tract of land surveyed in persuance of a warrant dated March 20, 1744, granted to William Lemond and others, in trust for the said congregation, containing 89 acres and 105 perches, and allowances as expressed in the patent granted by the Commonwealth of Pennsylvania under the hand of Thomas Mifflin, Esq., Governor, and the seal of the said Commonwealth, to the said John Carson, &c., and successors of said congregation, dated at Philadelphia, September 23, 1794, together with all the singular, &c., to have and to hold, &c. Attest, John Geddes, John Dunbar, John Carson."

The house in which Revs. William Linn and Samuel Wilson lived having passed out of the possession of the congregation, no necessity for a parsonage was felt during the ministry of Dr. Williams or Mr. McCachran, as they owned farms upon which they lived. After the location of Mr. Henderson this necessity arose. The congregation on January 26, 1854, authorized the trustees to sell the remaining quit rents on borough lots, and invest the proceeds of such sales in a lot on which a parsonage was to be erected. The lot was not, however, purchased until January 28, 1857, when the trustees bought from Peter A. Ahl, one acre of ground on what is now Parsonage Street, this ground included lots Nos. 55, 53, 51, 49, 47, and 32 feet in width of lot No. 45. The price paid was four hundred dollars. Immediately after the purchase of a lot a comfortable and commodious brick parsonage was built at a cost of twenty-three hundred and twenty-two dollars. This was improved in 1866, by the addition of a porch in front of the house, and in 1888 the property was enclosed by an iron fence.

RULING ELDERS OF THE CHURCH.

SABBATH SCHOOL AND SOCIETIES OF THE CHURCH.

The first elders of whom we have an account, we find taking part in a joint meeting of the sessions of the Big Spring, Middle Spring and Rocky Spring churches in 1743.* They were probably among the first ordained after the organization of the congregation. Their names were: David Killough and Samuel Lemond.

We find James Walker and Alexander McClintock, associated with William Lemond and David Killough, in obtaining a warrant for the glebe land in 1744, and presume they were also elders, but we have nothing definite to prove it.

The elders in 1790 and during the ministry of Rev. Samuel Wilson, were William Lindsay, John Carson, Robert Lusk, John Lusk, William Bell, Thos. Jacob, Samuel McCormick, Robert Patterson, John Robinson, Hugh Laughlin, John Bell, John McKeehan, David Ralston, John Caldwell, William Stevenson.

During the ministry of Rev. Joshua Williams, the following elders were ordained:

Nathan Ramsey, Alexander Thompson, Thomas McCormick, Isaiah Graham, Richard Woods, John McCune, James Brown, Atchison Laughlin, James Laird.

The following were ordained by Dr. Williams, Sept. 29, 1827:

Robert McElwain, Nathan Woods, Samuel McKeehan.

*Session Book of Middle Spring Church.

The following were ordained July 30, 1836:

David Ralston, William Davidson, James Laughlin, James McElhenny, Andrew Coyle, Samuel Davidson.

The following were ordained Nov. 17, 1848:

William Ker, William Green, James Fulton, Joseph Jacob.

The following were elected Nov. 22, 1858:

Thomas Stough, William Brown, Wm. Mills Glenn, Robert Mickey, James B. Leckey.

The following were elected Nov. 19, 1870:

George Gillespie, D. D. G. Duncan, and William Green, re-elected.

The following were elected Nov. 17, 1877, and ordained Feb. 16, 1878:

Samuel A. McCune, Peter Ritner, John Wagner, David A. McKinney, Edwin R. Hays.

The following were elected June 27, 1893:

Dr. John C. Claudy, James Cunningham, George W. Swigert, John F. Kendig, Dr. E. J. Zook.

The Sabbath School was organized in 1817. It was not exclusively Presbyterian. It was called a union school although most of its officers and teachers were Presbyterians. Rev. Alexander Sharp, D. D., then a young man attending Latin school in Newville, was the first superintendent. The following in the order they are given have been superintendents of the school. We have been unable to fix the exact date of the incumbency of all. Alexander Sharp in 1817; Nathan Reid, John Moore, several years prior to 1831; Andrew Thompson, James Laughlin, James R. Irvine, the first superintendent after the school was made exclusively Presbyterian; Andrew Coyle, W. B. Johnson, Joseph C. Williams,

John M. Davidson, J. Hunter Herron, in 1860; J. Blair Davidson, in 1862; James R. Brewster, in 1865; Thomas Stough, W. H. Thompson, David A. McKinney, 1877 to 1880; Thomas Stough, 1880 to 1892; Edwin R. Hays elected 1892 the present incumbent.

On July 5, 1814, a Ladies' Bible Society was organized under the name of the Newville Bible Society as an auxiliary of the Philadelphia Bible Society. As the society has always been officered by a Presbyterian it has been looked upon as an organization of that church. The society organized with fifty-six members each of whom were to pay an annual membership fee of one dollar. The treasurer was the principal, and for many years has been the only officer of the society. The treasurers have been in the order given, Mrs. Elizabeth Davidson, Mrs. Jane McCandlish, Mrs. Agnes Woodburn, Mrs. Ann Davidson, Mrs. Jane McFarlane, Miss Jennie W. Davidson and Mrs. Jane McCandlish the present treasurer.

The first Home Missionary Society of the church was organized February 14, 1867; Rev. P. H. Mowry, president. The Society of Hopeful Workers was organized 1871; Miss Mamie McCandlish was the first president. The Young Ladies' Branch of Workers, organized 1873, with Mrs. Margaret Stough as president. The Ladies' Foreign Missionary Society was organized Nov. 1, 1879; Mrs. J. B. Morrow was the first president. The Young Ladies' Branch of Hope, organized Nov. 15, 1878, with Mrs. J. B. Morrow as president. The Boys' Band organized March, 1878; Mrs. Jennie E. Hays, president. The Christian Endeavor Society was organized Dec. 8, 1889; Mrs. Belle McK. Hays Swope, was its first president.

SONS OF THE CHURCH WHO HAVE ENTERED THE MINISTRY.

James Graham was a son of James Graham who lived in Westpennsboro township. He was born October 16, 1775, and died June 5, 1848. He was graduated from Dickinson College, 1797. He read theology, and was licensed to preach in November, 1800. He accepted a call to the Beulah Presbyterian Church, in Allegheny County, Pa., and was ordained and installed pastor of that church October 18, 1804, and so continued until his death. He married Elizabeth Martin, of Sunbury, Pa., June 14, 1804.

Alexander Williamson was a son of David and Tamar Williamson. He was born in Mifflin township, September 17, 1797. He was graduated from Jefferson College in 1818. He entered Princeton Seminary in 1819, from which he was graduated in 1822. He died at Corydon, Ind., July 14, 1869, after having served faithfully, laboriously and with much self denial as a home missionary, in building new churches in a malarious region of country, for a quarter of a century.

McKnight Williamson, was a son of David and Tamar Williamson. He was born in Mifflin township on his father's farm, Feb. 28, 1800. He graduated at Jefferson College in 1820. He entered Princeton Theological Seminary in 1822, and graduated in 1825. His first pastorate was the Dickinson congregation, not more than a dozen miles from his home. He was ordained and installed there, Oct. 20, 1827. Most of his ministry was spent in the State of Ohio.

Moses Williamson, was also a son of David and Tamar Williamson. He was born on his father's farm near Newville, May 7, 1802. He made a public profession of his faith and was received into the Big Spring church in the seventeenth year of his age. He was graduated from Dickinson College in 1824. He entered Princeton Theological Seminary in 1825, from which he was graduated in 1828. He was licensed by the Presbytery of Carlisle, April 28, 1828. He afterwards spent six months in study at Andover Theological seminary, and subsequently became pastor of the Presbyterian church, at Cold Spring, Cape May Co., N. J., where he remained for over a half a century. He married Sept. 15, 1834, Emily H., daughter of Humphrey Huges, of Cape May. He died Oct. 30, 1880.

J. Davidson Randolph, was a son of Paul and Betsy (Lecky) Randolph. He was born May 16, 1831, died May 23, 1897. He graduated from the College of New Jersey, 1858, and from Princeton Theological Seminary 1861. He was licensed by the Carlisle Presbytery, June 13, 1860. He was ordained and installed pastor of the Presbyterian church at Frenchtown and Kingwood, May 16, 1864, and later served the congregations of Pittsgrove, Daretown, Christiana and Atglen, where he died.

William McCandlish, although not born within the bounds of the Big Spring Church, was reared here and can be called a son of the church. He was born in Scotland, Sept. 12, 1810. His father, Alexander McCandlish, came to this country in 1817, and settled near Newville, and died there in 1821. William, after many struggles against poverty, entered Jefferson College, from which he was graduated, 1834. He entered the Western Theological Seminary in 1834, graduating in 1837; licensed Sept. 1837, by the Presbytery of Carlisle; ordained May 1839 by the Presbytery of Wooster, O. He was actively engaged in the ministry of the Presbyterian Church for forty-five years and died in Omaha, Neb., Aug. 4, 1884.

Samuel Davidson, was a son of John and Nancy (Sterrett) Davidson, of Westpennsboro township. He entered the ministry of the Presbyterian Church and supplied the churches of Derry and Paxton, between 1790 and 1800. He died prior to 1800.

Williamson Nevin Geddes, Ph. D., son of Dr. John P., and Catharine I. (McClay) Geddes, was born in Newville, Pa., Dec. 28, 1836. He was graduated from Jefferson College in 1854, entered Princeton Theological Seminary, from which he graduated in 1858. He taught several high grade schools in Virginia, Maryland and New Jersey; was stated supply at Charlestown, W. Va., in 1869 and 1870; was ordained by the Presbytery of Carlisle, May 5, 1871; pastor of the Presbyterian Church in Waynesboro, Pa., in 1871. In 1872 he accepted the chair of Latin and mathematics in Hanover College Ind., where he remained until 1876. He was one of the editorial staff of the "Standard Dictionary" recently published.

John Hood Laughlin, son of John and Jane (Hood) Laughlin, was born at Newville, March 23, 1854. He was graduated from the College of New Jersey and from Princeton Seminary in 1877. He was ordained April 13, 1881, by the Presbytery of Carlisle, a missionary, and sailed for China September 1881, where he still labors. He married first, July 9, 1881, Annie Johnson who died in China, leaving an infant daughter. He married secondly, Aug. 17, 1886, Jennie Anderson.

PASTORS OF THE BIG SPRING CHURCH.

REV. THOMAS CRAIGHEAD.

Rev. Thomas Craighead belonged to a family of ministers. He was a son of Rev. Robert Craighead, a native of Scotland and pastor in Derry and Doneaghmore, Ireland. He was a brother of Rev. Robert Craighead, Jr., who was moderator of the Synod of Ireland. Thomas Craighead was born in Scotland and studied medicine there, but afterwards read theology under his father in Derry, and was licensed to preach the Gospel, was ordained and settled some ten or more years in Ireland. In consequence of the numerous grievances to which the Presbyterians were subject in Ireland, he joined a company of emigrants and came to America. He first settled in Freetown, Mass., where he continued for some time, but became dissatisfied because of a want of sufficient support. Cotton Mather, the distinguished minister of Boston at that time, urged his friends at Freeport to "provide for his continuance and spoke of him as a man of an excellent spirit, and should he be driven from among you it would be such a damage as is not to be thought of without horror." In January, 1724, he became a member of the New Castle Presbytery and accepted an invitation to preach at White Clay Creek and Brandy Wine. In 1733, he was called to Pequea, Penna., where he was very active in gathering and building up new congregations. He was released from Pequea September 19, 1736.

At a meeting of Presbytery, October 27, 1736, Rev. Thomas Craighead was appointed to supply Conodoguinet for six months. The following year he was called to supply the people of Hopewell, but was not installed until October 13, 1738, on account of the difficulty in locating the church on the Big Spring, and a trouble in his own family, he having without consulting his session suspended his wife from church privileges, because she failed to live in peace in the same house with her daughter-in-law. He did not live to minister to the congregation on the Big Spring more than seven months, but died suddenly the latter part of April, 1739, just after preaching an eloquent discourse to his people. His doctrinal views were in strict accordance with the Westminster standards, to which he was warmly attached, and which he had adopted both in the Presbytery of New Castle and Donegal as the confession of his faith. Mr. Craighead left four sons, Thomas, Andrew, Alexander and John. John was a farmer and lived south of Carlisle.

REV. JOHN BLAIR, D. D.

Rev. John Blair was born in Ireland in 1720, and came to this country when quite young, and most probably his father settled near Brandywine or Red Clay Churches in Chester County, Pa., as the name of William Blair occurs as an elder from there in 1729 and 1732. He and his brother Samuel received their classical and theological education under William Tennent at the Log College at Neshaminy, Bucks County, Pa. He was licensed to preach by the New Side Presbytery of New Castle, and was ordained pastor of the congregations of the Three Springs, Big, Middle and Rocky, December 27, 1742. During his pastorate here he made visits to Virginia, the last in 1746, preaching with great power and effect in various places, organizing several new congregations, and leaving where ever he went an abiding impression of his learning and piety. It is stated by some writers that he resigned his pastorate of the churches of the Three Springs December, 1748, but this is probably incorrect. Whilst the exact date of his resignation is involved in much uncertainty, the weight of evidence points to the year 1755. In 1757 he accepted a call to the church at Faggs Manor, Chester County, which had been made vacant by the death of his distinguished brother, Rev. Samuel Blair. Here he remained ten years, taking his brother's place both as pastor of the church and principal of the classical school which his brother had conducted. In 1767 he was chosen to fill the newly founded chair of divinity in Princeton College, and was also chosen vice-president, and was its acting president until Dr. Witherspoon entered upon his duties in 1769. It soon became evident that the fund contributed to endow the chair of divinity was insufficient for the support of the professor. Accordingly Dr. Blair resigned his position and Dr. Witherspoon performed the duties of both positions. Dr. Blair then accepted a call to Walkill, Orange County, N. Y., where he continued until his death, December 8, 1771, at the age of fifty-one. Dr. Blair was without doubt among the foremost preachers of his time. Dr. Archibald Alexander expressed the opinion that "Dr. Blair as a theologion was not inferior to any man in the Presbyterian Church in his day. He was a judicious and persuasive preacher, and through his preaching sinners were converted and the children of God edified. His disposition was uncommonly patient, placid, benevolent, disinterested and cheerful. He was too mild to indulge in bitterness or severity." Dr. Blair married the daughter of John Durburrow, of Philadelphia. The Rev. John D. Blair, D. D., of Richmond, Va., was his son. His daughter was married to the Rev. Dr. William Linn, one of his successors in the church of Big Spring.

His published writings are Animadversions on "Thoughts on the Examination and Trials of Candidates," "The Synods of New York and Philadelphia Vindicated," "A Treatise on Regeneration," "A Treatise on the Nature and Use of the Means of Grace."

REV. GEORGE DUFFIELD, D. D.

Rev. George Duffield was born in Pequea township, Lancaster County, Pa., October 7, 1732. He was the third son of George and Margaret Duffield who came to that place from the north of Ireland, between 1725 and 1730. His parents were of French Huguenot extraction, the family having first taken refuge in England and later settled in the north of Ireland. The name was originally Du Field. The subject of this sketch was prepared for college at the Academy of Newark, Deleware, and graduated at Princeton in 1752. He studied theology under Dr. Smith at Pequea; was tutor in Princeton College from 1754 to 1756, and was licensed by the Newcastle Presbytery, New Side, March 11, 1756. He was called to the churches of Big Spring and Carlisle, New Side, some time in 1757, but was not ordained until September, 1759. In 1763 Mr. Duffield was called to the second church in Philadelphia, which had been organized out of the followers of Mr. Whitefield, and of which Rev. Gilbert Tennent, one of the most remarkable preachers of that day was the pastor. This call was not accepted, and in 1766 it was renewed, but Presbytery declined to place it in his hands. In 1769 his relation with the Big Spring church was dissolved, and in August of that year a call was presented for one-third of his time from the newly organized congregation of Monaghan. This call was accepted and he was released from Big Spring and was installed there Nov. 14, 1769.

May 21, 1772, a call was presented from the Third Presbyterian Church of Philadelphia, which after much consideration was accepted. He was installed pastor of that church notwithstanding the opposition of its elders, the Presbytery and the trustees of the First Church, and continued in this relation until his death, February 2, 1790. His remains were buried beneath the central aisle of that church. Dr. Duffield was a man of ardent temperment, an earnest, zealous and popular preacher, in hearty sympathy with the great revival movement, and with the followers of Whitefield. He was equally zealous and patriotic in the cause of his country, and threw himself with all the ardor of his nature into the cause of independence. He was chosen Chaplain of the Continental Congress, and was often found following the army, doing all that he could to encourage, comfort and stimulate the soldiers, and in preaching to them the gospel and administering to them its consolations. Dr. Duffield was the first stated clerk of the General Assembly. He was twice married, first to a daughter of the Rev. Samuel Blair. She died September 25, 1757, at Carlisle. He married secondly Margaret, sister of General John Armstrong, of Carlisle. By this marriage he left two children, one of them being the father of the late Dr. Duffield of Carlisle and Detroit.

REV. WILLIAM LINN, D. D.

Rev. William Linn was born in Lurgan township, Franklin County, Pa., February 27, 1752. He was the oldest son of William Linn, a ruling elder in the Middle Spring Presbyterian Church. His mother is believed to have died in Shippensburg, November, 1755, where the family had taken refuge in consequence of the Indian raids at that time. His grand father had come from Ireland in 1732 and settled first in Chester County, and from thence had come, prior to 1750, to the Cumberland Valley and purchased and settled upon a tract of land where William was born. After persuing a preparatory course under Rev. George Duffield and in the school of Rev. Robert Smith, at Pequea, Mr. Linn entered Princeton College and graduated in the class of 1772. He studied theology under his pastor, Rev. Robert Cooper, D. D., and seems to have been licensed and ordained by the First Presbytery of Philadelphia, or that of New Castle, in 1775 or 1776, and was appointed Chaplain to the Fifth and Sixth Pennsylvania Battalions, February 15, 1776. Shortly after Magaws battalion was ordered to Canada, when Mr. Linn resigned because circumstances would not admit of his protracted absence from home. He received a call to the Big Spring Church, April 9, 1777, and was installed pastor of that church October 3, 1777. Here he continued until 1784, performing faithfully the duties of pastor and preacher. He was then elected principal of Washington Academy, Somerset County, Md. At the end of one year on account of sickness in his family he was obliged to resign and remove from that region. He accepted a call to the Presbyterian Church at Elizabethtown, N. J., in 1786, and in 1787 he was called to be collegiate pastor of the Reformed Dutch Church in the city of New York, which position he accepted and occupied until 1805. After entering upon his work here he was chosen the first Chaplain to Congress, May, 1789. In his position in New York, Dr. Linn rose to great eminence in the ministry, and attained a reputation for talents and eloquence second to no other minister at that time in the city. Dr. Linn resigned the pastorate in New York in 1805, on account of declining health, and removed to Albany, N. Y. He there engaged to supply the church, preaching once each Sabbath for one year. In the meantime he was chosen president of Union College, Schenectady, N. Y., but was unable to accept the position on account of rapidly failing health. He died in Albany, January, 1808. Dr. Linn was thrice married, first January 10, 1774, to Rebecca, daughter of Rev. John Blair, by whom he had seven children, one of which was Rev. John Blair Linn, D. D. He married secondly, Catharine, widow of Dr. Moore, of New York and had one son. He married thirdly, Helen Hanson, they had one son.

REV. SAMUEL WILSON.

Rev. Samuel Wilson was born 1754, in Letterkenny township, Cumberland, now Franklin County, Pa., in sight of the old Rocky Spring Church, in which his parents worshiped, and in the grave yard of which several generations of his family are buried. He was the fourth son of John Wilson, a farmer of Scotch Irish parentage, and his wife Sarah Reid. The youngest son of the family entered the army where he contracted camp fever and came home and died in 1778. Samuel attended his brother during his sickness and also contracted the disease and was very ill. During this sickness he resolved, if his life was spared, to devote it to the service of God in the work of the christian ministry. Accordingly, on his recovery, he relinquished farming and went to Princeton College, from which he was graduated in 1782. He studied theology under Dr. Cooper at Middle Spring; was licensed by the Presbytery of Donegal, October 17, 1786; called to be pastor of the Big Spring Church, and ordained and installed June 20, 1787. "He continued to labor faithfully, acceptably, and usefully in the Big Spring congregation until his death." Soon after his settlement in the ministry he married Jane, daughter of Archibald Mahon, of Shippensburg, Pa., and grand daughter of David and Martha Mahon, of Rai, County Donegal, Ireland. They had two children, John, who died January 30, 1809, aged sixteen years, and Jane, who married Dr. William M. Sharp, of Newville, and who died there July, 1876. A number of the great grand children, and great, great grand children of Rev. Samuel Wilson, are now members of the Big Spring Church. He died March 4, 1799, and rests beneath a large marble slab which the massive walls of the church he built in his early ministry shade from the slanting rays of the setting sun.

REV. JOSHUA WILLIAMS, D. D.

Rev. Joshua Williams was of Welsh descent. His grand father, Joshua, came to this country prior to 1764, and located in the Welsh settlement in Chester County, Pa. He had two sons, Louis and Joshua, both of whom served in the Revolutionary war. Louis married Mary Hudson and settled at Dillsburg, York County, Pa., where they raised a family of eleven children. The Rev. Joshua was the third son and was born March 8, 1768. He prepared for college at Gettysburg, Pa., under the tuition of Rev. Mr. Dobbin, and entered Dickinson College from which he was graduated 1795. He read theology under Rev. Dr. Cooper, at Middle Spring, and was licensed to preach the gospel by the Presbytery of Carlisle, in 1797. In the following year he was called to become the pastor of the churches of Paxton and Derry, and was ordained and installed by the Presbytery of Carlisle, October 2, 1799. After laboring there with increasing usefulness for two years, he received a call to the church of Big Spring, which he accepted, and was installed there April 14, 1802. Here he continued for twenty-seven years, the able minister and faithful pastor of this people, when, in 1829, in consequence of impaired health, he resigned.

It is said that "few men in the ministry of the Presbyterian Church of the eminent talents, learning, piety and usefulness of Dr. Joshua Williams, were so little known to the church at large. This was doubtless owing to the quiet and retired life which he lived, and to the absence in him of everything like a spirit of self assertion, or obtrusiveness. He was by nature possessed of an acute and vigorous intellect. His judgment was regarded as sound and discriminating, and he had a remarkable taste and aptitude for metaphysical reasoning. His mind was richly stored with the results of extensive reading, close observation and much reflection, all systematically arranged and at his command. As a preacher of the gospel, Dr. Williams was grave and solemn in manner and richly scriptural and instructive in matter. The great doctrines of the cross were not held by him as mere theoretical beliefs, but constituted the very life of his own soul. As a pastor he was regular and faithful in family visitation and in the catechetical instruction of all classes of people". He married, June 15, 1800, Eleanor Campbell, who died April 28, 1856, aged seventy-six years. They had six sons and three daughters. Dr. Williams died Aug. 21, 1838, and rests in the grave yard of the Big Spring Church, Newville.

REV. ROBERT M'CACHRAN.

Rev. Robert McCachran was descended from a Scotch ancestry. His great grand father, accompanied by his wife, four sons and one daughter, emigrated from Cantyre, near Campbellstown, Scotland, about 1725, and settled in the Forks of the Brandywine, Chester County, Pa. Robert McCachran, the second son of John McCachran and Isabella Cunningham, was born at the Forks of the Brandywine, Chester County, Pa., September 24, 1798. He early manifested a strong desire for a liberal education, and as there was no school in his immediate neighborhood where the higher branches of an English education were taught, he walked daily three miles in winter to a school affording those advantages. This he continued to do for some time, when a classical school was opened at Brandywine manor, by the Rev. John Grier. Mr. McCachran entered this school and remained there until its removal from the place, when he entered the Academy at West Nottingham, Md., in charge of Rev. James W. Magaw, a successful and popular educator in those times. At the end of the course of study in this Academy, Mr. McCachran entered the junior class in Dickinson College, Carlisle, where he received his collegiate training. After completing his course at Dickinson, he taught for a season in the Academy at Newark, Del., and then entered Princeton Theological Seminary in 1824, from which he was graduated in 1827. He was licensed to preach the gospel by the Presbytery of New Castle, April, 1827, and in the Autumn of the same year a field of labor was opened to him at Middletown, Deleware County, Pa. In connection with his work in this church, he gave half of his time to missionary work in Deleware and adjoining counties. He was ordained at New Castle, Del., May 19, 1829. In 1830, because of ill health, he resigned his charge. After his resignation he made a journey on horse back in quest of health and another field of labor, up through Lancaster, York, Cumberland and Franklin counties, preaching as the opportunity presented. He preached several sermons in the church at Newville, which had recently become vacant by the resignation of Rev. Joshua Williams, and so pleased were the people with his ministrations that they gave him a call which was accepted, and he was installed pastor of that church April 13, 1831. Mr. McCachran labored with great diligence and success in the Big Spring Church for twenty-one years, resigning October 8, 1851. He then turned his attention to the establishment of a classical school for the training of young men for college and the ministry. He erected a suitable building near Newville where he successfully conducted the school until 1864, when it was discontinued because of a loss of students occasioned by the civil war. "Mr. McCachran was a man of great simplicity of character. He was sincere in his religious convictions and conscientious in the performance of duty. He was well read in the ancient classics and in the works of the old divines of the seventeenth century. He was in the constant habit of daily reading the New Testament in the original Greek language. As a preacher he was simple, plain, scriptural and orthodox. He was generally regarded as excelling most of his brethren in the brevity, comprehensiveness and felicity of expression in his prayers." For many years he was stated clerk of the Presbytery, and always an active member of the standing committee on languages, and conducted his examinations with due consideration and acceptableness. In his private life he was quietly and unostentiously charitable to the poor, and especially so to the colored people, many of whom were greatly assisted by his counsels and liberality." It can be truly said of him that his entire life was in all respects most exemplary and blameless, and his end was in peace." He died February 25, 1885. On November 11, 1834, he married Jane Laughlin, who was born August 3, 1802, and died November 27, 1871. She was a daughter of Atchison Laughlin, a ruling elder in the church. To them were born two children, Mary and Robert, the latter is now a successful attorney-at-law in Newville, and represented his district in the Legislature of Pennsylvania from 1878 to 1882.

REV. JAMES S. H. HENDERSON.

Rev. James S. H. Henderson was born in Frederick County, Md., September 20, 1815. He pursued his theological studies in Union Theological Seminary, N. Y., and Princeton Seminary, N. J., graduating from the latter in the year, 1842. He was ordained by the Presbytery, of Nashville, Tenn., 1842, and spent some time in home missionary work. In 1844 he was installed pastor of the Presbyterian Church at Augusta, Ky., where he remained ten years. In 1852 he accepted a call to the Big Spring Church, Newville, Pa. He resigned the church at Newville in 1861, and removed to Montgomery County, Md., where he became stated supply of the church at Neelsville. He ministered to this congregation for nearly eighteen years, until his death, August 17, 1882. His ministry there was very successful, although the church at Neelsville was a small one. He organized a congregation at Boyds and these two became one pastorate. Both congregations built handsome church edifices prior to his death and were in a flourishing condition. He was married in 1842 to Rosanna J. Neel, daughter of James Neel, one of the original members of the church bearing his name, who with a daughter and six sons survive him. One of the latter is a clergyman of the Presbyterian Church.

REV. PHILIP H. MOWRY, D. D.

Rev. Philip Henry Mowry was born in Allegheny, Pa., March 6, 1837. His father, a graduate of the Western University of Pennsylvania, and of Jefferson Medical College, Philadelphia, practiced medicine in Allegheny from March, 1836, until his death, March 14, 1895. His grand father, Philip Mowry, was born in

Pittsburg, Pa., 1777, where his great grand father, Christian M. Mowry, a soldier of the Revolutionary war, settled but a short time before. His mother, A. Rebekah Riddle, was a daughter of James M. Riddle, a lawyer, born in the Cumberland Valley, and who settled in Pittsburg in 1812, after marrying Elizabeth Weaver, of Cumberland County, Pa. Rev. P. H. Mowry graduated from Washington College, Cannonsburg, in 1858, and from the Western Theological Seminary in 1861. On leaving the Theological Seminary he was called to the Fourth Presbyterian Church of Philadelphia and ordained by the Presbytery of Philadelphia, October 8, 1861, and at the same time installed pastor of the church. In October, 1863, he was called to the Big Spring Church, Newville, and entered upon his ministerial work here the following December. After a very successful pastorate of five years he resigned the Big Spring Church and accepted a call from the second Presbyterian Church of Springfield, Ohio. He remained in Springfield five years when he accepted a call to the First Presbyterian Church of Chester, Pa., entering upon his pastoral work October 1, 1873. There he remains greatly beloved by his people and respected by all. Dr. Mowry married, October 23, 1861, Catharine A. daughter of William H. Richardson of Greensburg, Pa. She died January 20, 1881, leaving children—Elizabeth, Henrietta, Robert Bruce, Fred, Philip, Rebecca and Mary. Dr. Mowry married secondly, April 18, 1889, Sarah W., daughter of William E. Du Bois, of Philadelphia.

REV. EBENEZER ERSKINE, D. D.

Rev. Ebenezer Erskine is a son of John Erskine and

his wife Margaret Trainor. John Erskine was the fifth in descent from Rev. Henry Erskine, father of Revs. Ebenezer and Ralph Erskine, founders of the Secession Church, of Scotland. He came from County Down, Ireland, to this country at the close of the Revolutionary war, and after remaining for a time in Philadelphia, settled in Ridley township, Deleware County, Pa. There the subject of our sketch was born, January 31, 1821. He prepared for college in the celebrated classical school of Joseph P. Engles in Philadelphia, and entered Jefferson College, in 1839, from which he was graduated in 1843. In 1844 and 1845 he was principal of the Pottstown Academy. After resigning this position, he entered Princeton Theological Seminary October, 1845, from which he was graduated May, 1848. He was ordained and installed pastor of the Penn Presbyterian Church, Philadelphia, September 11, 1849. There he remained until 1851, when he accepted a call to Columbia, Pa. He remained as pastor of the church at Columbia until 1857, when he resigned to accept a call to the Presbyterian Church at Sterling, Ill. He resigned the church at Sterling in 1865, to undertake, at the request of several of his ministerial brethren, the founding of a Presbyterian College in Northern Illinois. This led to the establishment by him of the "North Western Presbyterion" at Chicago, in the fall of 1865, of which he was editor and proprietor. This paper was a means of communication with the churches. The attempted founding of the college was delayed on account of the church controversies arising out of the civil war, the reunion of the two branches of the Presbyterian Church, and in relation to the Theological Seminary of the

Northwest. In 1869 he accepted a unanimous call to become pastor of the Big Spring Presbyterian Church in Newville, where he yet remains, faithfully discharging his pastoral duties. Dr. Erskine has occupied many positions of importance and responsibility in the Presbyterian Church. He has been moderator of the Synod of Harrisburg; moderator of the Synod of Pennsylvania; a member of five General Assemblies; a director in the North Western Theological Seminary, Chicago, from 1865 to 1869, and has been a director of Princeton Theological Seminary for the past twenty years. At the meeting of General Assembly at Baltimore, 1875, he was appointed a member of the committee of conference on fraternal relations between the General Assemblies north and south. At the meeting of General Assembly at Saratoga, in 1890, he was chairman of the committee on revision that reported the plan of revision to the General Assembly which was unanimously adopted. He was also author of the resolution instructing the committee on revision not to report anything that would impair the integrity of the Reformed or Calvinistic system as set forth in the confession of faith. He was also a member of the permanent committee on the revision of the Westminster Confession of Faith which continued its work for two years, and on its being reported to the General Assembly and handed down to the Presbyteries was not accepted. Dr. Erskine and Drs. Patton and Green of Princeton were among the conservative members of the committee and unfavorable to some of the changes recommended by the majority. In 1889 Dr. Erskine together with Dr. George Norcross and Rev. Mr. West published a history of the Carlisle Presbytery including biographical sketches of deceased members. This is a very full and complete work, the result of much pains taking labor, and a valuable contribution to the history of Presbyterianism in this country.

Possessing more than ordinary intellectual endowments, Dr. Erskine ranks high in the Presbyterian Church as a well read and sound theologion. He is a man of strong and decided convictions, and of great courage and strength of purpose. His sermons are full of thought and instruction; his matter solid and rewards the attention of those who are serious and thoughtful and who care more for sound scriptural and theological instruction, than for ornaments of rhetoric and mere empty declamation. He is noted for a remarkably clear voice, an earnest, persuasive and impressive manner well adapted to his matter. He is faithful and conscientious in the discharge of all his ministerial work allowing nothing to interfere with what he considers duty.

Dr. Erskine married, October 7, 1874, Helen M., daughter of James and Margaret (Sharp) McKeehan, a descendent of two of the oldest and most respected families in the vicinity of Newville. They have two daughters, Helen and Mary, residing at home.

IN THE GRAVE YARD.

The earliest burials clustered around the old oak tree with its broad spreading branches in the south-eastern part of the graveyard, and near where the old log church stood. To the superficial observer, there seems to be much unoccupied space there, but this is not the case. In nearly every foot of ground rests the remains of the pioneer settlers and their children, although no tablet marks their resting place. There are very few of the first and second generations of the residents of this section who sleep in marked graves. Among many we have in mind, we mention the Fenton family of thirty persons, the grave of not one of whom is marked. The first of the family was Samuel Fenton. His son Samuel was a soldier in the Revolutionary war, and his son James was a Colonel in the war of 1812. In the progress of time, the graveyard gradually extended towards the church, the lower or south and eastern part bordering upon the spring, being very rocky, was used as quarries from an early date, and thus became a source of revenue to the church. In 1868, that portion was sold off, leaving sixteen feet along the fence for a road. In 1853, the western side of the graveyard was made on a line with the eastern side of Corporation street. This change in the boundary, left a number of graves of colored people outside of the enclosure in that part of the street between the fence and the property now owned by Samuel Ernst. The first record we find of an enclosure, is Sept. 1795, when Archibald McCoy was paid for 348 perch of stone, at one dollar and forty cents per perch, for a graveyard wall. Four years later, the trustees "Resolved to cover the graveyard wall and enclose a yard around the meeting house." Some old persons remember when they were young, of seeing the remains of this wall on the south side of the graveyard, along the spring, near the water's edge, and to this day can be seen running east and west, through the graveyard, about forty feet from the present fence dividing the church from the graveyard, a ridge of stone covered with earth and grass, which was doubtless the foundation of the wall. This ridge extends from the eastern extremity of the graveyard, west to the Boyd lot where it is broken by the terracing of the lot.

OUR FATHERS' RESTING PLACE.

BY BELLE M'KINNEY SWOPE.

Tall trees lift up their towering heads
As if upon the sky to trace
Their shades, and o'er the church they shed
A stately dignity and grace.
Within those ancient walls of stone,
Each generation as it passed,
Found Christ's own blood could guilt atone,
At His blest feet their burdens cast,
And drifting silently away,
Time faded into endless day.

On the sloping turf by the old gray walls,
The sunlight casts its slanting beams
Across the path where the shadow falls,
And touches the graves with golden streams.
The soft wind sighing among the pines
Whispers of perfect peace o'erhead,
And the spring as onward it slowly winds
Murmurs a requiem for the dead.
Its waters caressing the grassy steep
Where heroes and loved ones sweetly sleep.

Life's turmoil in each year that passes,
Disturbs no rest in that calm spot,
And silently the waving grasses

Mark mounds of earth too soon forgot.
Some slumber on in nameless places,
Some lie 'neath monuments of stone,
And hearts were sore to lose the faces
That gather now around the throne.
Peaceful the soldier's quiet sleep,
Laurels of fame his winding sheet.

Oh, sacred spot of hallowed sorrow
Guard well the dust in thine embrace;
The brightness of a glad tomorrow
Dawns o'er our fathers' slumbering place.
Thrice holy sepulchre, to thy
Blest shadows tender memory twines,
Where pastors in thy bosom lie,
And consecrated earth enshrines.
Faithful they were who rest from the strife,
'Neath the shades where they offered the
Bread of Life.

Fair home for the reapers' treasured spoils
Life's sweetest hopes lie in thy breast,
And mortals cease from wearied toils,
For unto all He giveth rest.
Time steals no beauty and the air
Breathes heavenly benedictions there.

INSCRIPTIONS FROM TOMBSTONES OF PERSONS BORN PRIOR TO 1800.

Adams, Robert, b. Oct. 2, 1798; d. May 14, 1874.
Adams, Margaret, b. 1766; d. 1840.
Allen, John, b. 1791; d. Feb. 10, 1817.
Allen, James W., b. June 25, 1789; d. June 19, 1869.
Auxer, Elizabeth, wife of Geo., b. Oct. 2, 1796; d. April 11, 1845.
Barr, Sarah, dau. of Dr. John Geddes, b. 1802; d. Jan. 27, 1838.
Barr, Alexander, b. 1764; d. Sept. 4, 1831.
Bryson, William, b. 1728; d. June 13, 1800.
Brownson, Mary, dau. of Thomas, b. 1764; d. Sept. 3,

1807.

Brown, James, b. Dec. 31, 1778; d. Oct. 11, 1822.
Brown, Martha, wife of James, b. Aug. 10, 1792; d. Feb. 7, 1852.
Brown, John, b. Sept. 19, 1752; d. Jan. 10, 1842.
Brown, Margaret, wife of John, b. 1748; d. Sept. 17, 1836.
Brown, Mary, b. April 12, 1788; d. Sept. 16, 1862.
Brown, James, b. 1777; d. July 31, 1862.
Brown, Nancy, wife of James, b. July 5, 1800; d. Oct. 15, 1835.
Brown, William, b. 1797; d. May 13, 1864.
Brown, Jane, wife of William, b. Sept. 21, 1802; d. Mar. 10, 1877.
Brown, Rachel, b. 1769; d. Mar. 24, 1805.
Brown, Joseph, b. 1777; d. July 31, 1862.
Brown, Nancy, wife of Joseph, b. July 3, 1800; d. Oct. 13, 1835.
Bratton, Adam, b. 1744; d. June 6, 1820.
Bratton, Ann, wife of Adam, b. 1752; d. Dec. 26, 1840.
Bratton, Samuel, b. 1796; d. Aug. 16, 1864.
Bratton, William, b. 1791; d. Mar. 11, 1862.
Bratton, George, b. 1784; d. Sept. 13, 1860.
Bratton, Mary, b. 1786; d. July 23, 1857.
Bratton, Eleanor, dau. of Adam, b. 1780; d. Sept. 20, 1848.
Bratton, William, son of Adam, b. 1796.
Buchanan, Mary, b. 1763; d. Oct. 16, 1823.
Buchanan, William, d. July 7, 1843.
Buchanan, Ezekiel, d. Aug. 31, 1831.
Buchanan, Robert, d. May 3, 1833.
Buchanan, Elizabeth, d. Aug. 25, 1863.

PRESBYTERIAN CHURCH.

Buchanan, Gen. Thomas, b. 1747; d. Oct. 13, 1823. (A soldier of the Revolutionary War.)
Binner, Mary E., b. 1772; d. Aug. 1853.
Boyd, William, b. Jan. 5, 1778; d. Feb. 2, 1846.
Boyd, Martha, wife of William, b. Dec. 14, 1779; d. Apr. 8, 1848.
Butler, Samuel, b, Feb. 2, 1778; d. Apr. 27, 1859.
Butler, Sallie, wife of Samuel, b. Apr. 4, 1793; d. Mar. 15, 1881.
Carnahan, Judith, wife of Robert, b. 1763; d. May 21, 1835.
Carnahan, Mary, wife of William, b. 1793; d. Sept. 7, 1823.
Carson, Hannan, b. 1774; d. April 5, 1844.
Carson, Priscilla, b. 1791; d. Aug. 16, 1864.
Campbell, William, b. Oct. 26, 1789; d. Apr. 1, 1864.
Cobean, William, b. 1795; d. Aug. 6, 1859.
Cobean, Mary McFarlane, wife of William, b. 1805; d. Oct. 4, 1855.
Conway, Mary, b. 1765; d. May 8, 1823.
Cook, Samuel, b. 1799; d. July 18, 1841.
Cook, Jane, b. 1794; d. Aug. 31, 1843.
Cox, Mary, b. 1800; d. Dec. 3, 1866.
Davidson, George, b. Oct. 27, 1777; d. June 12, 1856.
Davidson, Jane, wife of George, b. Mar. 13, 1779; d. Dec. 6, 1863.
Davidson, Ann, b. Nov., 1788; d. Feb. 16, 1866.
Davidson, John, b. Dec. 15, 1786; d. Jan. 9, 1840.
Davidson, Eleanor R., b. Apr. 15, 1797; d. Jan. 3, 1877.
Davidson, James, b. 1790; d. Sept. 27, 1858.
Davidson, Ann, wife of James, b. 1794; d. June 8, 1827.
Davidson, Ann, wife of James, b. 1791; d. Sept. 17, 1867.

Davidson, William, b. Dec. 2. 1788; d. Aug. 25, 1843.
Davidson, Mary, wife of William, b. Nov. 18, 1796; d: Apr. 3, 1848.
Davidson, Alexander, b. June 14, 1787; d. Oct. 19, 1865.
Davidson; Jane, wife of Alex., b. Nov. 29, 1790; d. Aug. 19, 1879.
Davidson, John, b. 1743; d. 1823.
Davidson, John, b. Feb. 27, 1772; d. May 10, 1810.
Davidson, Elizabeth Young, wife of John, b. 1772; d. Sept. 14, 1823.
Denning, William, b. 1737; d. Dec. 19, 1830. (The maker of the first wrought-iron cannon of the Revolutionary War.)
Dougherty, George, d. aged 82 years.
Dougherty, Rachel, wife of Geo., b. 1789; d. 1856.
Duey, Conrad, b. 1769; d. Oct. 15, 1833.
Duey, Rachel, wife of Conrad, b. 1779; d. Feb. 22, 1854.
Dunbar, Isabella, b. 1799; d. Sept. 25, 1824.
Dunbar, Mary, b. 1772; d. Jan. 30, 1830.
Dunbar, John, b. 1767; d. Oct. 18, 1829.
Duncan, Eliza Smith, wife of Capt. David, b. June 8, 1789; d. Aug. 7, 1863.
Ewing, Elizabeth, dau. of Geo. Gillespie, b. 1790; d. Jan. 16, 1846.
Elliott, Nancy, b. 1772; d. Apr. 16, 1798.
Elliott, Thomas, b. 1787; d. Mar. 19, 1849.
Elliott, Mrs. Elizabeth, b. July 13, 1794; d. Feb. 19, 1859.
Ferguson, William, b. 1758; d. Apr. 23, 1834. (A soldier in Revolution, and maker of the carriages for the cannon of William Denning.)
Fulton, Francis, b. 1764; d. Oct. 16, 1843.

Fulton, Sarah, wife of Francis, b. 1768; d. Aug. 4, 1834.
Fulton, James, b. Oct. 10, 1795; d. Aug. 17, 1860.
Gailbraith, William, b. 1731; d. Nov., 1815.
Gailbraith, Sarah, wife of William, b. Oct. 4, 1748; d. Jan. 22, 1827.
Geddes, Dr. John, b. Aug. 16, 1766; d. Dec. 5, 1840.
Geddes, Elizabeth Peebles, b. Feb. 8, 1772; d. May 20, 1839.
Geddes, Dr. John P., b. Oct. 10, 1799; d. Dec. 8, 1837.
Geese, Christian, b. Jan. 17, 1788; d. Nov. 24, 1814.
Giffin, Catharine, b. 1786; d. Jan. 15, 1834.
Gillespie, Nathaniel, b. 1744; d. Aug. 16, 1824.
Gillespie, Martha, b. Apr. 20, 1747, d. June 25, 1819.
Gillespie, Ann, b. 1782; d. Nov. 16, 1827.
Gillespie, Nancy, b. 1786; d. Aug. 21, 1835.
Glenn, Alexander, b. Feb. 22, 1787; d. Nov. 13, 1835.
Glenn, Maria, wife of Alexander, b. May 17, 1792; d. May 28, 1841.
Graham, Martha, b. 1731; d. July 22, 1779.
Graham, James, b. 1725; d. Sept. 2, 1807.
Graham, Isaiah, b. 1769; d. Aug. 27, 1835.
Graham, Nancy, wife of Isaiah, b. Aug. 17, 1772; d. Feb. 17, 1841.
Graham, Nancy, b. June 17, 1798; d. Jan. 19, 1863.
Graham, Robert, b. 1800; d. Jan. 24, 1873.
Graham, Eliza, wife of Robert, b. 1799; d. Dec. 6, 1855.
Green, John, b. Aug., 1769; d. Feb. 12, 1846.
Harlan, James, b. 1791; d. June 21, 1832.
Harlan, George, b. Jan. 13, 1794; d. Mar. 11, 1873.
Harlan, Elizabeth H., wife of George, b. Apr. 9, 1811; d. Aug. 9, 1858.
Harlan, Ruth, b. Mar. 15, 1792; d. Feb. 2, 1854.

Hays, Patrick, b. 1766; d. July 28, 1856.
Hays, Margaret Mickey, wife of Patrick, b. 1770; d. Jan. 25, 1837.
Hanna, Samuel, b. 1792, d. Feb. 8, 1825.
Hanna, Else, wife of Samuel, b. 1772; d. Feb. 10, 1850.
Hanna, John, b. 1765; d. Oct. 11, 1823.
Hamil, Mary, wife of Wm., b. 1787; d. Oct. 13, 1811.
Hackett, Henry G., b. Feb. 12, 1792; d. Dec. 7. 1845.
Hackett, Mary, wife of Henry, b. Dec. 4, 1794; d. Sept. 28, 1854.
Harper, John, husband of Jean, who, his journey finished and got to his rest Sept. 12, 1804, aged 73 yrs.
Harper, Robert, b. 1770; d. Nov. 19, 1802.
Harper, Samuel, b. 1775; d. Apr. 15, 1802.
Harper, Sarah, wife of Samuel, b. 1768; d. Mar. 16, 1848.
Harper, David, b. 1774; d. June 3, 1801.
Harper, Maj. John, b. Nov. 29, 1793; d. Oct. 11, 1846.
Harper, Andrew, b. 1799; d. Jan. 19, 1827.
Harper, Elizabeth, b. July 1806; d. Oct. 10, 1827.
Harper, William, b. 1761; d. May 18, 1824.
Harper, Esther, wife of Wm., b. 1762; d. Apr. 13, 1827.
Harper, Jean, wife of John, b. 1735; d. Mar. 16, 1808.
Harper, James, b. 1757; d. Feb. 13, 1816.
Harper, Margaret, dau. of James b. 1798; d. Aug. 8, 1817.
Harper, John, b. June 22, 1795; d. June 5, 1847.
Harper, Margaret, wife of John, and dau. of John, of Adams Co., b. 1811; d. May 21, 1836.
Harper, Elzabeth,, wife of John, b. 1772; d. Mar. 27,

1813.

House, John, b. 1782; d. Nov., 1872. (A soldier of the War of 1812.)

House, Elizabeth, wife of John, b. 1784; d. 1863.

Huston, James, b. 1784; d. June 17, 1825.

Huston, James, b. 1782; d. June 17, 1823.

Hunter, Joseph, b. 1775; d. June 28, 1835.

Hood, Josiah, b. Aug. 11, 1794; d. Oct. 2, 1873.

Hood, Sarah, wife of Josiah, b. Sept. 28, 1794; d. Mar. 18, 1852.

Heffleman, Michael, b. Mar. 9, 1780; d. July 24, 1845.

Heffleman, Mary, wife of Michael, b. Dec. 22, 1785; d. Feb. 2, 1837.

Heap, John.

Irvine, Samuel, b. 1747; d. Mar. 9, 1806.

Irvine, Mary, wife of Samuel, b. 1744: d. Oct. 28, 1819.

Irvine, Miss Ruth, b. July, 1777; d. Dec. 21, 1859.

Irvine, Rosanna, wife of Samuel, b. 1797; d. April 4, 1834.

Irvine, Samuel, b. 1785; d. May 10, 1849.

Irvine, Isabella, wife of Samuel, b. 1803; d. July 12, 1839.

Irvine, Margaret McClelland; wife of Samuel, b. Sept. 21, 1803; d. Sept. 2, 1886.

Irwin, James, b. 1776; d. Feb. 22, 1854.

Irwin, Prudence, b. 1784; d. Oct. 20, 1818.

Jacobs, Adam, b. Oct., 1787; d. Aug. 17, 1872.

Jacobs, Marjory, wife of Adam, b. July 1, 1795; d. Apr. 30, 1865.

Jacobs, Sarah Lenney, wife of Adam, b. 1787; d. Aug. 30, 1834.

Jacob, Joseph, b. 1782; d. Oct. 9, 1864.

Jacob, Lydia, wife of Joseph, b. 1785; d. Dec. 20, 1849.
Johnson, John, b. 1780; d. Sept. 8, 1841.
Johnson, Elizabeth, b. 1788; d. Mar. 2, 1847.
Kelley, John, b. 1791; d. March 1, 1864.
Kelley, Grizelda, b. 1796; d. March 23, 1864.
Ker, Sarah, wife of Alex., b. 1784; d. June 29, 1838.
Ker, William, b. Jan. 1, 1755; d. Oct. 8, 1845.
Ker, William, b. Oct. 30, 1791; d. Sept. 20, 1874.
Ker, Eliza B., wife of William, b. Sept. 16, 1806; d. Dec. 24, 1844.
Kennedy, Thomas, b. 1744; d. 1831.
Kennedy, Margaret, wife of Thomas, b. 1759; d. Jan. 16, 1826.
Kilgore, William, b. 1756; d. Oct. 11, 1823.
Kilgore, Isabella, wife of William, b. Oct. 1761; d. Feb. 18, 1826.
Kilgore, Jesse, b. Dec. 13, 1773; d. Aug. 19, 1823.
Kilgore, James, b. March 20, 1771; d. Dec. 5, 1834.
Kilgore, Bobert, b. Sept. 7, 1799; d. Aug. 27, 1878.
Kinsley, John, b. 1780; d. Dec. 13, 1851.
Klink, George, b. May 23, 1792; d. Jan. 30, 1869.
Klink, Elizabeth, wife of George, b. 1795; d. March 24, 1875.
Knight, Thomas H., b. Nov. 8, 1795; d. Apr. 30, 1852.
Knight, Elizabeth, wife of Thomas, b. Mar. 11, 1805; d. Apr. 17, 1863.
Knettle, Henry, b. 1774; d. July 5, 1845.
Knettle, Hannah, wife of Henry, b. 1778; d. Oct. 27, 1854.
Koons, Isaac, b. Sept., 1792; d. Nov. 19, 1874.
Laughlin, James, b. Sept. 14, 1783; d. Feb. 11, 1851.
Laughlin, Atcheson, b. 1756; d. Jan. 11, 1825.

Laughlin, Mary, wife of Atcheson, b. 1760; d. Oct. 22, 1842.
Laughlin, William R., b. Feb. 6, 1784; d. Feb. 12, 1835.
Laughlin, James, b. April 18, 1770; d. 1852.
Laughlin, John, b. March 15, 1773; died at sea.
Laughlin, William b. Aug. 17, 1778; d. June 21, 1844.
Laughlin, James, b. Sept. 14, 1785; d. Feb. 11, 1851.
Laughlin, Agnes, b. Aug. 7, 1794; d. Aug. 18, 1871.
Laughlin, Elizabeth, b. Nov. 16, 1796; d. Feb. 21, 1864.
Laughlin, Atcheson, b. Feb. 8, 1799; d. July 7, 1876.
Laird, Catharine, b. June, 1764; d. June 13, 1850.
Laird, Hugh, b. 1787; d. Sept. 30, 1815.
Laird, Thomas, b. 1794; d. April 19, 1830.
Laird, James, Esq., b. 1753; d. Oct. 10, 1834.
Laird, Robert, b. 1789; d. Jan. 15, 1848.
Lenney, Isaac, b. 1793; d. Aug. 14, 1848.
Lenney, Hannah, wife of Isaac, b. 1797; d. Aug. 16, 1869.
Lenney, Elizabeth, b. 1782; d. Jan. 17, 1847.
Lenney, Sarah, wife of Adam Jacobs, b. 1787; d. Aug. 30, 1834.
Lenney, William, b. 1782; d. Oct. 20, 1823.
Lenney, Sarah, wife of William, b. 1789; d. March, 17, 1862.
Leckey, Sarah B., b. Sept. 1, 1789; d. Oct. 6, 1823.
Leckey, Alexander, b. 1740; d. Mar. 16, 1818.
Leckey, Elizabeth, wife of Alexander, b. 1765; d. Nov. 16, 1817.
Leckey, Daniel, b. Sept. 4, 1783; d. March 3, 1854.
Leckey, Ann Davidson, wife of Daniel, d. Sept. 5, 1843.
Leckey, Sarah; dau. of Alexander, b. July 5, 1787; d. Dec., 1859.

Leckey, Isabella, b. 1799; d. Dec. 1862.
Leckey, Sarah, b. July 5, 1787; d. Dec. 1859.
Lindsay, William, b. July 6, 1793; d. Jan. 23, 1838.
Lindsay, Mary Forbes, wife of William, b. April 27, 1786; d. Oct. 26, 1842.
Lindsay, Jane, b. Oct. 1760; d. May 4, 1837.
Logan, James, b. 1782; d. Oct. 26, 1828.
Logan, Alexander, b. July 22, 1795; d. Nov. 12, 1870.
Logan, Martha, wife of Alex, b. 1797; d. Nov. 7, 1873.
Mathers, William, b. 1760; d, Oct. 18, 1850.
McCachran, Isabella, b. at Abbington, near Philadelphia, Jan. 8, 1765; d. Jan. 12, 1851.
McCachran, Rev. Robert, b. Sept. 24, 1796; d. Feb. 25, 1885. (Pastor of Big Spring Presbyterian Church.)
McCachran, Jane Laughlin, wife of Rev. Robert, b. Aug. 3, 1802; d. Nov. 27, 1871.
McCachran, James, b. Jan. 1, 1797; d. Aug. 25, 1885.
McCachran, Rachel, wife of James, b. Feb. 1803; d. Dec. 22, 1859.
McCormick, Samuel, b. 1726; d. Sept. 4, 1803.
McCormick, Elizabeth, wife of Samuel, b. 1727; d. Oct. 7, 1811.
McCormick, Thomas, b. May 29, 1766; d. Jan. 16, 1835.
McCormick, Margaret Young, wife of Thomas, b. Jan. 20, 1766; d. Feb. 20, 1824.
McCandlish William, b. 1768; d. Apr. 9, 1827.
McCandlish, Jane, wife of William, b. 1781; d. Aug. 4, 1827.
McCandlish, Maria, wife of John, b. 1802; d. Oct. 1, 1827.
McCulloch, James, son of John. b. 1761; d. Aug. 13, 1825.

McCulloch, Jane Henderson, wife of John, b. 1773; d. June 24, 1847.
McCulloch, John, b. 1741; d. May 10, 1808.
McCulloch, Elizabeth Hueston, wife of John, b. 1740; d. 1813.
McCulloch, William, b. 1778; d. Nov. 8, 1824.
McCulloch, Sarah M., b. 1782; d. April 4, 1834.
McCulloch, John, of Dickinson, b. 1771; d. Feb. 5, 1847.
McCulloch, Mary Williamson, wife of John, b. 1773; d. Sept. 5, 1862.
McCulloch, David, b. Dec. 16, 1798; d. Nov. 22, 1859.
McCulloch, Betsy Coyle, wife of David, b. Sept. 3, 1804; d. Dec. 28, 1882.
McCulloch, Jane Dunbar, wife of John, b. 1805; d. March 7, 1838.
McCrea, William, b. 1759; d. 1837.
McCrea, Margaret, wife of William, b. 1759; d. 1822.
McCrea William, b. July 21, 1800; d. Oct. 25, 1885.
McCracken, Capt. William, b. 1753; d. Jan. 16, 1803. (A Revolutionary soldier.)
McDannell, Daniel, b. in Ireland, Nov. 11, 1722; d. March 27, 1789.
McDannell, Jane, wife of Daniel, b. in Ireland, Jan. 1, 1726; d. June 28, 1795.
McDannell, Mrs. Elizabeth, b. Oct. 18, 1790; d. May 25, 1866.
McDannell, Margaret, b. March 6, 1797; d. May 8, 1809.
McDannell, Daniel, b. July 18, 1751; d. June 26, 1811.
McDannell, Daniel; son of Daniel, b. March 23, 1792; d. Nov. 13, 1825.
McDannell, Jane, b. 1765; d. Feb. 18, 1842.
McDannell, John, b. 1729; d. Jan. 1, 1800.

McDowell, Margaret, b. Dec. 30, 1792; d. June 9, 1851.
McDowell, Elizabeth, b. Nov. 16, 1797; d. June 8, 1851.
McDowell, Mary, b. 1768; d. Dec. 24, 1834.
McDowell, Samuel, b. 1764; d. Apr. 24, 1830.
McDowell, Mary, b. Sept. 18, 1794; d. Apr. 28, 1863.
McDowell, John, b. 1778; d. Jan. 9, 1829.
McDowell, Margaret Laird, wife of John, b. Dec. 19, 1790; d. May 30, 1855.
McElwain, Robert, b. 1781; d. Jan. 18, 1853.
McElwain, Jane, wife of Robert, b. 1790; d. May 12, 1869.
McElwain, Andrew, jr., b. April 19, 1785; d. Aug. 10, 1840.
McElwain, Mary, wife of Andrew, b. July 16, 1798; d. Oct. 27, 1868.
McFarlane, William, b. 1757; d. Jan. 29, 1802.
McFarlane, Esther, b. 1769; d. Feb. 18, 1789.
McFarlane, Eleanor, b. 1776; d. Oct. 19, 1814.
McFarlane, Elizabeth, b. 1767; d. March 16, 1816.
McFarlane, James, b. 1757; d. Dec. 16, 1807.
McFarlane, Elizabeth, wife of James, b. 1764; d. March 26, 1814.
McFarlane, Robert, b. Nov. 15, 1784; d. April 24, 1838.
McFarlane, Lydia, wife of Clemens, b. Aug. 1799; d. March 20, 1846.
McFarlane, William, b. 1744; d. April 3, 1811.
McFarlane, Robert, b. Oct. 23, 1776; d. Sept. 14, 1847.
McFarlane, Jane, wife of Robert, b. Nov. 21, 1799; d. Feb. 1, 1882.
McFarlane, Jane, wife of Robert, b. 1787; d. March 11, 1833.
McFarlane, Rosanna, b. 1734; d. Nov. 26, 1812.

McFarlane, Patrick, b. 1727; d. March 16, 1792.
McIlhenny, Margaret, wife of Robert, b. 1792; d. Apr. 22, 1835.
McIntire, John, b. 1745; d. Aug. 16, 1830.
McIntire, Margaret, wife of John, b. 1756; d. Sept. 17, 1830.
McKeehan, Benjamin, b. Aug. 2, 1748; d. Oct. 23, 1814.
McKeehan, Margaret, wife of Benjamin, b. Feb. 22, 1758; d. Apr. 24, 1829.
McKeehan, Samuel, b. 1786; d. Dec. 12, 1870.
McKeehan, Deborah, wife of Samuel, b. 1789; d. April 30, 1867.
McKeehan, Robert, b. Oct. 13, 1784; d. April 26, 1863.
McKeehan, Mary Trego, wife of Robert, b. March 24, 1782; d. Feb. 28, 1854.
McKibben, Joseph, b. 1794; d. Nov. 13, 1836.
McKinstry, James, b. 1805; d. Jan. 30, 1846.
McMonigal, William, b. 1766; d. July 14, 1813.
McMonigal, Agnes, b. 1755; d. May 19, 1812.
McWilliams, Robert, b. 1786; d. Mar. 10, 1813.
Megaw, James, b. 1775; d. May 26, 1838.
Megaw, Sarah, b. 1770; d. May 24, 1846.
Mickey, Robert, b. Dec. 21, 1746; d. Dec. 3, 1827.
Mickey, Ezemiah, b. 1755; d. Dec. 8, 1830.
Mickey, James, b. 1795; d. 1835.
Mickey, Lucetta, wife of James, b. 1802; d. 1862.
Miller, Henry, b. Jan. 1, 1777; d. Jan. 23, 1838.
Morrow, John S., b. July 26, 1788; d. April 16, 1863.
Moffit, Robert, b. May 6, 1790; d. Sept. 14, 1856.
Nicholson, Richard, b. 1713; d. Dec. 18, 1792.
Nicholson, Mary, b. 1708; d. **Jan. 5, 1793,**

Nickey, Jacob, b. Jan. 4, 1797; d. Jan. 1, 1886.
Neal, James, sr., d. Feb. 27, 1793.
Neal, Sarah, wife of James, d. Sept. 13, 1814.
Over, Keziah, wife of Samuel, b. Sept. 23, 1800; d. July 28, 1861.
Pollock, Mary, wife of Joseph, b. 1758; d. Aug. 1838.
Pierce, Paul, b. 1716; d. June 7, 1794.
Pierce Joseph, b. 1756; d. Aug. 30, 1806.
Pierce, Jane, wife of Joseph, b. Dec. 1768; d. Feb. 25, 1827.
Patterson, Elizabeth, b. 1772; d. Mar. 8, 1798.
Patterson Andrew, b. 1730; d. Nov. 10, 1792.
Patterson, Mary, wife of Andrew, b. 1734; d. March 15, 1827.
Patterson, Thomas, son of Andrew, b. 1773; d. Dec. 10, 1822.
Patterson, Obediah, b. 1762; d. March 10, 1804.
Patterson, Ann, wife of Obediah, b. 1798; d. March 5, 1840.
Patton, Elizabeth, b. Jan. 3, 1797; d. Feb. 4, 1870.
Peebles, Capt. William, killed at the battle of Flat Bush, L. I., 1776.
Peebles, Capt. Robert, b. 1776; d. Jan. 7, 1830.
Phillips, Edward, b. 1796; d. Dec. 25, 1857.
Phillips, Jane, wife of Edward, b. 1793; d. Dec. 22, 1870.
Randolph, Mary Knettle, wife of John, b. 1800; d. Dec. 12, 1841.
Ralston, Mary, b. 1779; d. Feb. 13, 1852;
Ralston, David, b. 1783; d. March 8, 1849.
Ralston, Lacy, wife of David, b. 1790; d. Jan. 28, 1863.
Reed, James, b. 1789; d. May 12, 1842.

PRESBYTERIAN CHURCH.

Reed, Hugh, b. 1783; d. 1823.
Richy, William, b. 1760; d. Feb. 3, 1830.
Sharp, James, b. Jan. 27, 1774; d. Feb. 28, 1823.
Starrett, James, b. July, 1768; d. June 18, 1812.
Sterrett, David, b. April, 1767; d. July 26, 1825.
Starrett, Martha, wife of Robert, daughter of Thomas Woods, b. in Lancaster County, July 25, 1801; d. 1838.
Sterrett, David, b. 1746; d. Nov. 2, 1790.
Sterrett, David, b. Apr. 4, 1800; d. May 6, 1864.
Sterrett, Rebecca, wife of David, b. Aug. 11, 1802; d. Mar. 7, 1865.
Sterrett, Rachel, b. 1796; d. Dec. 28, 1823.
Steel, Robert, b. 1766; d. Aug. 17, 1836.
Steel; Mary, wife of Robert, b. Feb. 1, 1776; d. Aug. 19, 1859.
Stevenson, John, b. 1739; d. Aug. 19, 1777.
Stevenson, Rachel, wife of John, dau. of Alex. Scroggs, b. 1756; d. Apr. 30, 1780.
Stevenson, Jane, b. 1758; d. 1818.
Stevenson, William, b. 1741; d. Dec. 1, 1817.
Stevenson, Margaret, d. Apr. 1, 1821.
Stevenson, John, b. 1780; d. Jan. 1, 1835.
Stevenson, John, b. 1786; d. Feb. 14, 1835.
Stevenson, Mary, b. 1783; d. Feb. 11, 1837.
Stevenson, William, b. Sept. 22, 1792; d. Nov. 27, 1848.
Smith, Hugh, b. 1750; d. Mar. 17, 1823.
Smith, Elizabeth McCormick, wife of Hugh, b. 1764; d. May, 22, 1822.
Smith, Benjamin, b. 1747; d. Oct. 16, 1838.
Thompson, Matthew, b. 1754; d. Oct. 19, 1823.
Thompson, Joseph, b. 1786; d. Nov. 5, 1832.
Trego, Rebecca, wife of Moses, b; 1762; d. Oct. 7, 1823.

Wallace, John, b. 1744; d. Dec. 12, 1814.
Wallace, Agnes, b. 1767; d. May 28, 1827.
Wallace, Margaret, b. 1792; d. April 2, 1855.
Wallace, John, b. 1798; d. 1876.
Wallace, Mary, wife of John, b. 1801; d. 1887.
Wallace, Thomas, b. Nov. 27, 1792; d. Sept. 30, 1832.
Wallace, Mary, wife of Thomas, b. Nov. 22, 1796; d. Apr. 13, 1838.
Weakley, Samuel, b. 1755; d. Feb. 10, 1829.
Weakley, Hetty, b. 1755; d. Oct. 1, 1819.
Weakley, John, b. 1778; d. Nov. 22, 1826.
Weakley, Martha, b. 1778; d. Oct. 1, 1857.
Wilt, Peter, b. 1776; d. July 23, 1842.
Wilson, Samuel, b. 1748; d. Apr. 3, 1837.
Wilson, Matthew, b. 1746; d. Jan. 6, 1824.
Wilson, Rev. Samuel, b. 1754; d. Mar. 4, 1799. (Pastor Big Spring Presbyterian Church.)
Wilson, Jane, wife of Rev. Samuel, b. 1761; d. May 29, 1835.
Wilson, John, son of Rev. Samuel, b. 1793; d. Jan. 30, 1809.
Williamson, William, b. 1791; d. Apr. 24, 1837.
Williamson, Tamar, wife of David, b. 1763; d. Mar. 23, 1813.
Williams, Catharine, wife of George, b. Aug. 5, 1780; d. Mar. 5, 1862.
Williams, Rev. Joshua, D. D., b. 1767; d. Aug. 21, 1838. (Pastor Big Spring Presbyterian Church.)
Williams, Eleanor, wife of Rev. Joshua, b. 1780; d. Apr. 28, 1856.
Williams, James C., son of Rev. Joshua, b. 1801; d. 1822.
Whitley, Andrew, b. 1769; d. Dec. 7, 1848.

SOLDIERS BURIED IN THE GRAVE YARD.

Allen, J. K., Rebellion.
Boose, Jonathan, War 1812.
Brandon, Thomas, Rebellion.
Barr, John, Rebellion.
Barr, Alexander, Rebellion.
Brown, John, b. Sept. 19, 1752; d. Jan. 10, 1842, Revolution.
Brown, George, Co. E, 187 Pa. Inft.
Butler, Corp. Elliott, Co. A, 127 U. S. C. I.
Buchanan, Gen. Thomas, b. 1747; d. Oct. 13, 1823, Revolution.
Crawford, Sargt. G. W., Co. G, 45th U. S. C. Inft.
Denning, William, b. 1737, d. Dec. 19, 1830, Revolution.
Fenton, Samuel, Revolution.
Fenton, John, War of 1812.
Fenton, Col. James, b. 1776, War of 1812.
Fulton, Robert H., d. Aug. 16, 1891, Rebellion.
Fry, Capt. Jesse R., b. 1832; d. 1893, Co. D, 77th Regt. Pa. Vol., Rebellion.
Ferguson, William, Revolution.
Graham, Sargent George W., b. May 6, 1841; killed May 16, 1863.
George, S. C., Co. E, 127 Pa. Inft.
Hays, John S., b. 1842; d. Mar. 29, 1877. Sargt. 130 Reg. Pa. Vol.
House, John, b. 1782; d. Nov. 1872, War of 1812.
Hackett, Thompson, b. Dec. 28, 1844; d. Apr. 14, 1893, Rebellion.
Howard, Nicholas, d. Nov. 18, 1847, War of 1812.
Hood, Josiah, b. Aug. 11, 1794; d. Oct. 2, 1873, War

McElwain, Thomas, War of 1812.
McCullough, Leo, b. May, 27; 1842, Rebellion.
McWilliams, John, War of 1812.
Moffitt, David S., b. Sept. 18. 1818; d. May, 8, 1888, Rebellion.
McCracken, Capt. William, b. 1753; d. Jan. 16, 1803, Revolution.
Nehf, George, Co. I, 12 Reg. Pa., Reserv. Vol.
Neal, Col. Joseph, d. Mar. 25, 1838, War of 1812.
Perry, Abram, Co. K, U. S. C. Inft.
Peebles, Capt. William, killed at the battle of Flat Bush, L. I., 1776.
Peebles, Capt. Robert, b. 1776; d. Jan. 7, 1830, War of 1812.
Roberts, Capt. John, War of 1812.
Richardson, John H., Rebellion.
Stewart, Samuel I., Co. K, 158 Reg. Pa. Inft.
of 1812.
Ickes, Charles, Rebellion.
Jenkens, George, Co. B, 23rd U. S. C. I.
Johnson, William H., d. July 16, 1869, Rebellion.
Johnson, John Bell, U. S. N.
Kinsley, J. R., Co. H, 3rd Pa. Cal.
Kyle, Samuel, War of 1812.
Kennedy, John, War of 1812.
Knight, James, U. S. Navy, Rebellion.
Laughlin, William, killed at the battle of Fredericksburg, Dec. 13, 1862.
Martin, Sargent D. E., Co. I, 201 Pa. Inft.
McCune, J. A., Co. M, 7th Pa. Cal.
McElwain, Robert, b. 1781; d. Jan. 18, 1853, War of 1812.

Snowden, Sargt. Samuel S., Co. G, 8th U. S. C. Inft.
Snowden, James H., Co. A, 24th U. S. C. I.
Turbet, William, Mexican War.
Vanderbilt, C. H., Rebellion.
Zeigler, Samuel R., b. Oct. 22, 1846; d. Mar. 15, 1897, Rebellion.

APPENDIXES.

APPENDIX A.

In giving the adherents of the Big Spring Church in John Carson's district on page 30, the following persons were inadvertently omitted:

Samuel McCune	14,	Elizabeth Kilgore	70,*
Hugh McCune	12,	Jesse Kilgore	22,
John McCune	60,*	Robert Kilgore	19,
Mary McCune	40,*	William Kilgore,	
Adam Fullerton	16,	Isabel Kilgore	21,
James Fullerton	14,	Mary Hawks	12,
Alexander Fullerton	11,	James Mickey	24,
John McCune	9,	Agnes Mickey	19,
Robert McCune	7,	Joseph Parks	55,*
Samuel Weir	66,*	Rebecca Parks	50,*
Jane Weir	30,*	Thomas Parks	20,
George Weir	30,	Joseph Parks	18,
Margaret Weir	25,	Anna Parks	16,
Agnes Marten,		John C. Parks	14.
George, a Negro,			

APPENDIX B.

The Presbyterians of the Cumberland Valley.

An Address at the Celebration of the Founding of the Log College, at Neshaminy, Pa., September 5, 1889.

BY REV. EBENEZER ERSKINE, D. D.

Mr. Chairman and Christian Brethren:

There is an instinctive tendency in the human mind to trace all things to their natural and proper origin. Discoverers and explorers follow rivers to their sources. Naturalists seek to trace all animal and vegetable organisms to their original germs. Philologists run back words to their roots. The great problem of the ages, in all the speculative schools of thought has been, what is the origin of moral evil? What is the origin of the material universe?

It is under the influence of this principle of causation, of antecedent and consequent, that we are here gathered to-day to celebrate the founding of the Log College by the elder William Tennent, as the first academical and theological school within the bounds of the Presbyterian Church of the United States for the training of young men for the work of the ministry. On this historic spot, with all its interesting historic environments, we have assembled, that here, with uncovered heads we may acknowledge, with gratitude to God, the obligations we are under to the consecrated, self denying founder of an humble institution, which sent out an influence that has pervaded the church and the nation.

We are here not from any superstitious regard for this historic place; nor with any mere affectation of interest in these historic scenes which we do not feel; but to call to mind the life, character and labors of William Tennent, the history of the school which he here established, and to inquire what were the faith, the spirit and the principles which animated and governed him and which found expression in the young men of talent and energy whom he here trained. The orthodox, Calvinistic faith, the evangelical spirit, and the consecrated life of William Tennent, which he impressed upon and infused into the young men here trained, are what made the Log College so famous in the history of the Presbyterian Church. William Tennent lived in those he here trained, more than in his work as a minister of the Gospel or any other thing which he accomplished. From this school went forth young men who, like Barnabas, were full of faith and of the Holy Ghost. The character of the school in this respect was the secret of its great power for good. This line of thought I cannot further pursue. I have been asked by the committee in charge of these services to say something in regard to the Presbyterians of the Cumberland Valley, and their relationship to the Log College.

THE CUMBERLAND VALLEY.

Perhaps there are those here to-day who would like to know just where and what this Cumberland Valley is.

I answer, that it is a part of that extended valley which lies between two chains of that great Appallachian range of hills and mountains which runs in a northeasterly and southwesterly direction across the eastern half of this continent and which is from twelve to twenty miles in width, the whole length of it. Starting out from the southern part of the State of Vermont, under different names at different stages of its progress, it runs down through eastern New York, crossing the Hudson at Newburg; coming on through Pennsylvania, it crosses the Delaware at Easton, the Susquehanna at Harrisburg and the Potomac at Harper's Ferry; and running on down through Virginia, it crosses the James River at

Lynchburg and then runs around through Tennessee and on down into Alabama.

Now, that part of this extended valley which is called Cumberland Valley, is that part which lies between the Susquehanna and the Potomac rivers and takes its name from Cumberland County, the first county organized in it, and which name was taken from that of a county in the North of England, bordering on Scotland.

By many it has been much regretted that it had not been allowed to retain its original Indian name, that of the Kittatinny Valley, the valley of endless mountains.

ITS SCENERY, SOIL AND CLIMATE.

From the Susquehanna to the Potomac, the Kittatinny, or the North Mountain, as it is commonly called, lifts up its long and almost level line of summit to the height of from seven to twelve hundred feet above the surface of the valley, presenting to the eye all along, a varying aspect of extended forests with here and there intervening patches of rocks, the changing drapery of floating mists, the fleeing shadows of ever passing clouds, and all the diversified hues of spring, summer and autumn foliage. To the dwellers in the valley it is ever a most pleasing object of sight and very restful and grateful to the eye.

The South Mountain, which runs along the other side, slopes more gradually into the valley than the North and is broken into knobs and spurs with deep intervening recesses, and is alike an object pleasant to behold.

The surface of the valley itself, is varied by hills, plains and dales, and is noted for the fertility of its soil, for its numerous great and ever flowing springs and its clear running streams, for its abundant crops of grain and its pure and bracing atmosphere. In all these respects it is perhaps unsurpassed by any other valley of equal extent in any part of the American continent.

Attractive as this valley thus is, its settlement was delayed by reason of the Indian claim to it, which was not purchased until the year 1736 and also somewhat by reason of the controversy pending between the two Provinces of Pennsylvania and Maryland in relation to the boundary line between them which was not adjusted until 1737, nor confirmed by Mason and Dixon's survey until 1763.

EARLY SETTLERS.

By whom was this beautiful valley first settled? The answer is almost exclusively by the Scotch Irish Presbyterians, a people of the same race and of the same religious faith and worship with the founders and alumni of the Log College.

It is not for me to tell you in detail here to-day who the Scotch Irish Presbyterians were. That task has been assigned to our friend Dr. Muchmore, who has been everywhere and knows everybody, and like most editors, almost everything.

I must answer the question, however, who were the Presbyterians, that were the chief original settlers of the Cumberland Valley? In doing so let it suffice here to to say, that they were Scotch Irish Presbyterians; and that they were very much a Scotch colony, induced by James the First to settle on the forfeited lands of the Earls of Tyrone and Tyrconnel in the Province of Ulster, with its nine counties in the North or Ireland. The story of the English conquest of Ireland is one of great interest at the present time. When Pope Adrian in 1166 made a grant of Ireland to England, it was on two conditions. The first was that they were to have Ireland when they could get it. The second was that the Pope was to have an annual tax in perpetuity of a penny a family. This was the origin of Peter's pence, which they still continue to pay.

England found the native Irish a people hard to conquer and still worse to govern. Their troubles in this respect are still not ended. For a long time they tried to placate their Irish subjects by a liberal bestowment of titles of nobility, and restoration of lands, but in vain. For a period of more than three hundred years the English rule was limited to Dublin and its vicinity. Half of the people of Ulster perished in the successive rebellions and conflicts, they were wasted by wars, starved by famines, and reduced to the lowest state of poverty and wretchedness. Still they hated English domination. The break of Henry the Eighth with the Pope did not improve the situation. Elizabeth's distinctive Pretestantism made her reign still more offensive. It was not until the Scottish James came to the throne, and resorted to the old Roman policy of confiscation that Ulster was subdued. He confiscated five hundred thousand acres of land in various parts of the Province. On these lands the hardy and loyal Scotch gentry and people were induced to settle. To do so, they left the hills and glens and lowlands and mists of Scotland, where they had so heroically battled for the rights of conscience and the Crown rights of Christ, and came and sojourned for a time beneath the moister skies of Ulster, and there took on a milder type of character and a more evangelical and warmer type of religion, by reason of the gracious revivals of religion with which their churches were blessed. These were the Scotch Irish Presbyterians.

As soon as America was open for settlement, the Scotch and the Scotch Irish were among the earliest emigrants, and with their restless energy and spirit of adventure, they touched the American coast at almost every point from Nova Scotia, to which they gave its name, to the Carolinas. But their main settlements were in Pennsylvania and the Carolinas. The reason of this was, the laws of the Provinces of New York and Virginia, and their Provincial officers were unfriendly to the coming of any ministers except those of the Church of England. This was illustrated in the experience of the Rev. James Anderson, an able and thoroughly educated minister of the Church of Scotland, sent over in answer to overtures from Mr. Makemie, McNish and others, for the express purpose of settling in Virginia, but who after a stay of six months, for the reasons stated, abandoned the attempt and came north and settled in 1710, at New Castle, Delaware; and in 1716 was called to be the first pastor of the First Presbyterian Church in the city of New York; and on the other hand by the arrest, imprisonment and prosecution of the Rev. Mr. Makemie, the father of the Presbyterian Church in America, "as a roving minister" in the city of New York. The tidings of these things went back to Ulster and Scotland, and had the effect of largely preventing the people from going where they could not take their ministers with them. Wherever this people went, they brought their Presbyterianism with them.

The Scotch Irish were far more numerous among the earlier emigrants into Pennsylvania than the Scotch. Not being allied to Ireland by any long standing traditions or sacred memories, and being there greatly oppressed and harassed by the tyranny and exactions of a despotic and profligate monarch, and the restrictions and penalties imposed by an obsequious parliament, and by the intolerance and persecutions instigated by a haughty hierarchy, these things, with the rapacity and greed of the landlords, determined great and increasing numbers of them to come to America. And learning that under the liberal charter and the free laws of the Province of Pennsylvania, equal rights and all the advantages of civil and religious liberty were guaranteed alike to all the settlers, they were attracted in large numbers to the free Province of Pennsylvania.

As they left their homes with their families, for the reasons stated, to seek new homes across the seas and in the wilderness of another continent, the reasons actuating them had come to be in their minds solemn and grave considerations. They had suffered for the rights of conscience and liberty to worship God in both their former homes.

These early Scotch Irish Presbyterian settlers were generally agriculturists. When therefore they landed at Wilmington or Philadelphia, they were not drawn to the towns or cities, but went at once into the rural districts and settled generally on lands along the streams of water, or in vicinity of the great springs which abounded in the country; as along White Clay creek in Delaware, the Brandywine and Octorara creeks in Chester county, Pa., on the Neshaminy and other streams here in Bucks county, or farther on up as at the Forks of the Delaware in Northampton county; along the Pequea and Donegal streams and springs in Lancaster county, and on the banks of Swatara and Fishing creeks in what is now Dauphin county.

Then when encouragement was given and licenses were granted they began to cross over the Susquehanna at Harris's ferry, now Harrisburg, from 1726 to 1736. Crossing over at Harrisburg they settled along the Conodoguinet and about the Big Spring, Middle Spring, Falling Spring and Rocky Spring, in the central part of the valley, and on up along the Conococheague and its several branches, in the vicinity of what is now Chambersburg and Mercersburg.

Land warrants were sold from 1736 onwards. From that time a great tide of emigration set into all these regions in the valley. From thence this tide of emigration flowed on to the Potomac and on down the valley of Virginia into the Carolinas and Tennessee and across into Kentucky.

When the valley was thus fully open to settlement, its attractions were so great, that a large influx of people at once set into it. Those who came were principally immigrants from the north of Ireland, Scotch Irish Presbyterians, or people of the same nationality and of the same religious faith and order from the earlier settlements in the Province of Pennsylvania. They were generally substantial farmers, men of steady habits, hardy, energetic, industrious and enterprising, with sufficient capital for the improvement and extension of their farms. They selected their lands with a view to permanent residence and as future homes for their families. Many of the dwelling houses of these first settlers in Cumberland Valley were built of hewn logs, two stories high, well and strongly built, with several apartments above and below. As early as 1744, many stone houses of two stories were erected in different parts of the valley. Some of these are still standing, and are substantial and comfortable dwellings.

Nine-tenths of all who came thus into the valley at that period were Scotch Irish people. They were a people who had been trained up under the Westminster Confession of Faith and the Larger and Shorter Catechisms. They were generally an intelligent, sincere, honest, Christian people, with a religious character and life based upon the doctrines and duties set forth in the standards of the Presbyterian Church and diligently inculcated upon their minds from their youth up.

As the settlements progressed, congregations were organized. By 1740, there were about one thousand families in what is now Cumberland and Franklin counties, and out of these there were at that time eight or nine congregations organized. These were Silver's Spring and Meeting House (Carlisle), Big Spring (Newville), Middle Spring, Rocky Spring, Falling Spring (Chambersburg), Upper, Lower and West Conococheague (Mercersburg, Greencastle and Welsh Run).

It was within the bounds of the first of these last three congregations mentioned (Mercersburg, called after General Mercer who fell in the battle of Princeton), that the mother of our worthy and excellent Chief Magistrate, Mr. Harrison, who has honored us by his presence here to-day, and the part he has taken in these services, had her birth and religious training. All these congregations erected at once church buildings, and not satisfied with licentiates or untrained ministers, they all sought educated, well trained and settled pastors.

The early Presbyterian ministers of the valley were all, with but one exception, of Scotch or Scotch Irish antecedents and all graduates of some college or university. These people had been trained up under such ministers at their former homes and they would be satisfied with none other here. They were intelligent enough to know the difference between thoroughly educated ministers, men sound in the faith and skilled in matters of casuistry and those who were mere smatterers in divine knowledge and christian experience.

Simultaneously with the organization of churches, was the erection of school houses in every neighborhood, and the procuring of suitable schoolmasters, men of good moral and religious character and of the other necessary qualifications. In these schools the common branches of an ordinary English education were taught. In all of them the Bible was the standard daily reader and the Shorter Catechism was recited each day and reviewed on Saturday morning.

The government of this extended community in the early history of these settlements was largely patriarchal in its character. The father of each family was the prophet, priest and king of his own household. He taught and trained his family in the knowledge, worship and service of God. Subordination to parental authority was a matter of universal inculcation, and obedience to parents was the settled rule with respect to the youth of the entire community.

The great instrumentalities for the instruction and training of the young were the home, the school and the church. "Their religion," as Carlisle has somewhere said, "was the chief fact about them." It was the controlling thing in the family and in all their social intercourse and domestic relations. With them the "chief end of man," was practically to serve and glorify God. With Sir William Hamilton, they could have said that "the great end of man is man," realizing that the more highly and perfectly man was developed physically, intellectually, morally and spiritually, the more he would honor and glorify his Maker. "They were a people of a book, and that book was the Bible." It was read daily in the family at family worship, and in the schools, and not only read but ably and clearly expounded on the Sabbath. With Dr. Thomas Arnold, of Rugby (but not with his degenerate progeny), they regarded the school not merely as "a place where a certain amount of general learning might be obtained, but as a sphere of intellectual, moral and religious discipline, where healthy and vigorous characters are formed, and where the youth are trained for the duties, struggles and responsibilities of life." With them no system of education was complete, in which thorough moral and religious discipline was omitted. The great conservator and arbiter of right among them was the well regulated religious and moral sentiment of the community.

As these original settlers were chiefly farmers, they went on improving their farms, educating their children, and in providing for the subsistence of their families and the support of their schools and churches.

As I have said, in 1740 there were in Cumberland and Franklin counties about one thousand families and eight or nine organized churches, none of them nearer to each other than from eight to ten miles. In 1850, as shown by the census, there were in these two counties four thousand and eighty-nine farms, the greater part of which were still in the hands of the descendents of the original settlers.

Now the peculiarity of the Presbyterians of the Cumberland Valley is, that here for forty years was to be seen a Scotch Irish Presbyterian settlement more universal and extended, than was to be seen anywhere else upon this continent, a people not only of the same nationality but of the same religious faith and worship; of the same homogeneous tastes and dispositions, dwelling together in peace and harmony, and performing towards each other all the offices of good neighborhood; a people of great integrity and uprightness of character, of pure and lofty patriotism and of intelligent and consistent piety. Here was the Presbyterian Church of Ulster transferred to American soil, existing under a government where equal rights were guaranteed to all its citizens, a people knowing their own rights and respecting the equal rights of others. To what was their peculiarity as a religious community due? Is it to be ascribed to any peculiarity as to race or blood? to their Celtic sprightliness combined with their Teutonic obstinacy and firmness? to soil or climate? We answer no. Whatever may be due to these elements of soil, climate, race or blood, their chief peculiarity was due to the providential and religious training which they had received.

Coming as they did out of those fierce and protracted persecutions which they and their fathers had endured in Ireland and Scotland, they came with their Bibles and Confessions of Faith in their hands, and well stored away in their minds.

They came ready to inscribe in bold characters upon their banners here, the three great fundamental principles of Presbyterianism and also of religious and civil liberty, for which they had so bravely struggled, viz.: loyalty to Christ as the supreme and only head of the church, the parity of the ministry, and the right of every congregation to choose its own officers. Of the truth and importance of these fundamental principles, the Scotch and Scotch Irish Presbyterian ministers and people, were so fully pursuaded that no sacrifice was too great to be endured, rather than either renounce or betray them.

The Presbyterians of Scotland and Ireland having been called as they had been to contend amid the most cruel and bloody prosecutions, under which many thousands of them had sacrificed their lives for the supreme headship of Christ over his church, and as a consequence for its freedom from kingly and priestly domination, they became the foremost friends, advocates and defenders of religious and civil liberty, as against the usurpations and tyranny of both ecclesiastical and civil rulers.

The union of church and state had been so close and dependent, and the relations of religious and civil liberty so intimate in their bearing on each other, that those who contended for the former, soon forfeited the favor of the kings and prelates. No portion of the early settlers of this country so clearly comprehended the separate spheres of church and state, as the Scotch and Scotch Irish Presbyterians; and, as a consequence, while they were unwilling to allow the church to be interfered with or controlled by the secular power; so for fear of such usurpations as they had already suffered from, they would neither ask nor receive aid from the state nor submit to its dictation or authority in matters of religious faith and worship.

In their past experience, the natural and constant allies of civil despotism had been the Romish and Episcopal hierarchies, and the Presbyterians of Ireland and Scotland in their resistance to tyranny and oppression had suffered more from the latter than from the former, for the reason that the Episcopal Church was more frequently in the ascendancy and her prelates had much greater influence over their civil rulers and oppressors.

The greatest friends and promoters of religious and civil liberty in this land, history shows, were the Scotch and Scotch Irish Presbyterians, the Puritans of England, the Dutch of Holland and the Huguenots of France.

Presbyterianism, as it came therefore into the Cumberland Valley a century and a half ago, was not a thing crude in its principles and chaotic in its elements, but on the contrary was a clearly defined and thoroughly developed system of religious faith and order. It did not come here as something that was passive and plastic, to be determined in its character and history by the force of circumstances, or by the accident of its mere environment, but its earliest propagators came with positive opinions, with well settled principles and with deep and strong convictions of truth and duty and with clear conceptions of their mission in laying the foundations of the church in this new world.

The early Presbyterian ministers came with a system of doctrine that was distinct and sharply defined, with a form of government conformed to the word of God, and with a mode of worship that was at once simple, Scriptural and spiritual.

In tracing back, however, the lines of influence that entered into the formation of our earliest Churches and Presbyteries in this land, the student of history cannot stop at Ireland or Scotland or England or France or Holland. All the lines along which the faith of the Reformed churches and also of religion and civil liberty and popular education, are traceable, stop not in any of these countries, but all run through and beyond them to that valley which lies embosomed in the mountains of Switzerland and to the banks of that beautiful lake on which stands the city of Geneva, which has for its greatest distinction, and will have through all time, that it was the home and the scene of the labors and achievements of John Calvin, the great theologian of the Reformation. Here it was that John Knox, many learned English Puritans in the bloody times of Mary, as well as the Huguenots of France, fleeing from the persecutions at home, found their way, and there acquired a more thorough knowledge of the great doctrines of the Reformed faith and of the principles of religious and civil liberty, and there beheld a people governed by laws of their own making, a commonwealth without kings or nobles, a church without priests or prelates, and which acknowledged no head but Christ, and whose doctrines, government, laws and officers were all drawn directly from the word of God, and which had no authority to bind the conscience of any one, any further than they were sustained by the express statements of the Scriptures, or by plain inference from their expressed teaching.

It was thence that our earliest ministers received their chief impress. They were cast in the mould of that system of religious faith and worship known as the "Calvinistic," a system, says Froude, "which has ever borne an inflexible front to illusion and mendacity, and has preferred rather to be ground to powder like flint, than to bend before violence, or melt under enervating temptation." To Scotland belongs the great distinction of having perhaps more fully and clearly perceived and held fast the Reformed Calvinistic faith than any other country. Says Macaulay: "To the attempt to enslave Scotland, England owes its freedom," and it may be added, the United States their religious and civil liberty. This was due to their rigid adherence to the principles of Knox and Calvin. These were the principles which revolutionized Western Europe, emancipated the masses of the people from civil and religious despotism and secured civil and religious liberty for the United States of America.

Let some people think and talk as they may, the American revolutionary war was a Presbyterian war, waged chiefly by the English Puritans (half of whom were originally Presbyterians), and the Scotch Irish Presbyterians, for the securement of independence of Great Britain and the enjoyment of civil and religious liberty. As soon as the trouble rose at Boston, with the mother country, the cry rang out from the Presbyterians of North and South Carolina, Pennsylvania, New Jersey, Delaware, Maryland and Virginia in favor of independence. The immortal Witherspoon voiced the sentiment in the Continental Congress. Patrick Henry re-echoed it in the valley of Virginia. The Presbyterians of the Cumberland Valley rose up *enmasse* and ministers and people joined the war of independence. Generals Armstrong, Irvine and the gallant Mercer commanded the troops, Reverends John Steel and John Craighead went forth as captains of companies, and Drs. John King, Robert Cooper and George Duffield as chaplains in the army.

The reason of all this readiness to go, over and above the love of liberty and their sense of right and justice inspired by their religion and regulated by the Divine law, was that they held in remembrance the grievances which they had endured. They had come through the fires of fierce and prolonged persecutions. They had forsaken their homes as the President has so well said to-day "for God and liberty," and by the help of God, they were determined that the shackles of oppression should not be rivited upon them here.

Such is the estimate which in this brief and hurried survey, we place upon the character, principles and habits of the Scotch Irish Presbyterians of the Cumberland Valley. We do not claim for them perfection by any means. We do not deny that they had their defects, which neither we nor they would seek to palliate or justify. But like the sun, which has its spots, so whatever defects they may have had, they were all overpowered and obscured by the greater effulgence of the mass of excellencies which adorned their characters, and were exemplified in their lives.

Without any disparagement of the Quakers or the Germans, the other two general divisions of the early settlers in the Province of Pennsylvania, we speak thus more earnestly with respect to the Scotch Irish Presbyterians, from the conviction that as a people, justice has not yet been done them either in the history or the literature of the country.

THE LOG COLLEGE.

Now what of the relation of the Presbyterians of the Cumberland Valley to the Log College?

Soon after the withdrawal of the New Side party from the Synod in 1741, the people of Hopewell, which included Big Spring, Middle Spring and Rocky Spring congregations, and the New Side portions of Derry, Upper Pennsboro, Conococheague and other parts of congregations, sent supplications to the New Side Presbyteries of New Castle and New Brunswick for supplies, and Revs. Campbell and Rowland were sent to visit them.

Rev. John Rowland was an Alumnus of the Log College and licentiate of the Presbytery of New Brunswick. Although his licensure was irregular and became the occasion of a violent controversy, which issued in the division of the church, yet he was a strong and impressive preacher, and his ministry was extraordinarily blessed in what is now Lawrenceville and Pennington, New Jersey, to the bringing about of a great revival of religion in both congregations. When he came into the Cumberland Valley he came fresh from these revival scenes, and much in the spirit of Whitefield and the Tennents. Mr. Rowland's preaching is represented as having been with great power and marked results through all these congregations.

In 1742, Big Spring, Middle Spring and Rocky Spring churches united in calling Dr. John Blair, an alumnus of the Log College and licentiate of the Presbytery of New Castle to become their pastor. Mr. Blair continued pastor of these three congregations until 1748, and most probably until 1756, when the incursions of the Indians led to his withdrawal. In 1757 he succeeded his deceased brother Samuel, at Faggs Manor. In 1767 he was chosen Vice President and Professor of Divinity in Princeton College, from which position he modestly retired in 1769, in favor of Dr. Witherspoon. He died in Walkill, New York, in 1771 in the fifty-second year of his age.

John Blair, like his brother Samuel, was among the most talented and gifted ministers of his day. He is believed to have had no superior as a theologian at that time. He was a man of clear and strong convictions with respect to the doctrines of grace, and preached them with great clearness and force. His ministry to the three congregations in the Valley was eminently blessed to the awakening of the impenitent and the edification of the people of God. Its influence in favor of an orthodox faith and a warm evangelical piety, is felt in these congregations until this day.

Few men in the history of the church have had so many distinguished persons named after them. Dr. Samuel Stanhope and Dr. John Blair Smith were the children of one sister, and the Rices of Virginia were the children of another sister. Dr. William Linn was his son-in-law and Dr. John Blair Linn his grandson. Francis P. Blair, the editor of the Globe in Washington, and father of Montgomery and General Frank P. Blair, was also a grandson. In the inscription upon his tomb, he is spoken of as a man of genius, a good scholar, an excellent divine, an eminent Christian, a man of great prudence and a laborious and successful minister, who lived greatly beloved and died greatly lamented.

Rev. John Roan, an alumnus of the Log College, and a bold and fearless preacher was settled over the united New Side congregations of Paxton, Derry and Conewago in 1745, and labored there until his death in 1775, and lies buried in the graveyard at Derry. On his tomb is inscribed, "Here lies the remains of an able, faithful, courageous and successful minister of Christ." And finally, Dr. Benjamin Rush and Governor John Dickinson, pupils of Dr. Samuel Finley, an alumnus of the Log College, while at Nottingham, Maryland, and therefore grandsons of the Log College, were the founders of Dickinson College.

Few parts of the Church or country therefore received a more direct or deeper impress from the Log College than the Cumberland Valley.

Notwithstanding the distractions and the divisions occasioned by two violent religious controversies, the desolations caused by three protracted wars, and that greatest of all calamities, the loss of Dickinson College to the Presbyterian cause, the Churches of the Valley continue their existence and many of them have had a steady and solid growth. They have been distinguished all through their history generally for a strict adherence to the Westminster Standards, for a warm evangelical piety, for zeal in the promotion of revivals of religion, for their missionary spirit, and for their regard for higher Christian education. And although these churches have been subject to a constant depletion from the great attraction of the larger towns and cities of the older states; to a perpetual stream of emigration to the more fertile prairie lands and growing towns of the great west, and to the steady influx of the German population from the German settlements in the State, still the general roll of membership has not been diminished, and the highest point of Christian benevolence ever attained was reached the past year.

What Ulster has long been with respect to the whole religious world, the Cumberland Valley has been in relation to all parts of this wide spread land. A perpetual stream of emigration has gone out from it to strengthen the churches of the older towns and cities and to form new ones in all parts of the Great West.

CHURCH ORGANIZATION 1898.

PASTOR.
REV. EBENEZER ERSKINE, D. D.

RULING ELDERS.
EDWIN R. HAYS, ROBERT MICKEY,
JOHN F. KENDIG, GEORGE W. SWIGERT,
ELIJAH J. ZOOK, M. D.

TRUSTEES.
W. ALEXANDER McCULLOUGH, Pres.,
ROBERT H. SOLLENBERGER,
DANIEL LECKEY,
HON. HARRY MANNING,
ATCHISON LAUGHLIN,
W. LINN DUNCAN,
JOHN S. ELLIOTT.

TREASURER.
JOHN S. ELLIOTT.

CHOIR MASTER. **ORGANIST.**
WILLIAM J. LAUGHLIN, REBECCA WAGNER.

SUPT. OF SABBATH SCHOOL.
EDWIN R. HAYS.

ASSISTANT SUPT. SABBATH SCHOOL.
GEORGE W. SWIGERT.

SUPT. OF INFANT SCHOOL.
MRS. MARY ELLEN AHL.

SEXTON.
JOSEPH WILT.

INDEX

An asterisk indicates the name appears twice on the same page.

----, Bill 48
----, Catharine 79*
----, Ceasar 31
----, David 45
----, Dick 31
----, Elizabeth 81
----, Eve 45
----, Fan 47
----, George 180
----, Grace 42
----, Grant 44
----, Hall 45
----, Hannah 46
----, Jack 38, 45
----, Jane 53
----, Jonathan 28
----, Maragert 72
----, Mary 78, 81
----, Mat 36
----, Nancy 77
----, Ned 39
----, Phillis 28
----, Pomp 45
----, Rachel 44
----, Sal 33, 45, 47
----, Sally 72
----, Sandon 39
----, Tom 46
----, Walter 44
Abernethy, Rosanna 81
Ackman, John 28
Ackman, Mary 28
Adair, Rosian 36
Adams, Agnes 37
Adams, Ann 68
Adams, Elizabeth Barr 96*
Adams, Ephriam 89, 96*
Adams, Henry 71
Adams, J. 79
Adams, Jane 59, 75
Adams, Jane Eliza 71,
Adams, Jemima 96
Adams, Jennie 21
Adams, Jenny 37, 44

Adams, John 21, 37, 44
Adams, Margaret 161
Adams, Margaret Clark 96
Adams, Margaret J. 96
Adams, Martha 22
Adams, Martha S. 96
Adams, Matthew 59, 86
Adams, Mrs. 87
Adams, Rebecca 96
Adams, Richard 59, 86
Adams, Robert 68, 96*, 161
Adams, Samuel 37
Adams, Sarah G. 89
Adams, Susanna 96
Adams, Thomas 37, 71, 86, 87
Agnew, Nancy 50
Albert, Catharine 94
Albert, Elizabeth 74
Albert, John 89
Albert, Mary A. 91
Alexander, Anna 95
Alexander, Archibald 144*
Alexander, James 49
Alexander, Margaret 75
Alexander, Mary 63
Alexander, William 95*
Allen, Alexander 45
Allen, David 45
Allen, Elizabeth 45, 49
Allen, Hugh 45, 127
Allen, Isabella 45
Allen, J. K. 177
Allen, James 65, 96
Allen, James W. 161
Allen, Jane 65, 96
Allen, Jennet 45
Allen, Jenny 45
Allen, Jesse K. 96

Allen, John 45, 83, 161
Allen, Mary 65, 74
Allen, Nancy 32
Allen, William 65
Allison, John 18, 19
Allison, Mary 46
Allsworth, Mr. 43
Alter, Benjamin 71
Alter, Elizabeth 74
Alter, Susanna 78
Anderson, Hannah 34
Anderson, Isabel 21
Anderson, James 49, 185
Anderson, Jennie 141
Anderson, John 21
Anderson, Mary 54
Anderson, Rev. 58
Anderson, Samuel 21
Andrews, Ludwig 133
Appelby, ---- 52
Appleby, Eliza 37
Appleby, J. 37
Appleby, James W. 128
Appleby, Jane 37
Appleby, John 37
Appleby, Nancy 37
Appleby, William 37, 49
Applegate, John 70
Ardiler, Caleb 44
Ardiler, Jane 44
Armor, Samuel 71
Armstrong, ---- 54
Armstrong, Gen. 195
Armstrong, James 18, 49*
Armstrong, John 146
Armstrong, Margaret 146
Armstrong, Mary 51
Armstrong, Rebecca 33, 51
Armstrong, Robert 49
Armstrong, Sarah 51
Arnold, Thomas 190
Askin, Nancy 79

200

Asper, John 71
Atchison, Andrew Mitchel 95
Atchison, Benjamin 48
Atchison, Catherine 44
Atchison, Elizabeth 48, 75, 82
Atchison, Jacob 48
Atchison, James 48
Atchison, Joseph 49
Atchison, Nancy 95
Atchison, William 67
Aughinbaugh, Henry 133
Auld, Christina 28
Auld, David 133
Auld, Mary 28
Auld, Sarah 53
Auld, William 28, 126, 133
Auxer, Elizabeth 161
Auxer, Geo. 161

Baker, Jacob 71
Baker, Joseph 61
Baker, Samuel 71
Bales, Eliza 96*
Bales, Jane McFarlane 96
Bales, Thomas J. 96
Ballentine, George 71
Banks, Mr. 43
Barnes, Grizel 42
Barnes, Margaret 42
Barnes, Robert 42
Barnes, Thomas 42
Barr, Alexander 96, 161, 177
Barr, Andrew McElwain 97
Barr, Elizabeth 72, 89
Barr, Esther Thompson 97
Barr, Hugh 96*
Barr, Hugh A. 97
Barr, J. W. 97
Barr, James 65
Barr, Jane 89
Barr, John 50, 89, 177

Barr, John Geddes 96
Barr, Margaret L. 96
Barr, Maria 75
Barr, Martha 97*
Barr, Mary A. 96
Barr, Robert 46, 49, 83
Barr, Robert Lusk 96
Barr, Sally 77
Barr, Samuel 89
Barr, Sarah 96*, 161
Barr, William 71, 82, 96*, 97*
Bartnett, John M. 89
Barton, Gray 73
Basler, Thomas 71
Baxter, Alice 93
Baxter, Margaret A. W. 94
Bayle, Martha 31
Bayle, Samuel 31
Beale, Andrew 128
Beale, John 126
Beale, Robert 128
Beard, Anne 49
Beard, Elizabeth 49
Beard, James 49
Beard, Margaret 49
Beard, R. 126
Beard, Robert 49
Beaston, Jane 90
Beatty, James 84
Beatty, James, Jr. 65
Beatty, Margaret J. 81
Beatty, Mary 65
Beaty, Isabella 79
Beck, Philip 133
Bell, Andrew 19, 40
Bell, Ann 103
Bell, Betsy 40, 51
Bell, David 40
Bell, Elizabeth 34
Bell, George 34, 71
Bell, Ginny 23
Bell, Jane 34, 40, 77
Bell, Jenny 46
Bell, John 17, 18, 19, 33, 40, 46, 128, 136
Bell, Joseph 34, 49
Bell, Katherine 34
Bell, Margaret 52

Bell, Martha 46
Bell, Matty 40
Bell, Nancy 76
Bell, Peggy 40, 54
Bell, Robert 18, 34, 40, 49
Bell, Thomas 34
Bell, Walter 40, 83
Bell, William 34, 40, 50, 62, 85, 86, 136
Bell, William B. 103
Belt, Burt 89
Bender, Louisa 89
Bender, Mary A. 91
Benner, Joseph 71
Benson, John 61, 71
Berkley, Robert 71
Bessor, William 89
Best, Catharine 97
Best, Frances 97
Best, Henry 97*
Best, James 97
Best, Richard 97
Best, Robert 97
Best, Sarah E. 97
Bigler, Jacob 71
Bigler, John 71
Bigler, William 71
Binner, Mary 163
Black, Philip 89
Blain, Jean 22
Blain, John 71
Blain, Thomas 71
Blaine, Robert 49
Blair, ---- 49
Blair, Charity 48
Blair, Daniel 48
Blair, Francis P. 197
Blair, Frank P. 197
Blair, Isaiah 133
Blair, Jenny 48
Blair, John 12, 48, 143, 148, 196, 197
Blair, John D. 145
Blair, Montgomery 197
Blair, Mr. 13
Blair, Randle 48
Blair, Rannuel 20
Blair, Rebecca 148
Blair, Sally 62

Blair, Samuel 18, 124, 143, 144*, 146, 196, 197
Blair, William 141
Blankney, George 89
Blean, Isabella 78
Blean, Jane 89
Blean, Jesse 89
Boose, Jonathan 177
Bovard, Hannah 20
Bovard, Robert 17, 20
Bowan, Francia 92
Bowers, John 89
Bowman, Eliza 40
Boyd, Deborah 48
Boyd, Eleanor 49
Boyd, Elizabeth 66, 90
Boyd, George 49, 50
Boyd, James 49, 89, 97, 133
Boyd, Jane 61, 97
Boyd, John 21, 49, 86, 126, 133
Boyd, Martha 61, 163
Boyd, Rebecca 97
Boyd, William 61, 163
Boyle, Alex. 126
Boyles, Alexander 89
Brackenridge, Andrew 71
Brady, Hannah 53
Brady, Joseph 71
Brandon, Thomas 50, 177
Brannan James 41
Brannan, John 41
Brannan, Mary 41
Brannan, Thomas 41
Brannan, William 41
Brattan, Adam 30
Brattan, Anne 31
Brattan, Eleanor 82
Brattan, George 96
Brattan, Horace 31
Brattan, James Sharp 96
Brattan, John 126
Brattan, Martha 30
Brattan, Mary 82
Brattan, William 64, 126
Bratton, Adam 18, 85, 127, 162*

Bratton, Ann 162
Bratton, Eleanor 162
Bratton, George 89, 162
Bratton, John 128, 133
Bratton, Mary 162
Bratton, Samuel 162
Bratton, William 162*
Brewster, James R. 138
Brisby, Betsy 31
Brisby, John 31
Brisby, Nancy 31
Brisby, Sarah 31
Brisby, William 31*
Brittain, Ann 82
Brittain, Martha 81
Brittan, Eleanor 66
Brittan, Mary 66
Brittan, William 64
Brown, ---- 91, 94
Brown, A. 126
Brown, Adam 43
Brown, Agnes 30, 65, 89
Brown, Alexander 50
Brown, Ann 43, 74
Brown, Caroline 96
Brown, Catherine 18
Brown, Eleanor 62, 72
Brown, Elizabeth 43*, 50
Brown, Elizabeth A. 95
Brown, Elizabeth J. 96
Brown, Ellen D. 97
Brown, George 177
Brown, Hannah 43
Brown, James 84, 85, 127, 136, 162*
Brown, Jane 58, 68, 80, 91, 96, 162
Brown, John C. 97
Brown, John 17, 18, 20, 30*, 43, 62, 63, 71*, 86, 96*, 97, 127, 128, 162, 177
Brown, Joseph 43, 63, 83, 71, 89, 96*, 162,

Brown, Joseph Thompson 96
Brown, Katherine 34
Brown, Lacy 97*
Brown, Margaret 43, 79, 162
Brown, Margaretta 96
Brown, Martha 30, 93, 162
Brown, Mary 30. 43, 60, 67*, 162
Brown, Mary J. 97
Brown, Matthew 58
Brown, Nancy 23
Brown, Polly 51
Brown, Rachel 162
Brown, Samuel A. 97
Brown, Sarah I. 96
Brown, Thomas 89
Brown, Widow 63
Brown, William 30, 50, 68, 83, 96*,97*, 137, 162,
Brownfield, Elizabeth 54
Brownson, Mary 161
Brownson, Thomas 161
Browster, Alexander 36
Browster, Andrew 24
Browster, Ann 18, 36
Browster, William 24, 36, 49
Bryson, Hugh 46
Bryson, Margaret 46
Bryson, Mrs. 23
Bryson, Rebecca 50, 46
Bryson, Samuel 22, 46
Bryson, William 46, 127, 161
Buchanan, Agnes 32
Buchanan, Alex. 126
Buchanan, Elizabeth 64, 162
Buchanan, Ezekiel 162
Buchanan, Jane 67, 77
Buchanan, Margaret 60

Buchanan, Mary 64, 162
Buchanan, Nancy 65, 82, 94
Buchanan, Robert 32, 162
Buchanan, Sarah 65
Buchanan, Thomas 18, 19, 32, 163, 177
Buchanan, William 32, 162
Buhard, Brines 45
Burck, Rev. 58
Bush, John 89
Bush, Velotta 93
Butler, Elliott 177
Butler, Esther 95
Butler, John 71, 89
Butler, Sallie 163
Butler, Samuel 163

Caldwell, Ann 29
Caldwell, Anne 29
Caldwell, Elizabeth 29
Caldwell, James 29
Caldwell, John 29*, 126, 136
Caldwell, Mary 66
Caldwell, Samuel 29
Calvert, John 37
Calvin, John 193
Campbell, Barbara 75
Campbell, David 72
Campbell, Ebenezer 65
Campbell, Eleanor 151
Campbell, Elizabeth 79
Campbell, James 71
Campbell, Rev. 196
Campbell, William 163
Carithers, James 47
Carithers, Mary 36
Carlisle, T. Calvin 90
Carmer, George 133
Carnahan, ---- 127
Carnahan, Adam 47*, 71, 127
Carnahan, Agnes 47*

Carnahan, Elizabeth 47
Carnahan, James 47, 50
Carnahan, Jane 75
Carnahan, Joseph 46
Carnahan, Jude 67
Carnahan, Judith 46, 163
Carnahan, Margaret 65, 67, 77
Carnahan, Martha 46
Carnahan, Mary 163
Carnahan, Nancy 53
Carnahan, Robert 46, 50, 85, 163
Carnahan, William 46, 67, 72*, 163
Carothers, Andrew 72, 89
Carothers, Eliza 92
Carothers, Elizabeth 81
Carothers, James 72
Carothers, Jane 72
Carothers, John R. 72
Carothers, Josiah 72
Carothers, Martin 72
Carothers, Mary C. 72
Carrick, Katharine 53
Carson, Andrew 71
Carson, Elijah 50
Carson, Elisha 28, 86
Carson, Elizabeth 73*
Carson, Hannah 21, 28, 47, 163
Carson, Janet 47
Carson, John 27, 28, 85, 127, 133, 134, 136,
Carson, John E. 72
Carson, John, Jr. 21
Carson, Margaret 21, 82
Carson, Mary 47
Carson, Priscilla 28, 62, 82, 163
Carson, Ruth 43
Casey, John 89
Chapman, Mary 55

Chapman, Sally 46
Charlton, Robert 71
Clark, Agnes 32
Clark, Alexander 37
Clark, Henry 50, 72, 127
Clark, John 32, 133
Clark, Peter 72
Clark, Thomas 85
Clark, William 32*, 126
Claudy, Catharine 97*, 98
Claudy, George 89, 97*, 98
Claudy, John C. 137
Claudy, Margaret E. 98
Claudy, Samuel R. 97
Claudy, William B. 97
Clelland, Adam 37
Clelland, Jane 37
Clemmons, James 71, 84
Clendennin, James 72
Clendenning, John 59
Clendenning, Mrs. 59, 60
Cloyd, Jenny 51
Cobean, Mary McFarlane 163
Cobean, William 89, 163
Cochran, Stephen 89
Cole, Samuel 89
Conelly, Adam 31
Connel, Eliza 67
Connelly, Betsey 52
Connelly, Charity 32, 53
Connelly, Eliza 89
Connelly, Elizabeth 32
Connelly, James 32
Connelly, John 21, 126
Connelly, Joseph 63, 72, 84, 89, 126
Connelly, Mary 61
Connelly, Thomas 61
Connelly, William 23, 32, 63, 71, 84
Conner, Lavina 89

Conway, Mary 163
Cook, Alfred Dewey 97
Cook, Caroline 98
Cook, Elizabeth 71, 98
Cook, Felix 98
Cook, Fenix 89
Cook, George Grove 98
Cook, Jane 98, 163
Cook, Ruth 23, 40
Cook, Samuel 97, 98, 163
Cook, Thomas 72
Cooper, Andrew 83
Cooper, Benjamin 67
Cooper, Dr. 149
Cooper, James 89
Cooper, Jane 80
Cooper, John 85
Cooper, Margaret 72
Cooper, Rev. 58, 150
Cooper, Robert 195
Cooper, Sarah 67, 72
Cooper, William 63
Cope, ---- 89
Cope, Benjamin 72
Coulter, Joseph 72
Cowden, William 50, 133
Cowen, Elizabeth 64, 78
Cowen, Jane 65
Cowen, Martha 63
Cowley, Patty 29
Cox, Mary 163
Coyle, Andrew 97*, 137*
Coyle, David 97
Coyle, Eliza 97*
Coyle, John 97
Coyle, Martha Jane 97
Coyle, Mary W. 92
Coyle, Nancy 97*
Coyle, Robert Elliott 97
Coyle, Samuel McCord 97
Coyle, Scott 97*
Coyle, William H. 97
Craig, Mary 49
Craig, Peggy 54
Craighead, Alexander 10, 143

Craighead, Andrew 143
Craighead, George 71
Craighead, John 143, 195
Craighead, Robert 142
Craighead, Robert, Jr. 142
Craighead, Thomas, 10, 142, 143
Crain, ---- 89
Crain, Sarah 53
Crawford, Colonel 84
Crawford, D. 126
Crawford, G. W. 177
Crawford, Joseph 133
Crawford, Katherine 37
Crawford, Rachel 63, 82
Crawford, William 83
Creamer, Susanna 89
Cremer, Theodore H. 89
Crotzer, Catharine 79
Crow, Eleanor 49
Crow, George 50
Crow, John 72
Crowel, ---- 50
Crowel, Mrs. 64
Crowel, Rachel 74
Crowel, Samuel 50, 133
Crowel, Sarah 75
Crowell, James 72
Crowell, Jemima 82
Crowell, Rachel 51
Crowford, Nancy 51
Culbertson, Harry 65
Culbertson, Samuel 64, 72, 83
Cummins, Elizabeth 53
Cummins, Widow 126
Cunningham, Isabella 151
Cunningham, James 137
Cunningham, S. 17, 20

Dahr, Elenor 62
Dahr, Joseph 72
Dallas, William 90
Davidson, Alex. Leckey 98
Davidson, Alexander 72, 98, 164
Davidson, Ann 48, 66, 75, 138, 163*
Davidson, Arabella 99
Davidson, Catharine 98*
Davidson, David 62
Davidson, Eleanor 64, 75, 82, 98
Davidson, Eleanor R. 163
Davidson, Eliza 98*
Davidson, Elizabeth 23, 66, 98, 138
Davidson, Elizabeth Young 164
Davidson, Ellen Jacob 99
Davidson, Emily 65
Davidson, Francis 50
Davidson, George 62, 72, 163
Davidson, George E. 99
Davidson, George G. 99*
Davidson, Isabella 60, 98
Davidson, J. Blair 138
Davidson, James 42, 48, 66*, 72, 73, 83, 102*
Davidson, James Wilson 98
Davidson, Jane 62, 98, 99*, 163, 164
Davidson, Jennie W. 138
Davidson, John 18, 19, 23, 48, 50, 59, 66, 73*, 83, 85*, 86, 90, 98*, 124*, 126, 133, 141, 163, 164*
Davidson, John Blair 98

Davidson, John H. 99
Davidson, John Laughlin 68
Davidson, John M. 138
Davidson, John Young 98
Davidson, Lacy 60, 77
Davidson, Marjory T. 98
Davidson, Mary 64, 74, 78, 82, 98, 164
Davidson, Mary J. 89
Davidson, Mary Jane 98
Davidson, Matthew 48, 65, 73, 86, 98, 124
Davidson, Nancy 61, 76, 90, 98
Davidson, Nancy Sterrett 141
Davidson, P. 58
Davidson, Patrick 72
Davidson, Prudence 61
Davidson, Rebecca E. 98
Davidson, Robert 120
Davidson, Robert McFarlane 98
Davidson, Rosanna 98*, 99
Davidson, Ruth E. 91
Davidson, Samuel 73, 98*, 137, 141*
Davidson, Samuel Rankin 99
Davidson, Sarah Bella 91
Davidson, Sarah E. 98, 99
Davidson, Susan 61, 76
Davidson, William 59, 63, 65, 68*, 73*, 90*, 98, 9*, 137, 164
Davidson, William Miller 68
Davis, Charity 44
Davis, Hannah 71
Davison, Leacy 48
Davison, Samuel 83
Davison, Susan 60
De Peyster, Robert 90
Dearborough, I. 126
Dearmon, Margaret 55
Dearmond, William 72
Delany, Widow 75
Denison, Sarah 40
Denning, William 19, 164, 177
Denny, Margaret 89
Devenport, James 68
Devinport, William 31
Dickinson, John 197
Dickson, John 64, 73
Dickson, Sarah 76
Dickson, Widow 84
Dobbin, Rev. 150
Donald, Francis 18
Donaldson, Alexander 64
Donaldson, Jane 62
Donaldson, Martha 61
Donaldson, Thomas 73
Donnel, Francis 30
Donnelly, ---- 95
Donnelly, Mary 66
Dougherty, Catharine 62, 64, 77, 82
Dougherty, David 41
Dougherty, George 84, 164
Dougherty, Jane 80, 92
Dougherty, Maria 80
Dougherty, Rachel 164
Douglas, Agnes 34
Douglas, George 72
Douglas, John 34, 50
Douglas, Margaret 34
Douglas, Mary 34*
Douglas, Nancy 23
Douglas, William 17, 34*, 72, 124
Douglass, Margaret 51
Dowds, Robert 72
Doyle, John 127
Dridge, Mary 51
Drudge, Cassendannah 70
Drudge, Elizabeth 70, 90
Drudge, Henry 69*, 70*
Drudge, Jane 69
Drudge, John 69
Drudge, Margaret 74
Drudge, Mary 70
Drudge, Mary Ellen 70
Drudge, Rosanna 70
Drudge, Sarah 70
Drudge, Wilson 70
Drugon, Katharine 50
Du Bois, Sarah W. 155
Du Bois, William 155
Duck, Susanna 71
Duey, Conrad 164
Duey, Rachel 164
Duffield, George 14, 145*, 147, 195
Duffield, Margaret 145
Duffield, Robert E. 90
Duffy, Elizabeth 95
Duffy, Ellen 72
Duffy, John 73
Duffy, Mary 79
Dunbar, Abraham 59
Dunbar, David 164
Dunbar, Eliza Smith 164
Dunbar, Isabella 64
Dunbar, Jane 78
Dunbar, John 86, 133, 134, 164
Dunbar, Mary 64, 164
Dunbar, Robert 33
Dunbar, Rosanna 64, 74, 82
Duncan, D. D. G. 137
Duncan, Elizabeth 61
Duncan, Harriet 98
Duncan, James 50
Duncan, James Mitchel 98
Duncan, Jane 93
Duncan, John 98
Duncan, Joseph 61, 73
Duncan, Margaret 44, 76
Duncan, Mary 59, 91

Duncan, Nancy 81
Duncan, William 17, 20, 44, 50, 67, 72, 73*, 86, 127
Dunfee, John 90, 98*, 99
Dunfee, John Rankin 99
Dunfee, John T. 98
Dunfee, Mary 81
Dunfee, Mary E. 99
Dunfee, Sarah 98*, 99
Dunlap, Adella 99
Dunlap, Anna 99
Dunlap, Daniel 90, 98, 99*
Dunlap, Eliza 98
Dunlap, Frances 99*
Dunlap, James 90
Dunlap, Virginia 99
Dunlap, William 90, 98*
Durbara, Isaac 41
Durbara, Jane 41
Durbara, John 41
Durbara, Rueben 41
Durbarrow, ---- 50
Durburrow, John 145

Eager, Margaret 49, 50
Eccles, Nathaniel 86
Eckels, Nathaniel 24
Edmonston, Agnes 31
Edmonston, Joseph 31
Ege, Frances Hopkins 99
Ege, Jane 99*
Ege, Joseph 73, 99*
Ege, Mary A. 99
Ege, Mary E. 99
Elder, John 50
Eliot, Jenny 23
Elliott, A. 21
Elliott, Agnes 42
Elliott, Alexander 42, 84, 127
Elliott, Catharine 42, 91
Elliott, Elizabeth 93, 164
Elliott, Jannet 42
Elliott, John 90

Elliott, Katherine 60
Elliott, Margaret 80, 95
Elliott, Mary 79
Elliott, Nancy 92, 164
Elliott, Thomas 164
Emit, Sam'l 22
Emmett, Samuel 50, 127
Endsly, James 73
Engles, Joseph P. 156
Erskine, Dr. 157, 158
Erskine, Ebenezer 118, 155, 156
Erskine, Helen 158
Erskine, Henry 156
Erskine, John 155, 156
Erskine, Mary 158
Erskine, Ralph 156
Ervin, James B. 90
Espey, Ann 34*
Espey, Christian 51
Espey, Elizabeth 23, 34
Espey, George 126
Espey, James 34*
Espey, John 126
Espey, Margaret 34
Espey, Peggy 55
Espey, Rachel 34, 49
Espey, Robert 34, 62
Espey, Thomas 34, 126
Espey, William 34
Espy, Addah L. 69
Espy, Amy 73
Espy, Ann 21
Espy, Augustus A. 69
Espy, Elizabeth 23
Espy, George 69*, 73
Espy, John 32, 50
Espy, Mills B. 69
Espy, Robert 73
Espy, Theressa J. 69
Espy, Thomas 17, 84
Ewing, ---- 62
Ewing, Alexander 37
Ewing, Anna 37
Ewing, David 31

Ewing, Elizabeth 31, 52, 66, 79, 164
Ewing, James 37*, 73*
Ewing, Jane 37*, 65
Ewing, Jean 21
Ewing, John 17, 20, 37*, 67, 126
Ewing, Mariana 37
Ewing, Martha 21, 28, 37, 54
Ewing, Mary 37, 50
Ewing, Matthew 37
Ewing, Mrs. 87
Ewing, Nancy 37
Ewing, Ralph 62, 83
Ewing, Rebecca 37*
Ewing, Robert 37
Ewing, Sarah 37
Ewing, Thomas 37*
Ewing, W. 22
Ewing, William 37*, 87, 126

Fager, Rebecca 80
Falkner, Margaret 52
Farhner, Prudence 28
Farrier, David 73
Fenton, Ann 21, 41
Fenton, James 21, 41, 83, 84, 159, 177
Fenton, John 41*, 73, 177
Fenton, Mary 41
Fenton, Robert 41, 84
Fenton, Samuel 21, 41*, 159, 177
Ferguson, Catharine 73
Ferguson, David Morrow 100
Ferguson, Jane 95
Ferguson, Mary 100*
Ferguson, William 31, 86, 164, 177
Fertig, Mary 50
Filer, ---- 95
Filer, David 90*
Findlay, Samuel 28
Findley, Samuel 20
Finkenbinder, John 90

Finley, Major 22
Finley, Polly 22
Finley, Sam'l, 18, 51, 127, 133, 197
Fitzsimmons, Elizabeth 66
Fitzsimmons, Mary 93
Fitzsimmons, Patrick 66
Fleming, Eliza 63
Fleming, Elizabeth 76
Fleming, James 51, 60
Fleming, Jane 64
Flin, William N. 28
Flint, Elizabeth 60
Forbes, Mary 76
Forhner, Katherine 22
Forhner, Mary 22
Forhner, Priscilla 22
Forhner, Sidney 22
Fortner, Mary 71
Fosnaught, Jacob 68*
Fosnaught, Mary 68
Fosnot, Jacob 100
Fosnot, John C. 100
Fowler, Elizabeth 36
Fowler, John 36, 51
Fowler, Robert 36
Fox, John 51, 85
Fox, Rachel 59
Frank, Henry 90
Frazer, Wilson 90
French, Elizabeth 71
French, John 63
French, Martha 41
French, Mary 63
French, Samuel 67
French, William 66, 126
Frother, Joseph 51
Fry, Jesse R. 177
Fuhrhob, Godlieb 73
Fullerton, Adam 180
Fullerton, Alexander 180
Fullerton, Isabel 28
Fullerton James 180
Fullerton, Thomas E. 28
Fullerton, Thomas Elder 50

Fulton, Ann 74
Fulton, David 100*
Fulton, Elizabeth 75
Fulton, Elizabeth J. 99
Fulton, F. Huston 69
Fulton, Francis 62, 69*, 99, 164, 165
Fulton, Grizelda 100
Fulton, Houston 99, 100*
Fulton, Isabel 69
Fulton, Isabella 68, 78
Fulton, James 68, 73, 99*, 100*, 137, 165
Fulton, Jane 76, 99
Fulton, John 73
Fulton, Katharine 55
Fulton, Kezia 69
Fulton, Martha 100
Fulton, Mary 76
Fulton, Mary E. 100
Fulton, Matilda 69, 91
Fulton, Nancy 69, 73
Fulton, Robert 177
Fulton, Samuel H. 100
Fulton, Sarah 78, 99, 100*, 165
Fulwiler, Nancy 94
Furguson, William 100*

Gailly, Sarah 50
Galbraith, Eleo 37
Galbraith, Jane 81
Galbraith, Sarah 75, 165
Galbraith, William 165
Gallespie, Ann 42
Gallespie, D. 126
Gallespie, Elizabeth 42
Gallespie, Martha 42
Gallespie, Mary 42
Gallespie, Millie 42
Gallespie, Nancy 42
Gallespie, Nathaniel 42
Gallespie, Nelly 42

Gallespie, Robert 42
Gallespie, Samuel 42
Gamble, Anne 51
Gardner, Sara A. 95
Garman, John 90
Garnel, Benjamin 61
Garnel, Mary 61
Gaster, James 100
Gaster, John 90
Gaster, John Henderson 100
Gaster, Sarah 100
Gayman, ---- 90
Geddes, Catharine I. McClay 141
Geddes, Catharine 100*
Geddes, Charles King 100
Geddes, Eliza 63
Geddes, Elizabeth 23, 81, 82
Geddes, Elizabeth Peebles 165
Geddes, James 51
Geddes, John 23, 51, 85, 133, 134, 161, 165*.
Geddes, John P. 83, 100*, 141
Geddes, Margaret 81
Geddes, Martha 67
Geddes, Sarah 67, 71, 82
Geddes, Thomas M. 90
Geddes, William M. 100
Geddes, Williamson Nevin 100, 141
Gees, Elizabeth 54
Geese, Christian 74
Geese, Mary A. 80
George, David 85
George, Rachel 79
George, S. C. 177
George, Thomas 133
Gibson, Martha 32
Gibson, Patrick 32
Giffen, Betsy 31
Giffen, Elenor 31
Giffen, Robert 74
Giffen, William 17, 20, 31
Giffin, Catharine 165

Gillaspie, William 42
Gillespie, ---- 127
Gillespie, Albert Stewart 101
Gillespie, Alfred Ewing 100
Gillespie, Ann 62, 82, 165
Gillespie, David 51
Gillespie, Eleanor 71, 73, 81
Gillespie, Elizabeth 73
Gillespie, Elizabeth J. 101
Gillespie, Elleanor 33
Gillespie, Geo. 33, 164
Gillespie, George 22, 101*, 127, 137
Gillespie, James 17, 33
Gillespie, James Stewart 100
Gillespie, Jane 33
Gillespie, John A. 101
Gillespie, Lucinda 101*
Gillespie, Martha 22, 165
Gillespie, Mary 66
Gillespie, Mat. M. 33
Gillespie, Nancy 54, 62, 82
Gillespie, Nathaniel 22, 84, 165
Gillespie, Polly 71
Gillespie, Robert 22, 84*
Gillespie, Samuel 100*, 101*
Gillespie, Samuel S. 101
Gillespie, Sarah E. 101
Gillespie, Sarah I. 101
Gillespie, Thomas 127
Gillespie, Thomas G. 101
Gillespie, Widow 84
Gillespie, William 32
Gillsepie, Nancy 165
Gilmore, David McKinney 100
Gilmore, Eleanor 100, 101*
Gilmore, James 100, 101*
Gilmore, John 30
Gilmore, Lydia B. 101
Gilmore, Nancy Jane 101
Given, William 126
Givler, Benjamin 100*
Givler, Isabella 100*
Givler, Martha 100
Givler, Thomas McFarlane 100
Gladen, William 24
Glen, Alexander 35
Glen, David 74, 48
Glen, Elizabeth 35
Glen, Gabriel 30*
Glen, Jane 30
Glen, Jenny 30
Glen, John 35
Glen, Mary 48
Glen, Thomas 35*
Glen, William 30
Glendenning, James 51
Glenn, Alexander 21, 23, 51, 64, 100, 165
Glenn, Ann E. 92
Glenn, Anna M. 101
Glenn, Atchison L. 100
Glenn, David 86
Glenn, Elizabeth 87
Glenn, Gabriel 126
Glenn, James 73
Glenn, Jane Rachel 93
Glenn, Jean 21
Glenn, Maria 100, 165
Glenn, Mary 101*
Glenn, Mrs. 85
Glenn, Rachel 62, 74
Glenn, Rebecca 73
Glenn, Robert E. 101
Glenn, Thomas 21
Glenn, Thompson 82
Glenn, Thos. 124
Glenn, William 59, 73, 86
Glenn, William M. 101*
Glenn, Wm. Mills 137
Goffine, Agnes 47
Goffine, James 47
Goffine, John 47
Goodhart, Catharine 94
Goodling, Samuel 36
Goodman, Alfred 90
Gopock, Robert M. 46
Gordon, Jane 34
Gorly, James 32
Gorrel, Isabella 46
Gorrel, John 46, 83
Gourd, Elizabeth 79
Gourd, John 62, 69*
Gourd, Joseph 21, 37, 87
Gourd, Joseph D. 69
Gourd, Margaret 21*, 37, 69
Gourd, Martha 72
Gourd, Mary 62
Gourd, Mrs. 87
Gourd, Samuel 86
Gourd, William 69
Graham, Alfred Mateer 102
Graham, Arthur 31, 51, 64, 84, 101
Graham, Charles McFarlane 101
Graham, Eliza 165
Graham, Elizabeth 66, 75
Graham, Francis 51
Graham, George 74
Graham, George W. 177
Graham, Isaiah 23, 31, 51, 84, 136, 165
Graham, James 17, 19, 31*, 74, 84, 124, 126, 133, 139, 165

Graham, Jared 18, 30*, 84, 124
Graham, Jenny 30
Graham, John Davidson 100
Graham, Martha 52, 61, 165
Graham, Martha J. 89
Graham, Mrs. Isaiah 23
Graham, Nancy 64, 65, 82, 100, 101*, 102, 165*
Graham, Robert 74, 165
Graham, Samuel 66, 83
Graham, Susana 61
Graham, Susannah 31
Graham, Thomas 31, 73, 84
Graham, William 90, 100, 101*, 102
Graham, William Finley 101
Gray, Barton 61
Gray, Elizabeth 71
Gray, Fanny 78
Gray, James 90
Gray, John 64, 86, 87
Gray, Katherine 34
Gray, Margaret 62
Gray, Mrs. 87
Gray, Thomas 90
Greason, Samuel Carothers 74
Green, Barbara 101
Green, Dr. 157
Green, James 64
Green, John 23, 32, 51, 165
Green, John C. 102
Green, Joseph E. 101
Green, Mary 23, 63, 101*, 102*
Green, Mary G. 102
Green, Matilda L. 101
Green, Sally 23
Green, Samuel 101*, 102*
Green, William 60, 137*
Greenfield, Hugh 74
Greenwood, John 73
Greer, Patrick 133
Greer, Thomas 58
Grier, James 73
Grier, Jane 36
Grier, John 151
Grier, Sally 47
Grier, Thomas 18, 36
Griffin, Margaret 89
Grip, Eliza 89

Hackett, Henry C. 166
Hackett, Margaret 102
Hackett, Mary 102, 166
Hackett, Mary E. 102
Hackett, Robert 91, 102*
Hackett, Ross 102
Hackett, Thomas 91
Hackett, Thompson 177
Hadden, Jedidiah 63
Hadden, Thomas 51
Haden, Jedidiah 74
Hains, Aaron 46
Halbert, Joseph 34
Hall, Isabella 40
Hall, James 32
Hamil, Mary 166
Hamil, William 74
Hamil, Wm. 166
Hamilton, George 40
Hamilton, James 39, 128
Hamilton, John 74
Hamilton, Martha 60
Hamilton, Ruth 21, 40
Hamilton, William 190
Hammond, Edward P. 118
Hanna, Else 166
Hanna, James 51
Hanna, John 166
Hanna, Lydia 54
Hanna, Nancy 71
Hanna, Samuel 166
Hanna, William 46, 48
Hannon, Jennie 21

Hanson, Helen 148
Hard, John W. 74
Harlan, Caroline 102
Harlan, Catharine 102
Harlan, Eliza J. 102
Harlan, Elizabeth H. 165
Harlan, George 102*, 165
Harlan, Jacob W. 102
Harlan, James 165
Harlan, Jane E. 102
Harlan, John M. 69
Harlan, Mary C. 102
Harlan, Ruth 65, 69, 165
Harlan, Samuel A. 102
Harper, Andrew 166
Harper, Barbara 52
Harper, David 166
Harper, Eliza 95
Harper, Elizabeth 166*
Harper, James 166
Harper, Jane 78
Harper, Jean 166*
Harper, John 166*
Harper, Margaret 28, 49, 102, 166*
Harper, Maria 92
Harper, Mary 81
Harper, Nancy 53, 61
Harper, Robert 166
Harper, Samuel 166
Harper, Sarah 63, 166
Harper, Sarah A. 102
Harper, William 102, 166
Harris, ---- 91
Harris, Elizabeth 89
Hart, Sarah 89
Harvey, Andrew 133
Hawkes, John 51
Hawkins, Kate 91
Hawks, Mary 180
Hawthorn, James 33
Hawthorn, Margaret 32
Hawthorn, Samuel 33
Hawthorne, Samuel 17
Hays, Adam 32
Hays, Anne 32

Hays, Dorcus 81
Hays, Edwin R. 102, 137, 138
Hays, Ezemiah 80
Hays, Frances 60
Hays, Hannah 102*
Hays, Jennie E. 138
Hays, John 126
Hays, John S. 177
Hays, John Sharp 102
Hays, Joseph 32
Hays, Lucetta 90
Hays, Margaret 78
Hays, Margaret Mickey 166
Hays, Mary 72*
Hays, Mary A. 92
Hays, Patrick 74, 166
Hays, Robert 102*
Hays, Sally 80
Hays, Samuel 86
Hays, William T. 74
Heagy, David 74
Heagy, Eliza 65
Heagy, John 65
Heagy, Julia 94
Heap, John 15, 167
Heden. Mary 60
Hefflefinger, Adaza 94
Hefflefinger, Thomas 91
Heffleman, Eliza 90
Heffleman, Mary 167
Heffleman, Michael 167
Hemphill, James 51
Henderson, James S. H. 116, 153, 154
Henderson, Mr. 134
Henry, Patrick 195
Herron, J. Hunter 138
Herron, James 74
Herron, James Johnson 102
Herron, Margaret Davidson 102
Herron, Mary E. 102
Herron, Rebecca 93
Herron, Rev. 58
Herron, Thomas 74
Herron, William 102
Hershaw, Joseph 63

Hildebrand, Abraham 133
Hodge, Agnes 44
Hodge, John 44
Hodge, John, Sr. 17, 20
Hodge, William 17, 20
Holler, John 91
Holmes, George 51
Holmes, Hugh 133
Holmes, Susanna 66
Holms, John 74
Holt, Phebe 71
Homes, Nancy 37
Hood, Jane 141
Hood, Jane S. 102
Hood, John 91, 102, 103*, 141
Hood, John Wallace 102
Hood, Josiah 64, 69*, 167, 177
Hood, Margaret A. 69
Hood, Margaret Harper 103
Hood, Margaretta A. 95
Hood, Mary Jane 69
Hood, Sarah 102, 103*, 167
Hood, Walter L. 103
Hoover, Hannah 90
House, Elizabeth 167
House, John 167
Houston, Isabel 48
Houston, James 35, 48
Houston, Robert 48
Howard, Nicholas 177
Hudson, George 74
Hudson, James 74
Hudson, Jonathan 90, 102
Hudson, Martha E. 102
Hudson, Mary 150
Huges, Emily H. 140
Huges, Humphrey 140
Hughs, Nancy 23
Hughs, Thomas 51
Hume, James 74
Hume, James Davidson 103
Hume, William D. 91

Humes, Emma M. 102
Humes, Hetty 102, 103*
Humes, William 102, 103*
Hunter, ---- 49
Hunter, Agnes 30
Hunter, Elizabeth 38
Hunter, James 30
Hunter, Jan 29
Hunter, Jane 30*
Hunter, Joseph 29, 84, 167
Hunter, Lathey 30
Hunter, Lathie 30
Hunter, Nancy 71
Hunter, Sally 52
Hunter, W. 126
Hunter, William 18*, 29, 30*, 38, 127
Huston, Andrew 24, 36
Huston, Ann 77
Huston, James 18, 74, 86, 103, 124, 176*
Huston, Jane 36, 75
Huston, John 24, 36, 51, 127
Huston, John D. 103
Huston, Jonathan 74
Huston, Margaret 50, 64
Huston, Martha 32, 80
Huston, Mary 63, 72, 77
Huston, Nancy 32, 63, 76
Huston, Peggy 32
Huston, Robert 32
Huston, Samuel 74
Huston, Sarah 36
Hutchinson, Robert 126
Hutchison, Martha 23, 44
Hutchison, Mary 44*
Hutchison, Robert 18, 20, 44*
Hutchison, Rosannah 44
Hutchison, Susanna 23

Hutton, James 74
Hye, Martha 89

Ickes, Charles 178
Ingram, Mary 77
Ingram, Rachel 76
Irvin, Susan 67
Irvine, Catharine 79
Irvine, Gen. 195
Irvine, Isabella 103, 167
Irvine, James 20, 62, 74, 84, 103
Irvine, James B. 103
Irvine, James Davidson 103
Irvine, James R. 91*, 103, 137
Irvine, Margaret 103
Irvine, Margaret McCllelland 167
Irvine, Mary 167
Irvine, Mrs. 61
Irvine, Rosanna 167
Irvine, Ruth 167
Irvine, Samuel 74, 91, 103, 167*
Irvine, Sarah 103
Irvine, Susan M. S. 103
Irwin, Agnes 36
Irwin, Ann 77
Irwin, Eleanor 44
Irwin, Isabel 44
Irwin, James 44, 126, 167
Irwin, John 44
Irwin, Mary 44*
Irwin, Prudence 167
Irwine, Agnes 18
Irwine, James 17

Jack, Andrew 47
Jack, Cynthia 47, 51
Jack, Hannah 47
Jack, James 19, 47, 127
Jack, Jane 47
Jackson, John 75
Jacob, David 75
Jacob, Eleanor 69, 76, 94
Jacob, Elenor 31

Jacob, Eliza 81
Jacob, Elizabeth 22, 31, 94
Jacob, Elizabeth Ralston 69
Jacob, John 133
Jacob, Joseph 65, 103, 137, 167, 168
Jacob, Joseph A. 103
Jacob, Katherine 21
Jacob, Lydia 65, 168
Jacob, Mary 31, 50
Jacob, Thomas 20, 22. 31, 43, 74, 75, 85
Jacob, Thos. 136
Jacobs, Adam 167, 169
Jacobs, Garman 44
Jacobs, Jarman 18, 20, 126
Jacobs, Katherine 44
Jacobs, Marjory 167
Jacobs, Sarah Lenney 167
Jacobs, Thomas 126, 133
James, Henry 60
James, Jane 62
Jamison, Isaac 133
Jenkens, George 178
Johnson, ___ 48*
Johnson, Andrew 51, 91
Johnson, Ann 103*
Johnson, Annie 141
Johnson, Betsy 40
Johnson, Eliza J. 95
Johnson, Elizabeth 23, 51, 168
Johnson, Henry 91
Johnson, Hetty 89
Johnson, Isabella 67, 74
Johnson, James 17, 32, 84, 126*
Johnson, Jane 95
Johnson, Jean 48
Johnson, Jennie 22
Johnson, Jenny 32
Johnson, John 168
Johnson, John Bell 103, 178
Johnson, Margaret 48

Johnson, Margaret E. 91
Johnson, Martha 32
Johnson, Mary 22, 91
Johnson, Peggy 22, 32
Johnson, Robert 22, 116
Johnson, Robert B. 103
Johnson, Savilla 95
Johnson, Thomas 86. 48*, 126
Johnson, W. B. 137
Johnson, William B. 103*
Johnson, William H. 178
Johnston, Alexander 51
Johnston, Ann 36
Johnston, Isabel 82
Johnston, James 28, 33*
Johnston, Jane 32, 63
Johnston, John 32, 63*, 75*
Johnston, Margaret 28
Johnston, Mary 33
Johnston, Robert 28, 36
Jones, Hugh, 51
Jones, James 51
Jones, Margaret 75

Kean, John 75
Keans, John 91
Keeper, Augustus A. 91
Keizer, David 91
Kellen, Eliza 90
Keller, Sarah 90
Kelley, Alexander 103
Kelley, Ann G. 104
Kelley, Cornelius 91
Kelley, Emaline 103
Kelley, George 105
Kelley, Grizelda 104*, 105, 168
Kelley, Jane 103*, 104*

Kelley, John 127, 168
Kelley, John A. 104
Kelley, Joseph 127
Kelley, Margaret 104
Kelley, Mary A. 103
Kelley, Samuel Kennedy 104
Kelley, Sarah J. 103
Kelley, William 103
Kelly, Ann 35
Kelly, Christian 35
Kelly, Daniel 35
Kelly, Elizabeth 35
Kelly, Gusilla 65
Kelly, James 52
Kelly, Margaret 52
Kelly, Richard 35
Kelly, Robert 75
Kelly, William 35
Kelso, John 91*, 104
Kelso, Mary E. 104
Kelson, Matilda 104
Kelsy, George 33*
Kelsy, Jane 33
Kendig, John F. 137
Kennedy, Alexander Barr 103
Kennedy, Ann 47
Kennedy, Annie 94
Kennedy, Elizabeth 64, 77
Kennedy, James 75, 103*, 104*, 105*
Kennedy, James McFarlane 104
Kennedy, Jane 54, 94
Kennedy, John 52, 88, 104, 178
Kennedy, John G. 105
Kennedy, Margaret 104, 168
Kennedy, Maria 103*, 104*, 105
Kennedy, Mary Barr 105
Kennedy, Nancy 67, 76
Kennedy, Rev. 58
Kennedy, Robert 75, 104
Kennedy, Thomas 85, 103, 128, 168
Kennedy, William L. 105

Ker(r), Alexander 75, 168
Ker(r), David Sterrett 103
Ker(r), Eliza 103, 104
Ker(r), Eliza B. 168
Ker(r), Elizabeth J. 104
Ker(r), Mary I. 104
Ker(r), Matthew 52
Ker(r), Sarah 168
Ker(r), William 52, 75, 103, 104*, 137, 168*
Kieser, George 133
Kilgore, Elizabeth 104*
Kilgore, Elizabeth 65, 71, 180
Kilgore, Ezekiel 75, 83, 104*
Kilgore, Ezekiel J. 104
Kilgore, Harriet 91
Kilgore, Isabel 67, 180
Kilgore, Isabella 91, 94, 168
Kilgore, Jane 77
Kilgore, Jesse 75, 85, 104, 128, 168, 180
Kilgore, Jonathan 28
Kilgore, Mary 104
Kilgore, Mary E. 104
Kilgore, Nancy 75, 78
Kilgore, Nancy J. 104
Kilgore, Rob. 22
Kilgore, Robert 52, 128, 168, 180
Kilgore, Ruth 29
Kilgore, Samuel 75
Kilgore, William 85, 127, 168, 180
Kilgore, William M. 104
Killough, David 129, 136*
Kincade, Mary 71
King, Elizabeth 81
King, John 195
King, Mrs. 65

Kingborough, Agnes 60
Kingsborough, Nancy 76
Kinkaid, ---- 92
Kinkaide, James 75
Kinkaide, William 75
Kinsley, Charlotte 104*
Kinsley, George 104
Kinsley, J. R. 178
Kinsley, Jacob 75, 104*
Kinsley, John 168
Kinsley, John R. 104
Kirkpatrick, Elizabeth 53
Kirkpatrick, Hugh 45
Kirkpatrick, James 52, 86, 126
Kirkpatrick, Miss 43
Kishler, Jacob 91
Klink, Elizabeth 168
Klink, George 168
Knettle, George 105*
Knettle, Hannah 168
Knettle, Hannah M. 104
Knettle, Henry 84, 168
Knettle, James H. 105
Knettle, Jane E. 105
Knettle, Lauretta 105
Knettle, Mary 79
Knettle, Mrs. 62
Knettle, William 75
Knight, Elizabeth 168
Knight, James 178
Knight, Thomas 168
Knox, John 193
Koons, Isaac 91, 103, 104, 168
Koons, James 104
Koons, Jane 103
Koons, Joseph 104
Koons, Thomas 103
Koontz, Isaac 67, 68*, 75
Koontz, Jane 67
Koontz, Robert 68
Koontz, Sarah 67
Kyle, Samuel 178

Laird, Ann 65, 76
Laird, Catharine 169
Laird, Hugh 169
Laird, James 34, 84, 127, 136, 169
Laird, Jane 34
Laird, Mary 77
Laird, Matthew 67*
Laird, Robert 169
Laird, Susanna 67
Laird, Thomas 169
Landis, David 91
Landis, Nancy 89
Latshaw, Sally 75
Lauderdale, Sarah 52
Laughlin, Agnes 169
Laughlin, Alex. 18
Laughlin, Alexander 19, 45, 63, 85, 127
Laughlin, Ann 45
Laughlin, Atcheson 18, 20, 86, 44, 136, 153, 168, 169*
Laughlin, Betsy 52
Laughlin, Catherine 61, 75
Laughlin, Catharine A. 92
Laughlin, Charity 45, 60
Laughlin, Doctor 28, 127
Laughlin Elenor 28
Laughlin, Eliza 64, 82
Laughlin, Elizabeth 46, 169
Laughlin, Hannah 61, 75
Laughlin, Hugh 17, 19, 45, 46, 85, 127, 136
Laughlin, James 20, 44, 46, 126, 137*, 168, 169*
Laughlin, James, Jr. 63, 83
Laughlin, Jane 45, 78, 82, 153
Laughlin, Jas. 18, 86

Laughlin, John 21, 44, 45, 47, 59, 65, 75*, 85, 169
Laughlin, John Hood 141
Laughlin, Margaret J. 47, 65, 93
Laughlin, Maria 63
Laughlin, Mary 21*, 44*, 46, 81, 169
Laughlin, Matthew 22, 28, 52
Laughlin, Nancy 54, 64, 82
Laughlin, Paul 28
Laughlin, Phebe 22
Laughlin, Polly 60
Laughlin, Robert 46
Laughlin, Susana 45
Laughlin, Thomas 52*
Laughlin, William 20, 44*, 46, 66, 133, 126, 169, 178
Laughlin, William R. 169
Laughlin, Wm. 86
Layburn, Elizabeth 94
Layburn, Rachel 95
Leacock, Jane 53
Leacock, Priscilla 63, 81, 82
Leacock, Thomas 65, 76
Leburn, Robert 76
Leckey, A. 126
Leckey, Alexander 17, 34, 84, 169*
Leckey, Ann 62, 73, 82
Leckey, Ann Davidson 169
Leckey, Betsy E. 80
Leckey, Catharine 64, 68, 73
Leckey, Daniel 61, 75, 123, 169
Leckey, Elizabeth 34, 169
Leckey, Emily 66
Leckey, George 61, 75, 76
Leckey, Isabel 66
Leckey, Isabella 170
Leckey, James B. 137

Leckey, Mary 72, 82
Leckey, Prudence 74
Leckey, Sarah 61*, 82, 169, 170
Leckey, Sarah B. 169
Lee, Dianna 75
Lee, John 67, 75
Lee Samuel 105
Lee, Sarah Jane 90
Leecock, William 52
Leeper, James 37*
Leeper, Martin 37
Leeper, Mary 37
Leeper, Sally 38
Lefevre, David 105
Lefevre, David Alter 76
Lefevre, George 126
Lefevre, Isaac Lawrence 105
Lefevre, Kitty A. 105
Lefevre, Mary A. 105
Lefevre, Mary E. 105
Lefevre, Peter Wilt 105
Lehmon, Catharine 80
Leiper, William 133
Leman, Martha 28
Leman, Samuel 28
Leman, William 28*
Lemmond, William 129, 136
Lemon, ---- 91
Lemon, Elizabeth 36
Lemon, Jane 36
Lemon, John 45
Lemon, Polly 36
Lemond, John 124
Lemond, Nancy 49
Lemond, Samuel 136
Lemond, William 134
Lenney, Elizabeth 169
Lenney, Hannah 169
Lenney, Isaac 169
Lenney, Sarah 169*
Lenny, William 91, 169
Lieper, Charles 17
Liggat, ---- 49
Liggate, Nancy 51
Lightcap, Elizabeth 47, 52
Lightcap, Godfrey 47

Lightcap, Levi 47
Lightcap, Mary 47, 54
Lightcap, Nancy 47
Lightcap, Samuel 23, 47
Lightcap, Solomon 17, 20, 47* 127
Lightcap, Thomas 47, 75
Lightcap, William 47, 52
Lightel, George 30
Lightel, Sarah 30
Lindenburg, Charles 91
Lindsay, James 22, 66, 91
Lindsay, Jane 61, 67, 170
Lindsay, Lacy 75
Lindsay, Mary Forbes 170
Lindsay, Nancy 32*, 51, 65, 71, 82
Lindsay, Robert 32, 54, 84
Lindsay, Samuel 18, 32*, 63, 75, 82, 126
Lindsay, William 18, 29, 32, 62, 76, 83, 84, 136, 170
Lindsey, Joseph H. 105
Lindsy, Jane 32, 59
Lindsy, Jenny 32
Lindsy, Mrs. 68
Linn, John 76
Linn, John Blair 148, 197
Linn, Rev. 58
Linn, Samuel 15, 16, 75*, 134, 145, 147, 197
Little, George 18
Logan, Alexander 170
Logan, Ann 73
Logan, George 76
Logan, James 67, 76, 170
Logan, Martha 170
Logan, Robert 58
Long, Elizabeth 40
Long, John 85

Long, Rebecca 59
Longwell, Sarah 73
Love, James 32
Love, John 32
Love, Margaret 32
Love, Thomas 32
Lowery, Isaac 76
Lowry, Mary 50
Lowry, Nancy 37
Lowry, Samuel 40
Lowry, Sarah 63
Luper, Charles 19
Lusk, David 18
Lusk, Jane 39
Lusk, John 18, 24, 136
Lusk, Martha 133
Lusk, Mary 65
Lusk, Robert 38, 128, 133, 136
Lusk, Thomas 133
Lusk, William 18, 24, 65, 127
Lynch, Elizabeth 63
Lyone, James 12
Lytle, Annie M. 105
Lytle, George 75
Lytle, Martha 62
Lytle, Sarah E. 105
Lytle, William 105*

Macfee, William 77
Magaw, James W. 152
Mahon, Archibald 149
Mahon, David 149
Mahon, Elizabeth 74
Mahon, Jane 149
Mahon, Martha 149
Majoirs, Elizabeth 42
Majoirs, Isaac 42
Majoirs, Nancy 42
Makemie, Mr. 186
Markward, Isaac 92
Marshall, John 53
Marshbank, James 31
Mart, Alexander G. 93
Marten, Agnes 180
Martin, ---- 50
Martin, D. E. 178
Martin, Eliza J. 91

Martin, Elizabeth 22, 71, 139
Martin, Hannah 76
Martin, Jane 39
Martin, Jared Jr. 22
Martin, John 39, 53, 76*, 83, 105
Martin, Jonathan 85
Martin, Joshua 77
Martin, Letitia 71
Martin, Mary 39, 92
Martin, Nancy 55, 80
Martin, Paul 83, 126
Martin, Rosanna 39
Martin, Sarah 81
Martin, Sarah E. 105
Martin, Thomas 39, 45, 83*
Mason, Elizabeth 39
Mason, Isaac 53, 133
Mason, John 133
Mason, Thomas 76
Mateer, Andrew 77
Mateer, Mary 93
Mathers, Eleanor 43
Mathers, Isabella 43, 79
Mathers, James 60
Mathers, Jennet 43
Mathers, John 43, 64, 77*, 83
Mathers, Joseph 43, 86, 126
Mathers Martha 41, 80
Mathers, Mary 21*, 41
Mathers, Robert 46, 53, 77
Mathers, Samuel 18, 20, 43, 86, 126
Mathers, Susan 105
Mathers, Thomas 41, 43, 105, 127
Mathers, William 41, 84, 170
Mathias, Mr. 130
Matthews, Edward 93
Matthews, William 84
Matthias, Samuel 135
Mauer, Susan 91
Maxwell, George 76
Maxwell, John 77
Mayes, Samuel 52

McAlister, Leacy 79
McAllister, Lacy 43
McBeth, Alexander 60, 86
McBride, ---- 59
McBride, Alexander 36, 87, 127
McBride, Alexander, Jr. 18, 24*
McBride, Andrew 106
McBride, David 69, 106
McBride, Deborah 76
McBride, Hannah 106
McBride, Jane 65. 68, 69
McBride, John 62, 63
McBride, Margaret 72, 82
McBride, Mrs. 59
McBride, Nancy 78
McBride, Robert 61, 69, 77, 86
McBride, Secustus 69
McBride, Tabitha 36, 77
McBride, William 64
McCachran, Isabella 170
McCachran, James 170
McCachran, Jane 107
McCachran, Jane Laughlin 170
McCachran, John 151
McCachran, Mary 93, 107, 153
McCachran, Mr. 133, 134
McCachran, Rachel 170
McCachran, Rebecca J. 90
McCachran, Rev. 152
McCachran, Robert 78, 88, 93, 95, 107*, 151, 153, 170*
McCaleb, J. 78
McCall, Ezra 133
McCandlish, Alexander 140
McCandlish, Andrew 64
McCandlish, Jane 138, 170

McCandlish, John 78, 170
McCandlish, Mamie 138
McCandlish, Margaret 82
McCandlish, Maria 170
McCandlish, Mary 94
McCandlish, Mattie 93
McCandlish, Thomas 92
McCandlish, William 140, 170
McCann, Sarah 55
McCanon, Rosanna 78
McCarroll, Sarah 92
McCarron, George 82
McCasland, Martha 46
McCausland, Mark 52
McClaran, Thomas 53
McCleary, John 52
McClellan, Anne 32
McClellan, Elias 76
McClellan, Jenny 32
McClellan, John 62
McClelland, John 77
McClelland, William 78
McClintock, Alexander 41, 129, 136, 137
McClintock, David 133
McClintock, Elizabeth 43
McClintock, Sarah 41
McClure, Andrew 34
McClure, Betsy 34
McClure, Elizabeth 64
McClure, Jennet 34
McClure, John 40
McClure, Margaret 18, 34*, 54
McClure, Martha 38
McClure, Mary 32, 76
McClure, Nancy 34, 51
McClure, Polly 64
McClure, Robert 34*, 127
McClure, Theo. 23
McClure, Walter 46
McConel, Charles 36

McConel, Eleanor 36
McConel, Isabel 36
McConel, Jenny 36
McConel, Martha 36
McConel, Mary 36
McConnel, ---- 53
McCord, Andrew 62
McCord, James 61, 76, 77, 123
McCord, Lacy 90, 95
McCord, Mary 92
McCord, Robert 77, 78
McCord, Rosanna 62
McCord, Susan 123
McCormick, Ann 42
McCormick, Eliza 67, 80
McCormick, Elizabeth 42, 170
McCormick, Esther 45
McCormick, Hugh 175
McCormick, Jane 22, 42, 52
McCormick, Joseph 84
McCormick, Joseph 22, 42, 53
McCormick, Leary 23
McCormick, Margaret Young 170
McCormick, Maria 78
McCormick, Mary 66
McCormick, Robert 45, 53
McCormick, Samuel 17, 20, 40, 66, 78, 127, 136*. 170
McCormick, Susan 62
McCormick, Thomas 22, 42, 78, 83, 136, 159, 170
McCoy, Archibald 124, 159
McCoy, Archy 133
McCoy, Daniel 92, 109
McCoy, Joshua 92
McCoy, Margaret 109
McCoy, Rosanna 63
McCoy, William A. Shannon 109
McCracken, Elizabeth 28
McCracken, Jane 59
McCracken, Jenny 28

215

McCracken, Martha 28, 78
McCracken, Rachel 82
McCracken, Samuel 59
McCracken, William 18, 20, 28, 171, 178
McCrea, Catharine 74
McCrea, Margaret 171
McCrea, W. H. 40
McCrea, William 171*
McCulloch, David 171
McCulloch, Elizabeth 36
McCulloch, Elizabeth Hueston 171
McCulloch, James 36, 127, 170
McCulloch, Jane Dunbar 171
McCulloch, Jane Henderson 171
McCulloch, John 83, 78, 170, 171*
McCulloch, Mary Williamson 171
McCulloch, Robert 36
McCulloch, Sarah 171
McCulloch, Tabitha 78
McCulloch, Thomas 78
McCulloch, William 83, 171
McCullouch, Betsy Coyle 171
McCullough, Archibald 24
McCullough, Elizabeth 18, 53
McCullough, James 92, 93
McCullough, Jane 82
McCullough, John 78
McCullough, Leo 178
McCullough, Rachel 77
McCullough, Robert 93
McCullough, Sally 74
McCullough, Samuel 92, 133
McCullough, T. Henderson 93
McCullough, W. Linn 92

McCullough, William 77*
McCullough, William H. 93
McCune, ---- 128
McCune, Ann 107
McCune, Cyrus 110
McCune, Eliza 89
McCune, Ellen Culbertson 106
McCune, Ezemiah 107
McCune, Hannah 65, 67
McCune, Hannah M. 108
McCune, Hugh 85, 100, 106*, 108*, 110, 107, 180
McCune, Isabel 28
McCune, Isabella 50, 73
McCune, J. A. 178
McCune, James 126
McCune, Jane 80, 89
McCune, John 28, 62, 85, 105, 106, 127, 136, 180*
McCune, Joseph 78
McCune, Margaret 67
McCune, Margaretta 106
McCune, Mary 85, 180
McCune, Mary A. 90, 105, 106, 107, 108, 109,
McCune, Peggy 28
McCune, Rebecca 107
McCune, Robert 28, 85, 180
McCune, S. Elder 93
McCune, Samuel 53, 85, 108, 180
McCune, Samuel A. 137
McCune, Samuel Brady 109
McCune, Sarah J. 89, 105
McCune, Thomas 78
McCune, William 63, 92, 107, 108, 109
McCune, William B. 107
McCurdy, Agnes 49
McCurdy, David 37*, 52

McCurdy, Elizabeth 37
McCurdy, James 37, 128
McCurdy, Janet 37
McCurdy, Mrs. 37
McDannel, Daniel 123
McDannel, Elizabeth 171, 89
McDannel, Jane A. 110
McDannel, John 171
McDannel, John Martin 109
McDannel, Margaret 171
McDannel, Mary 109, 110
McDannel, William 86, 92, 109, 110
McDannell, Catherine 89
McDannell, Daniel 171*
McDannell, Jane 171*
McDermond, Henry 133
McDermond, Joseph 77
McDonald, Anne 79
McDonald, Catharine 75
McDonald, Daniel 77*
McDonald, Esther 79
McDonald, John 126
McDonald, Mr. 43
McDonald, Sarah 76
McDonald, Thomas 127
McDonald, William 127
McDonnel, ---- 94
McDowell, Elizabeth 172
McDowell, John 77, 126, 172
McDowell, Margaret 172
McDowell, Margaret Laird 172
McDowell, Mary 49, 172*
McDowell, Nancy 50
McDowell, Samuel 172
McDowell, Sarah 72
McElhenney, Martha 91

216

McElhenny, Elizabeth 107
McElhenny, Hugh 45, 83
McElhenny, James 106*, 107, 137
McElhenny, Joseph 83
McElhenny, Margaret 45
McElhenny, Margaret J. 106
McElhenny, Mary 45
McElhenny, Rebecca 45
McElhenny, Robert 77, 107, 173
McElhenny, Samuel 45, 128
McElheny, Jane 66
McElheny, Joseph 66
McElheny, Samuel 23
McElrow, Hugh 76
McElvain, Alice 70*
McElvain, Andrew McKinney 70
McElvain, Andrew Thompson 70
McElvain, Elizabeth Bell 70
McElvain, Ellen 106
McElvain, James 70*, 105
McElvain, James R. 105
McElvain, Jane 70
McElvain, John S. 92
McElvain, Margaret Bell 70
McElvain, Marjory Ellen
McElvain, Mary 94
McElvain, Mary E. 92
McElvain, Mary Jane 70
McElvain, Mary Nicholson 70
McElvain, Richard 70*
McElvain, Robert McCachran 106
McElvain, Rosanna 70*
McElvain, Ruth Rosanna 70
McElvain, Sarah 106
McElvain, William 106
McElvain, William S. 70
McElwain, Andrew 38, 39, 52, 128
McElwain, Andrew, Jr. 172
McElwain, Elizabeth 39
McElwain, Elsey 66
McElwain, Isabella 90
McElwain, James 39, 66, 83
McElwain, Jane 39, 62, 71, 80, 172,
McElwain, Margaret 50
McElwain, Mary 39*, 52, 53, 66, 79, 172
McElwain, R. 52
McElwain, Robert 39*, 62, 76, 83, 106, 128, 136, 172, 178
McElwain, Ruhanna 80
McElwain, Ruth 71
McElwain, Sarah 64
McElwain, Susanna 64
McElwain, Thomas 178
McElwain, William 64
McEntire, Elizabeth 44, 53, 64
McEntire, Mary 64
McEntire, Mrs. 60
McEntire, Sarah 22
McEntire, Thomas 64
McFaden, John 53
McFarland, Margaret 18
McFarlane, Jane 72
McFarlane, Alexander 41, 78
McFarlane, Andrew 32
McFarlane, Ann 31, 41
McFarlane, Anna M. 109
McFarlane, Betsy 22
McFarlane, Clemens 78, 106*, 172
McFarlane, Daniel Ligget 105
McFarlane, Eleanor 172
McFarlane, Eliza 62, 66
McFarlane, Elizabeth 31*, 32*, 41, 74, 172*
McFarlane, Esther 172
McFarlane, Hannah 31
McFarlane, I. G. 109
McFarlane, J. G. 110
McFarlane, James 10, 31, 41, 32, 77, 84, 85, 123, 126, 172
McFarlane, James Graham 110
McFarlane, Jane 60, 106*, 138, 172*, 138
McFarlane, Jane M. 106
McFarlane, John 32, 41*, 84, 128
McFarlane, John E. 108
McFarlane, John Finley 109
McFarlane, Lydia 106*, 172
McFarlane, Lydia B. 108
McFarlane, Margaret 21, 31, 41, 63, 106, 109, 110
McFarlane, Martha 105
McFarlane, Mary 31, 41, 54, 89
McFarlane, Patrick 173
McFarlane, Robert 31, 32, 76, 77, 84, 92, 106, 108, 127, 172*, 108
McFarlane, Rosanna 22, 86, 90, 172
McFarlane, Sarah 32
McFarlane, Widow 126
McFarlane, William 17, 20, 32, 40, 41, 63, 86, 126, 133, 172*

McGaw, Elizabeth 106*, 107, 108*
McGaw, George W. 108
McGaw, Isabella 106
McGaw, James 106
McGaw, John 108
McGaw, Samuel 106*, 107, 108*
McGaw, Sarah M. 106
McGaw, Scott 107
McGinness, J. H. W. 92
McGlaughlin, ---- 52
McGlaughlin, Daniel 52
McGlaughlin, Sarah 46
McGoffine, ---- 22
McGoffine, ---- 53
McGoffine, James 22
McGonegal, William 133
McGovern, Ann 30
McGovern, James 30
McGovern, Mary 30
McGuffin, James 85
McGuffin, Mary 45, 61*, 77
McGuffin, Thomas 126
McGuffine, Jane 28
McGuffine, John 46
McGuffine, Joseph 28
McGuffine, Mary 28
McGuffine, Robert 28
McGuffine, William 28, 46, 52
McGuffog, James 127
McGuffog, William 127
McGuire, Daniel 23
McGuire, Thomas 76
McIlhenny, Margaret 173
McIlheny, Samuel 133
McIlwain, William 133
McIntire, John 29, 173
McIntire, Margaret 173
McIntire, Sally 29
McKain, Elizabeth 82
McKane, Mrs. 65
McKean, Margaret 17, 20

McKean, William 53
McKee, Alexander 92
McKee, James 78
McKeehan, ---- 92
McKeehan, Albert 108
McKeehan, Alexander 20, 48*
McKeehan, Benjamin 48, 49, 86, 92, 105, 107, 126, 173
McKeehan, Betsy 22, 49, 53
McKeehan, Caroline 109*
McKeehan, David 106
McKeehan, Deborah 62, 82, 123, 173
McKeehan, Eleanor 105*, 106, 107*, 108*
McKeehan, Eliza A. 94
McKeehan, Elizabeth 48*, 49
McKeehan, Ellen 108
McKeehan, Emily 90
McKeehan, Emma 110
McKeehan, George 19, 48*, 86, 109, 126, 133*
McKeehan, Grissy 72
McKeehan, Helen M. 158
McKeehan, James 48, 49, 86, 126, 158
McKeehan, Jane 74
McKeehan, Jane M. 108
McKeehan, Jennire 72
McKeehan, Jenny 48
McKeehan, John 17, 19, 48, 49, 53, 66, 77, 86, 105*, 106, 107*, 108*, 124, 136
McKeehan, John, Jr. 60
McKeehan, Joseph 92, 108
McKeehan, Lydia 74
McKeehan, Margaret 23, 49, 52, 81, 92, 105, 173
McKeehan, Mark 67, 77

McKeehan, Martha 62
McKeehan, Mary 48*, 49, 71, 73, 76, 92, 105*, 107*, 108, 110,
McKeehan, Mary Ann 48
McKeehan, Mary Trego 173
McKeehan, Nancy 49, 50
McKeehan, Peggy 49
McKeehan, Rebecca J. 108
McKeehan, Robert 76, 92, 109*, 110, 173
McKeehan, Samuel 48, 62*, 76, 123, 136, 173
McKeehan, Sarah J. 95
McKeehan, Tabitha 66, 81
McKein, Elizabeth 44
McKein, Mary 44
McKein, William 44
McKibben, Chambers 77, 82
McKibben, Elizabeth 81
McKibben, Isabella 67
McKibben, Jere 127, 133
McKibben, Jeremiah 19, 47, 85
McKibben, John 77
McKibben, Joseph 18, 66, 78, 83, 92, 107*, 173
McKibben, Keziah 82
McKibben, Mary 47
McKibben, Nancy 107
McKibben, Polly 74
McKibben, Rebecca 79
McKibben, Susan M. 107
McKibben, Tabitha 66
McKimmins, Gabriel 21
McKinney, ---- 71
McKinney, Andrew 76
McKinney, David 123
McKinney, David A. 110, 137, 138

McKinney, Grizelda 54
McKinney, Lydia B. 92
McKinney, Maria 110
McKinney, Mary 76
McKinney, Rachel 110*
McKinney, Thomas 93, 110*
McKinnie, Mary 73
McKinsey, Jane 22
McKinstre, Susanna 51
McKinstry, Alexander 76
McKinstry, James 78, 87*, 173
McKinstry, Mrs. 87
McKnight, Jane 73, 82
McKnight, Margaret 64, 82
McKnight, Mary 64, 82
McLandburg, John 53
McLane, William 77
McLaughlin, Daniel 127
McLaughlin, Daniel Harper 109
McLaughlin, Eliza 109
McLaughlin, Emaline 109
McLaughlin, Lavina 109
McLaughlin, Margaret A. 108
McLaughlin, Maria 108, 109*
McLaughlin, Robert 109
McLaughlin, Samuel 92, 108, 109*
McLaughlin, Susan 109*
McLaughlin, William 92
McLaughlin, Zachariah 109
McMonigal, Agnes 173
McMonigal, William 173

McMullan, Elizabeth 39
McMullin, Rebecca 45
McNair, Mary 72
McNeil, Samuel 77
McNichols, William 21
McNickle, Jane 73
McNish, Mr. 186
McPherson, Hannah 77
McQuire, Daniel 133
McQuon, James 18
McRory, Samuel 52
McTeer, Agnes 30
McTeer, John 30
McWilliams, Albert 109
McWilliams, Eliza 68
McWilliams, Esther 64
McWilliams, Hetty 91
McWilliams, Hetty G. 68
McWilliams, James 68
McWilliams, Jane 109
McWilliams, John 61, 68*, 76, 178
McWilliams, Mary 74
McWilliams, Mary A. 68
McWilliams, Robert 173
Means, Allen 46
Means, John 62
Means, Joseph 32
Means, Nancy 32
Means, Nathan 60, 87
Mechey, Mary 90
Megaw, David 13
Megaw, James 173
Megaw, Sarah 173
Melroy, Eliza E. 67
Meradith, Margaret 78
Mercer, ---- 90
Mercer, Gen. 195
Michal, John 53, 85
Michels, James 107
Michels, Jane 107*
Michels, Samuel 107
Michels, William 107
Mickey, Agnes 180
Mickey, Andrew 127

Mickey, Benjamin 107, 108*
Mickey, Benjamin J. 108
Mickey, David 85
Mickey, Eleanor 62*
Mickey, Eliza 107, 108*
Mickey, Elizabeth 65, 109, 110*
Mickey, Ezemiah 92, 173
Mickey, Hannah 53
Mickey, Hays 106
Mickey, Jacob 174
Mickey, James 85, 127, 173, 180
Mickey, John E. 110
Mickey, Laura A. 110
Mickey, Lucetta 106, 173
Mickey, Margaret 73, 74, 107
Mickey, Nancy 62, 74
Mickey, Rebecca S. 108
Mickey, Robert 84, 109, 110*, 123, 127*, 137, 173
Mickey, Sarah 93
Mickey, Sarah Belle 109
Mickie, Agnes 28
Mickie, Andrew 28
Mickie, David 28
Mickie, Eleanor 28, 51
Mickie, Hannah 28
Mickie, Isamiah 28
Mickie, Mary 28
Mickie, Robert 28*
Mickie, Thomas 28
Middleton, Andrew 92
Mifflin, Thomas 134
Miller, ---- 93
Miller, ---- 94
Miller, Henry 173
Miller, John 48, 86
Miller, Joseph 92, 107
Miller, Lewis 107
Miller, Lydia 78
Miller, Maria 93
Miller, Mary 73, 106
Miller, Mr. 43

219

Miller, Rachel 106
Miller, Rebecca 67
Miller, Samuel 34, 68, 106
Miller, Sarah J. 93
Miller, Thomas 78
Miller, Titus 133
Miller, William 48, 86
Milligan, William 18
Mills, Rachel 30
Milroy, William Rodman 76
Mitchel, Andrew 53
Mitchel, Elizabeth 44
Mitchel, Eve 44
Mitchel, Ezekiel 42
Mitchel, James 42, 44*, 66*
Mitchel, Jane 66
Mitchel, John 36, 42*, 43*,
Mitchel, Lacy 43
Mitchel, Margaret 42
Mitchel, Mary 42, 44*, 70
Mitchel, Mrs. 83
Mitchel, Rebecca 44
Mitchel, Samuel 42
Mitchel, William 78
Mitchell, Isabella 77
Mitchell, John 18, 20, 128
Mitchell, Samuel 128
Mitten, Mary 94
Mitten, William 124
Moffit, David S. 178
Moffit, Robert 173
Monemy, ---- 50
Monroe, John 126
Montgomery, Ann 60, 76
Montgomery, David 83
Montgomery, Eleanor 66
Montgomery, Eliza 93
Montgomery, Elizabeth 63
Montgomery, Hannah E. 110
Montgomery James 23, 61, 76
Montgomery, James Ramsey 78
Montgomery, Jane 63
Montgomery, John 63*, 76
Montgomery Martha 60
Montgomery, Rachel 110
Montgomery, Rebecca 76
Montgomery, Robert 93, 110
Montgomery, Thomas 45
Montgomery, William 46, 77
Montroe, John 40
Montroe, Margaret 40
Montroe, Mary Ann 40
Montroe, Rueben 40
Montroe, William 40
Moody, Joseph 92
Moon, Gilbert 86
Moor, Elizabeth 31, 49, 80
Moor, Isabel 46
Moor, James 22
Moor, Margaret 31
Moor, Samuel 53
Moore, Catharine 148
Moore, Eleanor 79
Moore, Eliza A. 92
Moore, Elizabeth 77
Moore, John 77, 78, 133, 137
Moore, Martha 105
Moore, Mary 105
Moore, Saml. 43
Moore, Thomas 43
Moorhead, Mr. 43
Mophet, Jane 42
Mophet, Pebe 42
Mophet, Rebecca 42
Mophet, William 42
Morain, John 47*, 127
Morain, Sarah 47
Morris, Francis 44
Morris, Mary 37
Morrison, Elizabeth 45
Morrison, Ezra 63, 66
Morrison, Mary 21, 45
Morrison, Robert 21, 45*, 53
Morrison, William 45
Morrow, ---- 54
Morrow, Ada 110
Morrow, Andrew 63
Morrow, David 85
Morrow, Eleanor 65, 77
Morrow, Eliza 108
Morrow, Elizabeth 89
Morrow, Emma 108
Morrow, Hannah 39
Morrow, James 46, 76
Morrow, Jane 77, 91, 107
Morrow, John 39, 83, 128
Morrow, John Benton 108
Morrow, John S. 107*, 108*, 110, 173
Morrow, Mary 39, 60, 66, 80
Morrow, Mrs. J. B. 138*
Morrow, Rachel 107*, 108*, 110
Morrow, Samuel 46, 85, 127, 133
Morrow, William 65, 77, 85
Morrow, William Stevenson 107
Morton, Joseph 22
Morton, Thomas 22
Mowry, Christian M. 155
Mowry, Elizabeth 155
Mowry, Fred 155
Mowry, Henrietta 155
Mowry, Mary 155
Mowry, P. H. 138
Mowry, Philip 155
Mowry, Philip H. 116, 154*
Mowry, Rebecca 155
Mowry, Robert Bruce 155
Moyer, Samuel 22
Mullin, William 92
Murdock, John 78
Murdock, Robert 53

Murphy, Philip 53, 86
Murphy, Rebecca 65
Murray, David 32
Murray, Mary 89
Myers, Benjamin 92
Myers, Dorothy 90
Myers, Henry 93
Myers, Jacob 78
Myers, Jeremiah 92
Myers, Margaret 93
Myler, Elizabeth 50

Nagle, Lizzie R. 95
Nave, George 93
Neal, James Sr. 174
Neal, Jenny 54
Neal, Joseph 178
Neal, Sarah 174
Neel, James 154
Neel, Rosanna J. 154
Nehf, George 178
Nelson, John 79
Nettle, George 93
Nevin, John W. 88
Nicholdson, James 45, 85
Nicholdson, John 53
Nicholdson, Mary 45*
Nicholdson, Richard 45
Nicholson, James 126, 133
Nicholson, Mary 173
Nicholson, Richard 173
Nickle, John 133
Nickle, William 79
Nisbit, Esther 45
Nisbit, Fisher 79
Nisbit, Wm. 45
Niven, David 78
Niven, John 78
Noble, Daniel 79
Norcross, George 157
North, Andrew 93
Norton, Betsy 36
Norton, Sarah 36, 75, 87
Norton, Thomas 24, 36*, 78, 87, 127
Nyas, Mary 95

O'Neal, John 17
O'Neill, John 34
Officer, Alexander 17, 34, 124
Officer, David 21
Officer, James 17, 34
Officer, Mary 34*
Officer, Robert 21, 128, 133
Officer, Sally 55
Officer, Thomas 84
Ogler, David 133
Oliver, James 64
Oliver, John 79
Orr, Eleanor 79
Orr, Isabella 54
Orr, John 79
Over, Keziah 174
Over, Samuel 174
Owens, Albert 110
Owens, Benjamin F. 110
Owens, Hannah 110
Oxor, Elizabeth 72
Oxor, George, 79
Oxor, John 79

Painter, Mary 74
Palm, Adam 79
Palm, Elizabeth 41
Parker, Mrs. 43
Parks, Anna 180
Parks, David 28
Parks, John C. 180
Parks, Joseph 18, 19, 127, 180*
Parks, Rebecca, 28, 180
Parks, Thomas 180
Parks, William 28
Paten, Fanny 39
Paten, Francis 39
Paten, James 39
Paten, John 39*
Paten, Joseph 39
Paten, Mary 39
Paten, Robert 39
Paten, Thomas 39
Paten, William 39
Patrick, James 133
Patterson, Andrew 39, 83, 124*, 174

Patterson, Ann 36, 87, 174
Patterson, Anne 53
Patterson, Deborah 35, 51
Patterson, Elizabeth 36, 174
Patterson, Esther 36
Patterson, James 39*, 41, 79, 93
Patterson, John 54
Patterson, Mary 36, 39, 41, 174
Patterson, Nancy 41*
Patterson, Nathan 39, 54
Patterson, Obediah 23, 35, 53, 174
Patterson, Robert 17, 18, 19, 34, 54, 79, 124, 136
Patterson, Samuel 39
Patterson, Samuel H. 110
Patterson, Sarah 35, 36, 39, 68
Patterson, Thomas 36, 174
Patterson, Wallace 41
Patterson, William O. 110
Patterson, Zacheus 35
Patton, Andrew 54
Patton, Dr. 157
Patton, Elizabeth 174
Patton, Hezekiah 22
Patton, Hugh 17, 19
Patton, James 22
Patton, Janet 31
Patton, John 85
Patton, John 22, 31, 53, 54, 126
Patton, Margaret 31
Patton, Maria 81
Patton, Mary 31, 44, 54
Patton, Morgan 79
Patton, Robert 31
Patton, William 31*
Peebles, Eliza 82
Peebles, Elizabeth 51

Peebles, Martha 64, 77, 82
Peebles, Robert 54, 84, 174, 178
Peebles, Sarah 94
Peebles, William 174, 178
Peeple, Jane 72
Peeples, John 23
Peeples, Mary 80
Peeples, Robt. 23
Pennwell, Thomas 54
Penwell, Prudence 31
Peoples, Betsy 28
Peoples, Robert 28
Perry, Abram 178
Peters, John 93
Philips, Edward 110*
Philips, John G. 110
Philips, Nancy I. 110
Phillips, Edward 174
Phillips, Jane 68, 174
Pierce, Andrew 79, 110
Pierce, Jane 74, 174
Pierce, Joseph 174
Pierce, Paul 61, 82, 174
Pierce, Rebecca 65, 110
Pierce, William 110
Pilgrim, Henry 93
Piper, Andrew 110*
Piper, Elder 110
Piper, Eliza 110
Piper, Elizabeth 82, 110
Piper, James 79, 110
Piper, John A. 110
Piper, Maria E. 110
Piper, Nancy 52
Piper, Phebe 52
Piper, Thomas 65
Pipet, William 86
Plunkett, Isaac 54
Pollack, Jas. 20
Pollock, Catharine 61, 74
Pollock, Elizabeth 62, 75, 82
Pollock, Jos. 18
Pollock, Joseph 31, 124, 174

Pollock, Mary 23, 31, 74, 174
Porter, Elizabeth 52
Porter, Jane 54
Porterfield, William 21, 53, 133
Purdie, James 42
Purdie, John 42*
Purdie, Margaret 42
Purdie, Mary 42
Purdie, Rachel 42
Purdie, Thomas 42
Purdy, --- 21
Purdy, James 23, 84
Purdy, John 128
Purdy, Rachel 76

Quigley, James 54

Rainey, James 54
Ralston, Agnes 43
Ralston, Amy 44
Ralston, Andrew 42, 43*, 123
Ralston, Ann 43
Ralston, David 19, 17, 42, 43*, 44, 66, 79, 85, 86, 111, 126, 136, IV, 174
Ralston, Elenor
Ralston, Elizabeth 44
Ralston, Ellen 111
Ralston, James 43
Ralston, Jane 43
Ralston, Lacy 66, 174
Ralston, Margaret 43, 44
Ralston, Mary 43, 44, 174
Ralston, Mary E. 111
Ralston, Nancy 44
Ralston, Sally 44
Ralston, Sarah 43
Ramp, Emily 91
Ramp, Mary A. 93
Ramsey, Agnes 36
Ramsey, Anne 39
Ramsey, David 39*, 128
Ramsey, Eliza 87

Ramsey, Elizabeth 36
Ramsey, Hugh 42
Ramsey, James 24
Ramsey, Janet 36
Ramsey, Margaret 36, 42, 87
Ramsey, Mary 23, 36, 39
Ramsey, Matthew 126
Ramsey, Miss 23
Ramsey, Nathan 24, 36, 87, 136
Ramsey, Sarah 39
Randles, Margaret 51
Randolph, Alexander L. 111
Randolph, Amelia 111
Randolph, Betsey Lecky 140
Randolph, Hannah M. 94
Randolph, J. Davidson 140
Randolph, John 79
Randolph, Mary 90
Randolph, Mary Knettle 174
Randolph, Nancy 72
Randolph, Paul 88, 111, 140
Rankin, A. 111
Rankin, Mary J. 111
Rankin, William F. 111
Ray, James 63
Ray, William 79
Rea, Adaline 111
Rea, John McKeehan 111
Rea, Joseph 111
Reauge, Mary 126
Reauge, Samuel 126
Reed, ---- 51
Reed, David L. 93
Reed, Eleanor 44
Reed, Hugh 175
Reed, James 86, 93, 174
Reed, John 20, 40, 44
Reed, Sally 44
Reed, Sarah 40
Reed, Tabitha 67
Rees, John 79
Reid, Eleanor 21

Reid, John 17, 21, 126
Reid, Mary 73
Reid, Sarah 149
Reif, Nathan 137
Reigh, Elenor 37
Reigh, Mary 37
Reigh, Samuel 37
Reynolds, David 79
Rheme, Barbara 71
Rhine, Stephen 85
Richards, Andrew T. 111
Richards, Robert 93, 111
Richards, Susan 111
Richardson, Catharine A. 155
Richardson, James 93
Richardson, John H. 178
Richardson, William 94
Richardson, William H. 155
Richie, Agnes 66
Richie, Elizabeth 110*
Richie, Isabella 67
Richie, Mary 71
Richie, Nancy 71
Richie, William 79, 110
Richy, James 79
Richy, William 175
Riddle, A. Rebeckah 155
Riddle, James M. 155
Ridsbaugh, Barbara 51
Rightmier, Betsy 80
Rightmyer, Lewis 84
Rightmyer, Mary 70
Riley, John 79
Rine, David 61
Ripet, Widow 59
Rippet, Elizabeth 48
Rippet, John 48, 126
Rippet, Mary 48
Rippet, Rebecca 48, 51
Ripton, Elizabeth 81
Ripton, John 79
Ripton, Peter 79
Ripton, Widow 86

Ritner, Peter 137
Roan, John 197
Roan, Ruth 82
Roberts, Andrew 79, 111*
Roberts, Catharine 111*
Roberts, Elizabeth 79, 111
Roberts, John 54, 85, 111, 178
Roberts, Josephine 94
Roberts, Martha 60
Roberts, Nancy 23, 75
Roberts, Nathaniel 127
Roberts, Robert Gillespie 111
Roberts, William H. 111
Robertson, Thomas 79
Robinson, Esther 46*
Robinson, John 46*, 127, 136
Robinson, Mary 46
Robinson, Ruth 54
Robinston, James 17
Robison, Margaret 49
Rodgers, Catharine 89
Rodman, Rachel 54
Ross, Alexander McWilliams 111
Ross, David 63
Ross, Eliza 63
Ross, Hetty 111
Ross, James 66, 85
Ross, John 62, 79, 111
Ross, Joseph 79
Ross, Louisa 79
Ross, Simon 79
Rouse, Elizabeth 75
Rowland, Rev. 196
Royal, ---- 91
Rudgers, Whilhemina 94
Runsher, M. A. 94
Rush, Benjamin 197
Russel, Fauster 93
Russel, Mary 61
Russel, William 79, 85

Russell, Jane 95
Rutgers, Lucetta 94
Ryan, Jane 73

Sailor, Isaac 94, 112
Sailor, Lucetta 112
Sailor, William J. 112
Sanders, William 94
Saunders, Sarah 78
Sawyer, John 62
Sayers, Margaret 31
Saylor, Isaac 112
Saylor, Lucetta 112
Saylor, Rebecca J. 112
Scoby, Elizabeth 75
Scott, Felix 133
Scott, John 54
Scott, Miss 43
Scouller, John 80
Scouller, William 58, 94
Scroggs, Alex. 175
Scroggs, Allan 54
Scroggs, Elizabeth 81
Scroggs, Jane 77
Scroggs, Moses 80
Scroggs, Rachel 71
Scroggs, Sarah 72
Seelly, William 54
Seitz, Abraham 112
Seitz, John Wilson 112
Selfridge, ---- 60
Sensebaugh, Elizabeth 77
Shannan, Andrew 41
Shannan, John 45
Shannan, Joseph 46
Shannan, Sarah 41
Shannon, Agnes 41
Shannon, Ann 41
Shannon, David 29
Shannon, Elizabeth 79
Shannon, Hugh 80
Shannon, Isaac 21, 45, 54
Shannon, James 54, 80
Shannon, Jane 45, 76
Shannon, Jean 21

Shannon, John 22, 41, 63, 83, 84, 126
Shannon, Joseph 22, 39
Shannon, Leonard 29, 54, 133
Shannon, Margaret 22
Shannon, Mary 22*, 39, 45, 53
Shannon, Nancy 23
Shannon, Robert 18, 19, 45, 127
Shannon, Samuel 29
Shannon, Sarah 29, 45, 54, 77, 82
Sharp, Alexander 83
Sharp, Alexander McNitt 111
Sharp, David 54
Sharp, Elizabeth 49, 111
Sharp, James 60, 84, 175
Sharp, James W. 129
Sharp, Jane 89
Sharp, John 80*
Sharp, Margaret 158
Sharp, Martha 61, 71
Sharp, Mary 61, 71
Sharp, Nancy 75
Sharp, Samuel 94
Sharp, Samuel H. 111
Sharp, William 80
Sharp, William M. 149
Sharpe, Alexander 137*
Shaw, Charles 59
Shaw, James 94
Shaw, John 80
Shaw, John F. 111
Shaw, Joseph 86
Shaw, Peter Wilt 111
Sheldon, Susan 79
Shelly, James 83
Shepherd, Virginia E. 90
Shields, James 80
Shields, John 63
Shields, Margaret 66
Shover, B. 94
Shulenberger, Henry 80
Shullenberger, Adam 94
Shuman, Leonard 86
Sibbet, Margaret 67
Sibbet, Samuel 60, 86
Sibbet, Thomas 65
Silver, Samuel 133
Singleton, Mary A. 90
Skelly, David 80
Skelly, Jane 111
Skelly, Margaret J. 111
Skelly, Robert 80, 111
Skiles, David 80
Skiles, Elizabeth 90
Skiles, Mary J. 92
Skiles, Rebecca C. 92
Smiley, Francis E. 118
Smith, Archibald, 54
Smith, Benjamin 175
Smith, Elizabeth 43
Smith, Elizabeth McCormick 175
Smith, Esther 90
Smith, Eva 73
Smith, George W. 80
Smith, James 112*
Smith, James Houston 112
Smith, Jane 68
Smith, John 28, 43, 80, 86, 94,
Smith, John Blair 197
Smith, Joseph 80
Smith, Lacey J. 111
Smith, Margaret J. 112
Smith, Mary 43
Smith, Matilda 112*
Smith, Robert 43, 147
Smith, Sarah 43
Smith, Sarah I. 112
Smith, William 43, 80
Snodgrass, Benjamin 94
Snodgrass, William 94
Snoke, ---- 94
Snowden, James H. 179
Snowden, Samuel S. 179
Snyder, Jacob 94
Snyder, Jonathan 80
Sourpike, Daniel 133
Spangler, Samuel 80
Spear, Elizabeth 95
Spear, Susan 93
Spence, Anne 52
Sponseler, Jane 111
Sponseler, Widow 111
Spree, John 94
Sprigs, David 94
Stanhope, Samuel 197
Stanton, William 94
Starrett, James 175
Starrett, Martha 175
Starrett, Robert 175
Stars, John 41
Steel, James 94
Steel, John 88, 195
Steel, Mary 54, 175
Steel, Robert 54, 94, 175
Steen, James 45
Stephens, William L. 80
Stephenson, Elizabeth 39, 50
Stephenson, James 54, 83
Stephenson, Jane 39, 60, 92
Stephenson, Mary 60, 78
Stephenson, William 39, 83
Sterret, Bryce 39
Sterret, David 38, 39
Sterret, Elizabeth 39
Sterret James 54
Sterret, John 39
Sterret, Mary 38
Sterret, Rachel 39
Sterret, Robert 39
Sterret, William 39
Sterrett, Benjamin 54
Sterrett, Brice 133

Sterrett, David 67, 83, 175*
Sterrett, Eliza 67, 75
Sterrett, Elizabeth 54
Sterrett, Rachel 66, 175
Sterrett, Rebecca 175
Sterrett, Wilson 80
Sterrit, Eliz. 22
Sterrit, Mrs. 21
Sterritt, David 111
Sterritt, Isabella 111
Sterritt, Rebecca 111
Stevens, William 127
Stevenson, ---- 80
Stevenson, Hugh 175
Stevenson, James 80
Stevenson, Jane 175
Stevenson, John 175*
Stevenson, Margaret 175
Stevenson, Mary 175
Stevenson, Rachel 175
Stevenson, William 136, 175*
Stevick, David 126
Stevick, Jacob 94
Stewart, ---- 93
Stewart, Benjamin 127
Stewart, Caroline E. 112
Stewart, Eleanor 45
Stewart, Elizabeth 79
Stewart, James 45
Stewart, Jane A. 112
Stewart, John 112
Stewart, John M. 112
Stewart, Lucinda 95
Stewart, Mary E. 112
Stewart, Mitchel 94
Stewart, Nellie 128
Stewart, Rebecca 112
Stewart, Samuel I. 178
Stewart, Susan E. 112
Stewart, Widow 53

Stickfield, Michael 94
Stoneberger, William 94
Stough, Eliza 89
Stough, Jacob 66
Stough, Margaret 66, 138
Stough, Samuel 80
Stough, Thomas 137, 138*
Stow, John 80
Straw, William 94
Stuart, James 80
Stuart, Mary 79
Sturges, Jane 77
Sturm, David 80
Sully, George 45
Swigert, George W. 137
Swiler, Christopher Hume 111
Swiler, James 111, 112
Swiler, Sarah E. 112
Swope, Belle McK. Hays 138

Talbart, John 33
Talbert, Sarah 90
Taylor, Andrew 23, 54
Taylor, Elenor 41
Taylor, George 41*
Taylor, Mary 41
Taylor, Mr. 43
Taylor, Nancy 41
Tennent, Gilbert 145
Tennent, William 143, 181, 182*
Thomas, Martin 53
Thompson, ---- 62
Thompson, Alex. 133
Thompson, Alexander 18, 19, 23, 47, 85, 112*, 128, 15, 137
Thompson, Alice 82
Thompson, Andrew 41*, 59, 66, 84, 85, 128
Thompson, Ann 46
Thompson, Charles 95

Thompson, Eleanor 66, 73
Thompson, Elizabeth 64, 92, 112
Thompson, Ellen S. 112
Thompson, Ellenor 46
Thompson, Ellis 67
Thompson, Esther 66
Thompson, Hannah 41, 53
Thompson, Hugh 23, 41, 47, 81, 85, 94
Thompson, James 94
Thompson, James W. 41
Thompson, Jane 46
Thompson, John 81, 94, 112
Thompson, Joseph 64, 175
Thompson, Leacy 47, 52
Thompson, M. 22
Thompson. Margaret 91
Thompson, Margaret A. 112
Thompson, Mary 41, 64, 82
Thompson, Mary Ann 41
Thompson, Matthew 46, 54, 59, 85, 94, 112, 133, 175
Thompson, Nancy 74
Thompson, Peggy 23, 80
Thompson, Rachel 93
Thompson, Rhoda 62
Thompson, Robert 60
Thompson, Robert Houston 112
Thompson, Rosanna 73
Thompson, Samuel 23, 41
Thompson, Sarah 112
Thompson, Susan 75
Thompson, Susanna 47
Thompson, W. H. 138
Thompson, Widow 90
Thompson, William 46*, 85, 127, 128
Thornton, Nancy 66
Topley, Absalom H. 95

225

Torbet, George 113
Torbet, Joseph Wallace 113
Torbet, Miss 90
Torbet, Robert 94
Torbet, Tabitha 113
Trainor, Margaret 156
Treat, William 94
Trego, James S. 95
Trego, Joseph 113*
Trego, Julia R. 113*
Trego, Margaret 113*
Trego, Mary 76
Trego, Mary E. 113
Trego, Moses 175
Trego, Rachel R. 113
Trego, Rebecca 175
Tritt, Elizabeth 112
Tritt, George W. 113
Tritt, Jane M. 113
Tritt, Julia 113*
Tritt, Martha E. 113
Tritt, Samuel 94, 112, 113*
Tritt, Samuel R. 112
Tritt, Sarah E. 112
Tritt, Whilemina 112*
Tritt, William 112*
Turbet, William 179
Turner, Eleanor 73
Turner, James 18, 48, 126
Turner, John 24, 43, 126, 133
Turner, Joseph 24, 43, 81
Turner, Mary 43, 48
Turner, Sally 43

Uhler, Sarah 78
Underwood, Jane E. 113
Underwood, John 81
Underwood, William E. 113

Van Horn, Annie 37
Van Horn, Joseph 37
Vanard, Letitia 113
Vanard, Wilson 113

Vanbeaver, Isabella Oliver 113
Vanbeaver, Jane E. 113
Vanbeaver, Joseph 113*
Vanbeaver, Mary E. 113
Vanbeaver, Rebecca 113*
Vanderbilt, C. H. 179
Vanderbilt, Cornelius 54, 61, 84, 113*
Vanderbilt, Eleanor 62, 72
Vanderbilt, Eliza 66
Vanderbilt, Elizabeth 77
Vanderbilt, James 95, 113,
Vanderbilt, Jane E. 113
Vanderbilt, John 113
Vanderbilt, Mahala 113
Vanderbilt, Widow 60
Vanderbilt, William A. 113
Vandyke, William 62, 81
Vanhorn, Joseph 54, 127
Vanhorn, Mr. 130
Vanlever, Isabella 93

Wagner, John 137
Wagstas, Charity 36
Wagstas, William 36
Walker, ---- 50
Walker, Alexander 81
Walker, Andrew 20, 30, 128
Walker, Betsy 30
Walker, D. 128
Walker, David 81
Walker, Elizabeth 30*, 73, 93
Walker, Hannah 30
Walker, Isabel 30
Walker, James 30*, 41, 48, 127, 129, 136

Walker, Jane 30*, 41, 54
Walker, John 30, 86, 128
Walker, Joseph 18, 30*
Walker, Lucy 82
Walker, Margaret 30*, 73, 76
Walker, Mary 21, 30*, 50
Walker, Matthew 127
Walker, Rachel 30*, 50
Walker, Robert 18, 30*, 81, 127
Walker, Samuel 30, 128
Walker, Thomas 64
Walker, Widow 84, 128
Walker, William 18, 30*, 85, 128
Wallace, Agnes 50, 176
Wallace, Ann 62, 82
Wallace, Elizabeth .41
Wallace, Hugh 55, 133
Wallace, John 41, 176*
Wallace Margaret 176
Wallace, Mary 65, 176*
Wallace, Patrick 55
Wallace, Samuel Gowdy 114
Wallace, Sarah A. 91
Wallace, Thomas 61, 81, 83, 95, 114*, 176
Wallace, William Harper 69
Wallace, William Laird 114
Waltenberger, J. D. 133
Ward, Hester 72
Warner, Philip 61
Warrington, William 30
Watson, Anna M. 115
Watson, Beaty 114
Watson, Christian 95

Watson, Eliza J. 114*
Watson, George 95, 114*, 115,
Watson, John M. 114
Watson, Martha J. 114
Watson, Sarah 114, 115
Watson, William E. 114
Waugh, Samuel 58
Weakley, Alexander 86
Weakley, Hetty 176
Weakley, Isaac 81
Weakley, James 81, 83
Weakley, John 176
Weakley, Martha 67, 176
Weakly, Margaret 80
Weaver, Ann 95
Weaver, Anna 80
Weaver, Elizabeth 155
Weaver, John H. 95
Weidner, James 95
Weily, John 133
Weir, George 180
Weir, Jane 180
Weir, Margaret 189
Weir, Samuel 180
Welcome, David 95
Wells, Sally 73
West, Rev. 157
Whisler, Elijah 95
Whistler, ---- 91
Whistler, Christopher 95
White, Elizabeth 65
White, Robert 95
Whitecap, Eliza 92
Whitelock, Eliza 50
Whitely, Andrew 176
Wier, Alexander 46
Wier, Samuel 127
Wightman, William 81
Wigley, Joseph 81
Wilkison, Dolly 94
William, James C. 83
Williams, Catharine 176
Williams, Dr. 68, 88, 134, 151

Williams, Eleanor 176
Williams, George 176
Williams, James C. 176
Williams, Jane C. 82
Williams, Jane G. 65
Williams, Jane Whiteside 114
Williams, Joseph H. 114
Williams, Joseph C. 95, 137
Williams, Joshua 58*, 59, 70, 123, 136, 149, 150*, 152, 176*
Williams, Joshua D. 67
Williams, Lewis 86
Williams, Lewis H. 67, 81, 114
Williams, Louis 150
Williams, Mary 61, 66
Williams, Mary C. 81
Williams, Rachel 60
Williams, Rev. 58
Williams, Samuel M. 114
Williams, Sarah I. 114
Williams, Tabitha 114
Williams, William 61, 81
Williamson, Alexander 64, 139
Williamson, Betsy 79
Williamson, David 19, 23, 45, 77, 85, 128, 133, 139*, 176
Williamson, Eliza 77
Williamson, James 64
Williamson, John 61
Williamson, Mary 75
Williamson, McKnight 139
Williamson, Moses 65, 139
Williamson, Samuel 45, 59, 85
Williamson, Tamar 23, 123*, 176

Williamson, William 176
Willis, Mary 71
Willis, Rachel 72
Wills, David 81
Wills, Eliza 66
Wilson, ---- 80
Wilson, Adam 23
Wilson, Ann 47, 94
Wilson, Elizabeth 31
Wilson, Irving 95
Wilson, James 18, 31
Wilson, Jane 63, 80, 82, 149, 176
Wilson, John 148, 149, 176
Wilson, John S. 114
Wilson, Joseph 47*, 95, 128
Wilson, Letitia 85
Wilson, Margaret 31
Wilson, Mary 22, 31*, 65, 114
Wilson, Matthew 18, 31, 84, 127, 176
Wilson, Molly 78
Wilson, Mr. 86, 129
Wilson, Mrs. 95
Wilson, Rev. Mr. 130
Wilson, Robert 58, 81*
Wilson, Samuel 16, 17, 18, 19, 24*, 26, 31, 33, 49, 55, 58, 123, 124*, 127, 129, 133, 134, 136, 148, 176*
Wilson, Sarah 78
Wilson, Thomas 133
Wilson, William 18, 31, 47, 58, 126
Wilt, Catherine S. 114
Wilt, Eleanor 67
Wilt, Eliza J. 114
Wilt, Esther 67
Wilt, Hanna(h) 114*
Wilt, Hetty 80
Wilt, Jane Mary 113
Wilt, John 47, 67, 81, 113
Wilt, Mary 113*
Wilt, Mary H. 76

Wilt, Peter 66, 113*, 176
Wilt, Rachel A. M. 114
Wilt, Sarah 91
Wilt, William 113*
Wise, Michael 95
Witherspoon, Dr. 144
Withrow, Samuel 81
Withrow, William 81
Wolf, Elizabeth 80
Wolff, George 95
Woodburn, Agnes 138
Woodburn, Ann 114
Woodburn, Benjamin 95
Woodburn, Emily 73
Woodburn, George 81, 114
Woodburn, George W. 83
Woodburn, James 55, 81, 85, 95, 114, 126, 133
Woodburn, James H. 114
Woodburn, Jane 72, 73, 114
Woodburn, John 95
Woodburn, John J. 114
Woodburn, Joseph A. 114
Woodburn, Laura 114
Woodburn, Margaret 78, 82
Woodburn, Mary 114
Woodburn, Matthew 55
Woodburn, Skiles 81
Woodburn, William 81
Woodrow, Enoch 95
Woodruff, Anthony 55
Woods, Dorcas J. 114
Woods, Eliza 63
Woods, Elizabeth J. 115
Woods, Isabel 32
Woods, James Woodburn 115
Woods, Jane 32, 36, 87, 115*
Woods, Jenny 36
Woods, John 32, 36, 95
Woods, Joseph 32

Woods, Margaret, 114
Woods, Margaret A. 91, 115
Woods, Martha I. 114
Woods, Martha L. 114
Woods, Mary 36, 52, 60
Woods, Matthew 81
Woods, Nathan 36, 60, 87, 136
Woods, Paxton 115*
Woods, Polly 32
Woods, Richard 17, 32, 86, 126, 136
Woods, Robert 32
Woods, Samuel 24, 36, 113, 125,
Woods, Samuel A. 115
Woods, Thomas 24, 175
Woods, Thomas Jacob 115
Woods, W. 124
Woods, William 36*, 113, 114*, 115, 124
Woods, William, Jr. 24
Work, Alexander 22, 47, 133
Work, Betsy 23
Work, Elizabeth 47, 52
Work, F. 21
Work, James 47, 59, 85, 114
Work, James Scott 114
Work, John 47, 114, 127
Work, Letitia 67
Work, Letty 54
Work, Margaret 114*
Work, Mary 47
Work, Rosanna 22
Work, S. 47*
Work, Susanna 23, 47, 53, 67
Work, Thomas McFarlane 114
Work, William 47
Wright, Jennet 46
Wright, John 46
Wright, Margaret 46

Wylie, S. S. 12
Wynkoop, Maria 71

York, Nancy 66
Young, Betsy 50
Young, John 55
Young, Margaret 53
Young, Mary A. 74
Young, Sarah 76

Zeigler, Dr. 115
Zeigler, Jacob 122
Zeigler, John 95
Zeigler, Nancy Herron 115
Zeigler, Samuel R. 179
Zeigler, Sarah 115
Zook, E. J. 137
Zug, John 95

www.ingramcontent.com/pod-product-compliance
Lightning Source LLC
Chambersburg PA
CBHW070655100426
42735CB00039B/2152